AF710345

WITHDRAWN

Speech Communication

VOL. 1

Speech Wave Processing and Transmission

PROCEEDINGS

of the Speech Communication Seminar,

Stockholm, April 1–3, 1974

Edited by

GUNNAR FANT
Royal Institute of Technology
Stockholm

Almqvist & Wiksell International
Stockholm

A Halsted Press Book
John Wiley & Sons
New York – London – Sydney – Toronto

© Almqvist & Wiksell International
Stockholm, Sweden

All rights reserved

First published in Sweden by
Almqvist & Wiksell International
Stockholm

ISBN 91-22-00008-9

Published in the Western Hemisphere and
the United Kingdom by
Halsted Press,
a Division of John Wiley & Sons, Inc.
New York

Library of Congress Cataloging in Publication Data

Speech Communication Seminar, Stockholm, 1974.
Speech wave processing and transmission.
(Its Speech communication; v. 1)
"A Halsted Press book."
1. Speech processing systems-Congresses.
I. Fant, Gunnar. II. Title.
TK7882.S65S65 1974, vol. 1 001.54'2'08s [621.38] 75-26696
ISBN 0-470-25425-4

TK
7882
.S65
S65
1974
v. 1

Printed in Sweden by
Almqvist & Wiksell, Uppsala 1975

Table of contents

Vol. 1 SPEECH WAVE PROCESSING AND TRANSMISSION

---

* these papers were not published in the preprint version

FOREWORD

The Speech Communication Seminar in Stockholm, August 1-3, 1974 (SCS-74) was an international meeting of experts involved in various aspects of the study of human speech covering physiology, acoustics, transmission and perception with applications in man-machine speech communication systems and aids for people with hearing and speech defects.

The Proceedings of SCS-74, SPEECH COMMUNICATION, in four volumes, include the same material as was distributed to participants ahead of the meeting and an additional number of contributions including chairmen's reviews received during and after the Seminar. No attempt was made to transcribe and document the discussions. There are in all 136 contributions divided on the four sessions as follows:

I. Speech Wave Processing and Transmission
II. Speech Production and Synthesis by Rule
III. Speech Perception and Automatic Recognition
IV. Speech and Hearing. Defects and Aids. Language acquisition

This material represents a unique inventory of current research in the field with emphasis on scientific methods and functional models of human performance. Speech communication science is in a stage of an active development and expansion and we have been fortunate to collect a substantial number of contributions from works which have only recently developed and are less well known.

We want to thank all contributors for their prompt and willing cooperation and the chairmen for their valuable reviews and evaluations of the progress in the field.

January 1975

For the Organizing Committee of the
Speech Communication Seminar 1974

Gunnar Fant　　Arne Risberg
Si Felicetti

CHAIRMAN'S COMMENTS ON SESSION 1

J. N. Holmes,
Joint Speech Research Unit,
Eastcote Road, Ruislip, Middlesex, U.K.

These notes record my own personal recollections and opinions about the discussions in Session 1, and have been written completely independently of my co-chairman, Manfred Schroeder. I have not attempted to make a summary of all the points mentioned, and these comments will, without doubt, reflect my own personal bias.

The Session opened with a long discussion of linear predictive analysis and coding, which is currently regarded as one of the most important techniques in speech processing. Manfred Schroeder outlined the history of LPC, of which the early schemes transmitted a coded error signal and gave very good speech quality at 7-10 kilobits/s. Since then lower-bit-rate schemes which use conventional vocoder methods of providing excitation for synthesis have not consistently given such good performance on a wide range of speech material. The essential difference between the two approaches is that in the medium bit-rate systems the deficiences of the all-pole model of speech production are compensated for, within the limits of coding accuracy, in the transmitted error signal. In the low-bit-rate systems no such compensation is possible, and speech will be inadequately represented in respect of vocal cord excitation effects and non-ideal vocal tract configurations. Because of the great sensitivity of the real part of pole coordinates to the properties of the signal being analysed, these deficiencies frequently cause the synthesized speech to have grossly incorrect formant bandwidths.

There was much discussion about how things could be improved by adding zeros to the re-synthesis transfer function. Bishnu Atal presented his view that the necessary poles could be determined first, and afterwards an optimum set of zeros could be defined, without influencing the derived pole positions. This view was not generally supported by the meeting, and a widespread opinion seemed to be that optimum placement of the poles depended on the zero positions, and so iterative calculation was necessary for the best solution. Walter Lawrence put in a valuable comment that one should not, in considering these processes, lose sight of the physical significance of the zeros one was trying to determine.

There was no disagreement that linear predictive analysis was capable of providing meaningful speech data in a computationally efficient way. However, it seemed obvious that an analysis-by-synthesis method has the advantage of being capable of incorporating sensible speech constraints, at the expense of more computation.

A discussion followed on determining vocal tract shapes from the speech wave. Linear predictive analysis gives a straightforward method of deriving an area function of an unbranched tube, but the even components of an expansion of the area function depend on formant bandwidths, which are not normally accurately known. The use of articulatory constraints can help greatly to overcome this limitation, but it has been demonstrated by Bob Crichton of Cambridge University that even with the limitation of a simple assumption about the vocal tract losses it is possible to obtain shapes which are sensible enough to be useful for some purposes (in his case for teaching the deaf). Atal described a new general way of relating articulatory to acoustic parameters, which may have considerable value.

Louis Pols made a brief presentation about the value of his principal spectrum component representation for synthesis. I had the impression that this approach is very suitable for providing a reasonable acoustic description of speech which will contain the main features necessary for correct identification of sounds, although it would not be accurate enough for producing natural-sounding speech. On the other hand, as an analysis method for automatic speech recognition and related operations it is an extremely efficient method of description which will preserve almost all the important features of the speech. On examining the shape of Pols' components I was left with the impression that some regular functions, such as Fourier components of the third-octave representation, might be almost as good.

A very important part of the Session was the series of demonstrations of various speech coding systems. Ben Gold had arranged some live real-time demonstrations from Lincoln Laboratory. In these demonstrations one male and one female talker spoke through the speech coding systems, and the output was transmitted to Stockholm over the international telephone system. It was obvious that it was possible for both talkers to converse through a low-bit-rate predictive coding system, but in the circumstances of the demonstration it was impossible to judge how performance would compare with other types of vocoder. The impressive feature about these demonstrations was the successful implementation of a number of complete systems in real-time using a fast programmable digital processor.

Recordings were played of a number of other systems processing the speech material distributed for the Seminar. John Makhoul's demonstration of a straightforward simulated LPC at about 2600 bits/s sounded excellent. A part of this excellence was the result of a complete absence of pitch errors: some gross pitch errors in the automatic analysis had been corrected by hand. The best channel vocoders were also very good at about the same digit rate, and the performance of the two types of systems was sufficiently close in general acceptability for it to be impossible to evaluate their relative merits without proper subjective tests. Such tests would need to include users' opinions under normal conversational conditions.

There were some Bell Laboratories demonstrations of waveform coding at medium-to-high bit rates. These showed that adaptive differential PCM could give substantially perfect speech at 32,000 bits/s, and very good results at 24,000 bits/s.

It is probably useful at this stage to summarise the present standing and future potentialities of various vocoder systems and LPC techniques. My own views, which may of course be shown to be wrong within a very short time, are given below.

CHAIRMAN'S COMMENTS ON SESSION 1

I think that at the moment low-bit-rate LPC systems are capable of about the same level of overall performance as the best channel vocoders; as such they can provide usable communication links, but with significant degradation compared with a normal analogue telephone channel. The speech quality faults of the two families of systems are very different. Spectrograms of LPC speech tend to be too 'clean' looking, with clear formants, whereas channel vocoder spectrograms often have a 'moth-eaten' appearance, but still result in equally acceptable speech. This acceptability of some channel vocoders is possibly accounted for by the fact that the familiar distortion of room reverberation causes somewhat similar effects to the spectrum. The choice between the two types of system for any practical requirement depends at the moment on problems of implementation and the electronic technologies available. Channel vocoders can be made with simple analogue circuits, and at present are probably much cheaper. However, assuming digital technology continues to make its expected advances, it is probable that most future vocoders will be implemented digitally; if so, the elegant mathematics of the LPC approach may well lead to the cheapest solution.

I doubt whether the performance of the channel vocoders will ever be significantly better than has been achieved already, and I think the same is true of LPC unless considerable extra complexity is added. Possible lines for investigation could be

(i) using the residual signal from the analysis to specify excitation properties (I do not just mean for 'pitch extraction', although it is likely to prove useful for this purpose also);

(ii) adding zeros to the spectrum description;

(iii) constraining the transfer function to take into account known speech constraints.

All of these proposed extensions would cause more complexity, perhaps to such an extent that the implementation difficulty will become comparable with that of formant vocoders. Our own work at JSRU, described in the Seminar Proceedings, has shown that excellent speech quality for parallel-formant synthesis can be achieved at 1200 bits/s. With the powerful analysis techniques now generally available it seems likely that a major step forward in formant tracking will make complete formant vocoders competitive in quality with the other systems, but at a lower digit rate.

Looking further into the future I do not expect to see articulatory models being usefully exploited for analysis-synthesis systems for a long time. The complexities and uncertainties of deriving articulatory information from the speech wave for a wide range of speech sounds (as distinct from vowels only as in most current work) are too great. I think that for many years low-bit-rate speech systems will concentrate directly on the acoustic properties of speech, gradually exploiting more of our knowledge about the acoustic description of speech signals, and about the ear's tolerance to acoustic distortion.

CHAIRMAN'S COMMENTS ON SESSION 1 *

M. R. Schroeder, Drittes Physikalisches Institut,
University of Goettingen, F. R. Germany

It is said of speech researchers who build their own synthesizers that they become so accustomed to the poor vocal quality of their machines that they never realize how unspeakably awful their grunting pets sound. I have myself fallen victim to this illusion more than once. I remember when, in 1955 or 56, I had completed (soldering iron in hand) my own first channel vocoder - boasting all of six single-tuned filters for analysis and a similarly meager helping of poles for the synthesizer. Its sound quality was quite good (a certain resistance matrix operating on the channel signals saw to that) but whether it was speech quality can never be known because the squawky contraption was soon "salvaged" beyond salvation (and keeping good laboratory notebooks was never my idea of obliging big business or mollifying Ma Bell). As to intelligibility, my electronic creation simply had none. (If the concept of negative intelligibility had been more fully accepted in speech research, who knows, my 6-channel rack might have excelled in that direction.)

But I was completely unaware of this sorry situation. In fact, having people count (in English, from "one" to "ten")* over the contraption (and knowing it was counting, but not realizing the implications of this knowledge) so convinced me of the machine's merits that I immediately called my director of research (Axel Jensen, of television fame - television system design, that is) who appeared posthaste, a whole line of supervision in tow, to witness the purported breakthrough. Never, I believe, have the capabilities of a great Dane for polite comment been more severely taxed - and found wanting.

Unfortunately, this "scenario" has not remained unique in my Bell career (interspersed, though, by some happier moments such as those provided by the voice-excited vocoder and the cepstrum).

My ears, like those of so many others in the speech processing field, had become accustomed to the buzz and mush of synthetic speech, until - after a dozen years' immersion in electronic accents - I, at long last, turned definitely allergic to them (coincident, by the way, with my finally succumbing to the Jersey ragweed scourge).

* In other climes, according to a very competent speech source (decorated, parenthetically, by a Nobel Prize - although not for the spoken word and without the usual speech), highly predictable newspaper excerpts have been used as test material.

CHAIRMAN'S COMMENTS ON SESSION 1

It occurred to me that, in order to progress further in speech processing, we should

1. Use more appropriate models of speech production, and, realizing that no model could be perfect,

2. Leave room for error, i.e., preserve some description of the extent to which the model failed to account for the speech signal at hand.

Thus was born, in 1967, in collaboration with Bishnu Atal, the Adaptive Predictive Coding of Speech Signals[1, 2] which, it may be recalled, incorporated two predictors: one based on an all-pole model of speech production (utilizing short-delay correlations) and another based on the quasi-periodicity of voiced speech segments to exploit long-delay correlations.

In our first simulations, we settled on 8 predictor coefficients (2 each for 3 formants and 2 more thrown in as a sop to glottal excitation and lip radiation). In addition, there was one parameter for the pitch-period and a differential gain factor to account for growing and decaying amplitudes of pitch periods at the beginnings and ends of voiced segments. (Interestingly, a large part of the aperiodicity of voiced speech signals simply stems from the waxing and waning of amplitudes when voicing starts and stops.)

There was no voiced-unvoiced decision - I had learned long ago that decision processes incorporated the unfortunate possibility of mistakes - and the pitch-period parameter was permitted to adjust itself to a convenient value (in terms of low error energy) even for unvoiced sounds.

The unpredictable error was quantified to one (sign) bit per sample and the error energy was utilized as an 11th parameter, along with the 10 prediction parameters, for synthesis. The dichotomized error signal constituted the excitation signal.

The measured signal-to-distortion ratio averaged about 20 dB (considerably less for unvoiced segments). But, to our astonishment (and joy), the synthetic speech sounded nearly perfect. One had to resort to headphone listening in a quiet environment in order to discern any distortion at all, a distortion which sounded more like 30 or 40 dB below the signal level. This first impression was later confirmed in formal comparison tests which showed the one-bit predictive coder to be superior to 5-bit log-PCM speech.[3]

Where did this bonus in signal-to-noise ratio come from? We still do not know. Part of the reason may be that some of the error energy occurs during unvoiced sounds where the ear is known to be more tolerant of error than our definition (waveform difference) implies. As a matter of fact, as an illustration, take an unvoiced segment and Hilbert-transform it: the ear cannot tell the difference, it is completely indifferent to a 90°-degree phase shift in a noise-like stimulus. Yet, by our error criterion, the signal-to-noise ratio is not even 0 dB (-3 dB, to be exact).

But most of the error energy occurs during the (linearly) unpredictable transitions from one speech sound to the next and perhaps our ears are less sensitive to waveform distortion during those transitions. This hypothesis is amenable to formal confirmation (or rejection) and not irrelevant to a better understanding of speech perception.

For transmission and storage purposes this original linear prediction scheme was not very efficient: almost 7000 bits/sec were required for the error signal alone. Several simple-minded attempts at reducing this higher bit rate failed - except one: replacing all error samples by random bits. It gave high-quality, whispered speech.

I believe that the search for more efficient excitation is far from being complete. Today we are limited to a choice of either high-bit-rate excitation derived in a decision-free manner (as in the voice-excited vocoder and the original predictive coder) or low-bit-rate excitation schemes requiring decision processes and therefore liable to making errors. There is no theorem forbidding intermediate-rate (or even low-rate) excitation schemes that function essentially error-free.

While I was looking the other way (east, as a matter of fact, having left Bell Labs for Europe), Atal and Hanauer[4] dropped the room-for-error philosophy and came up with a predictive vocoder that sounded remarkably good for high-quality input speech. Later experiments with low-quality inputs showed noticeable distortions. This finding poses another question yet unanswered: what is the best analysis-synthesis process for a given input speech quality? Some speech signals we have to cope with (in conference telephony, for example) have reverberation, in other words: spectral zeroes (really more spectral zeroes, considering that nasals are already beset with zeroes). Until now we have handled zeroes by a thinning-out of poles (see Fig. 1 in Ref. 5). But more zeroes require many more poles and a pole-plus-zero model may be more efficient than an all-pole model. In his oral presentation during Session 1 in Stockholm, Atal showed how much better the spectral zeroes of a nasal /n/ are represented by the inclusion of 7 zeroes (14 additional parameters) in the predictor. By contrast, 13 additional prediction coefficients in an all-pole predictor still did not represent the zeroes well.

Another problem that will require more than lip service in the future is the nonstationarity of speech signals. Liporace's[6] serious consideration of this aspect of speech in linear estimation is a welcome contribution.

Makhoul[7], during Session 1, gave a succinct overview of linear prediction and demonstrated its merits vis-à-vis analysis-by-synthesis.

Apart from these developments, linear prediction has led to a number of other applications, notably in articulatory analysis which may turn out to be as important as efficient transmission and storage. Examples of such applications are the method for extracting pitch information and closed-glottis intervals described during Session 1 by Strube[8] and the relationship between predictor coefficients and vocal tract area functions.[9,10,11] In this area (of articulatory analysis) we may witness some of the most welcome (and urgently needed) advances - both for a better understanding of speech production and such applications as speech recognition and speaker verification using articulatory tracking.[12,13]

The importance of articulatory knowledge for automatic speech synthesis need hardly be stressed. It is clear that many coarticulatory effects, for example, are most naturally described in terms of articulatory models. But even vocal-tract area-functions reflect enough of the articulatory dynamics and constraints to be quite useful in speech synthesis. And this seems to be true even if the "area-functions" are derived (from predictor coefficients) by making certain, rather drastic, simplifying assumptions about the vocal tract losses and wall impedances. Even these so-called pseudo-area functions, a sort of footpath between acoustic and articulatory descriptions, have been usefully employed in a "tongue-reading" aid for deaf speech training[14] and speech synthesis by word concatenation.[15]

In word-concatenation synthesis a vocabulary of words, spoken in isolation, is analyzed and stored in terms of pseudo-area coefficients. For the actual synthesis of connected phrases, prosodic features are supplied by rule and the transitions between successive words are effected by interpolating the pseudo-area coefficients. Even at this early stage, and with a very limited effort, this type of synthesis works surprisingly well. In fact, the author asked J. Olive to synthesize for him the introduction to a talk on speech to an IEEE group in Philadelphia. The major limitation is (and probably always will be) the size of the vocabulary (about 1000 words at present) and "New Jersey," for example, had to be rendered as "New Joy See," - with no apparent ill effects on the audience.

In my opinion, the most impressive advance in converting speech signals into articulatory data is the work by Atal[16] in which predictive analysis and nonlinear regression techniques are combined to yield incredibly close articulatory matches for synthetic speech. Jansen,[17] too, finds how well nonlinear regression works among acoustic parameters.

If nonlinear regression can be made to work for articulatory parameters of human speech (the required training data could come from Fujimura's[18] surfacing computer-controlled dynamic cineradiography), then the future of speech research cannot fail to be very bright and rewarding.

References

1. B.S. Atal and M.R. Schroeder, Predictive coding of speech signals, Proc. 1967 Conf. on Communication and Processing, Cambridge, Mass., 1967, pp. 360-361.

2. B.S. Atal and M.R. Schroeder, Predictive coding of speech signals, Reports of the 6th International Congress on Acoustics, Tokyo, Vol. II, Paper C-5-4, 1968.

3. B.S. Atal and M.R. Schroeder, Adaptive predictive coding of speech signals, Bell Syst. Tech. J. Vol. 49, pp. 1973-1986,1970

4. B.S. Atal and S.L. Hanauer, Speech analysis and synthesis by linear prediction, J. Acoust. Soc. Am., Vol. 50, pp. 637-655 1971.

5. B.S. Atal and M.R. Schroeder, Recent advances in predictive coding - applications to speech synthesis, Speech Communication Seminar, Stockholm, 1974, Vol. 1, pp. 27-31.

6. L.A. Liporace, Linear estimation of speech signals, Speech Communication Seminar, Stockholm, 1974, Vol. 1, pp. 33-34.

7. J. Makhoul, Linear prediction vs. analysis-by-synthesis, Speech Communication Seminar, Stockholm, 1974, Vol. 1, pp.35-43.

8. H.W. Strube, to be published in J. Acoust. Soc. Am., 1974.

9. B.S. Atal, Determination of the vocal-tract shape directly from the speech wave, J. Acoust. Soc. Am., Vol. 47(a), p.65, 1970.

10. H. Wakita, Direct estimation of the vocal tract shape by inverse filtering of acoustic speech waveforms, IEEE Trans. Audio and Electroacoustics, Vol. AU-21, pp. 217-427, 1973.

11. H.W. Strube, Dissertation, Drit. Physik Inst., Goettingen, 1974.

12. T. Nakajima, H. Omura, K. Tanaka and S. Ishizaki, Estimation of vocal tract area functions by adaptive inverse filtering methods and identification of articulatory model, Speech Communication Seminar, Stockholm, 1974, Vol. 1, pp.11-20.

13. D. Lloyd Rice, Articulatory tracking of the acoustic speech signal, Speech Communication Seminar, Stockholm, Aug. 1-3, 1974, Vol. 1, pp.21-26.

14. R.G. Crichton and F. Fallside, The development of a deaf speech training aid using linear prediction analysis, Speech Communication Seminar, Stockholm, 1974, Vol. 4, pp. 35-40.

15. J.P. Olive, Speech synthesis by rule, Speech Communication Seminar, Stockholm, 1974, Vol. 2, pp. 255-260.

16. B.S. Atal, Towards determining articulator positions from the speech signal, Speech Communication Seminar, Stockholm, 1974, Vol. 1, pp. 1-9.

17. L.P.C. Jansen, Relations between some of the parameters of vowel sounds, Speech Communication Seminar,Stockholm,'74,Vol.1.,p.65

18. O. Fujimura, H. Ishida, and S. Kiritani, Computer controlled dynamic cineradiography, Ann. Bul. Res. Inst. Logopedics and Phoniatrics, U. of Tokyo, No. 2, p. 6, 1968.

Speech Communication Seminar
Stockholm. Aug. 1–3, 1974

SOME COMMENTS ON LINEAR PREDICTIVE CODING *

Bernard Gold, M.I.T. Lincoln Laboratory, Lexington, MA 02173, USA

Abstract

At the Stockholm Speech Communication Seminar, the subject of Linear Predictive Coding (LPC) received intensive scrutiny. It is commonly accepted by speech scientists that Homer Dudley's invention of the channel vocoder was a landmark event in speech research and its practical consequences. Will LPC prove to be of comparable importance? The following offering, needless to say, does not provide a definitive answer to such a question, which only time can provide, but some attempt has been made to assess the implication of present LPC efforts within the context of today's digital technology.

I. Introduction

Over the past five years, a new generation of speech bandwidth compression workers has arisen, conditioned primarily by the linear prediction analysis of speech initiated by Atal[1]. Whereas many of these younger people may think of linear predictive coding (LPC) as the way to approach problems in speech bandwidth compression, speech recognition, speaker verification, etc., some of us 'older' folk can look at LPC in broader perspective. There are several strands connecting LPC to other methods; perhaps the most obvious has to do with the relationships and comparisons of LPC to channel vocoders. The word 'prediction' in LPC has caused some confusion which we can try to resolve by exploring the relationships between LPC and some of the recent adaptive delta modulation schemes, for which predictors play an important role. Beyond this, we should examine LPC ideas in the context of some of the relevant older techniques needed to realize a complete bandwidth compressor; most important are the excitation problems of pitch extraction, voice excitation and spectrum flattening and the parameter coding problems.

The field of digital modems and transmission systems has advanced to the point where it is no longer necessary to limit our thinking to 2400 bit systems. It is now practical to consider bit rates from 1 through 32 kilobits per second (KBS). Removal of this 2400 KBS restriction means that a greater variety of source coding speech terminals become of practical interest. Prevention of future obsolence of speech terminals thus becomes a very important factor when considering speech terminal implementation.

The first part of this review gives a brief LPC summary and comparison of some LPC variations. We then discuss LPC in the context of the insights available to us from the channel vocoder field as well as the ideas of predictive speech coding. Finally, we summarize our own view of the implementation problem and its implication for practical speech communications systems.

II. Markel vs. Atal

In a later section we will examine how present LPC algorithms evolved from classical speech compression problems; in this section we will attempt

---

* not published in the preprint version

to summarize the present state of LPC. Figure 1 represents a 'canonic' form of a narrow band LPC system. Those familiar with channel vocoders will recognize that LPC differs in the method of extracting vocal tract parameters and in the specific way of modelling the synthesizer. These are very important differences but before we examine them in greater detail, we should realize the profound similarity between LPC and channel vocoders; that in both cases, speech is analyzed into its two major components, the vocal tract carrying spectral information and the vocal cord or excitation information. Thus far, all narrowband (2-6 KBS) LPC analysis has focussed on the vocal tract component so that all the difficulties inherent in the channel vocoder excitation problem remain with us in LPC work.

It is easiest to begin by referring to the LPC synthesizer. Atal's major assumption was that the human vocal tract could be modelled as a time-variable <u>all-pole</u> (digital) linear filter. His second important assumption was that a properly chosen least mean squared error criterion was suitable for speech analysis. Given these assumptions, Atal deduced an elegant method of obtaining the parameters of the synthesizer in terms of the measured auto-covariance matrix of the speech wave. Stated in mathematical terminology, we know that the output of an all-pole synthesizer can be written,

$$s(n) = \sum_{r=1}^{p} a_r s(n-r) + x(n) \tag{1}$$

where p is the number of poles, x(n) is the excitation signal and a_r (r=1, 2... p) represent the parameter coefficients. In LPC terminology, s(n) is the 'predicted' value of the nth speech sample based on the p previous samples of the speech s(n-1), s(n-2) ... s(n-p). Minimization of the mean squared difference (over some suitable time interval) between s(n) and $\sum_{r=1}^{p} a_r s(n-r)$ leads to the LPC solution. In this formulation, the excitation signal x(n) is not taken into account and thus appears as part of the error signal. The two correlation matrices shown in Figure 2 help illuminate the difference between the Atal or auto-covariance method and the Markel[2] or auto-correlation method, whereas Table I below states some of the differing aspects of the two approaches. Perhaps the most important advantage of the Markel approach is the ease with which the stability problem can be handled for finite word length arithmetic.

TABLE I

Atal	Markel
a. Non-Stationary	a. Stationary
b. Non-Toeplitz Matrix	b. Toeplitz Matrix
c. Does not always yield a stable synthesizer	c. Insures stability for infinite word length arithmetic
d. Does not require a window on data	d. Requires a window on data

IV. Synthesizer Structures

Any linear system can be completely specified via its poles and zeros (plus a gain factor). The reason for using an all-pole synthesizer and thus excluding the possibility of zeros lies in the relative resultant simplicity of the analysis procedure. There is also a large body of theoretical and empirical evidence in favor of an all-pole model for non-nasalized vowels. However, this model is by no means the accepted one for consonants and nasalized vowels. Furthermore, many other linear models are possible, as indicated in Table II; all of these systems are not merely academic and are actively being pursued.

TABLE II

a.	Serial Formant Synthesizer (LPC)	variable poles, no zeros
b.	Parallel Formant Synthesizer	variable poles, variable zeros
c.	Channel Vocoder	fixed poles, variable zeros
d.	Homomorphic Vocoder (12)	no poles, variable zeros
e.	Trivox Vocoder (15)	fixed poles, variable poles, variable zeros

V. Prediction vs. Modelling

The terminology of LPC has been the cause of some confusion. In speech processing, the word 'prediction' is usually associated with the type of system shown in Figure 3. In concept, if the 'predicted' signal s(n) is a 'good prediction' then the quantized error signal e (n) should carry less information and thus require a narrower bandwidth transmission channel than the original signal s(n). This idea is basic to a wide variety of delta modulation systems[3]. In these systems, no assumption is made about the separability of excitation function and vocal tract functions and in particular there is no need to extract separate pitch information. Typically, adaptive delta modulation (ADM) systems wherein the quantizer adapts to the error signal work well at rates between 15 and 30 KBS. Prior to Atal's LPC work, he and Schroeder[4] developed an adaptive predictive coding (APC) algorithm for which the linear predictor shown in Figure 3 was more directly oriented towards the properties of the speech signal. Thus, their predictor included a network with the transfer function $1 - \alpha z^{-N}$ where N was computed from a simple pitch extraction operation and was a correlation measurement. A 'correct' value of N and α during periodic sounds should greatly reduce the error signal size. However, an occasional wrong computation of these parameters would not (as in vocoders) create big 'gliches' because the error signal was able to compensate. A 6.6 KBS system based on these ideas has recently been implemented in real-time and is described in some detail by Goldberg[5]. Our purpose in this section is primarily to explain how the misnomer 'linear predictive coding' evolved from the more appropriately named earlier APC system of Atal and Schroeder. Perhaps a better name for LPC would be Serial Formant Vocoder with Parameters Extracted by Least Squares Analysis or (for short) Least Squares Formant Vocoder.

VI. Is An All-Pole Model Adequate?

This is an interesting and perhaps controversial issue. Fant's work in synthesis indicates that consonants and nasalized vowels do not, by and large, obey the equations of an all-pole model. However, we also know that, given enough poles, zeros of a system may be adequately represented and vice versa. At the same time we must admit that it is difficult to assess human perception sensitivities to errors in modelling different sounds. Thus we are faced with the canonic vocoder problem of trying it out. On this basis, LPC has certainly won a wide degree of acceptance. Many who have heard LPC systems appear convinced that LPC somehow duplicates the timbre of the speakers voice, as opposed to channel vocoders, which are claimed to introduce their own peculiar quality into the synthetic speech. No comprehensive intelligibility comparisons have yet been performed on LPC vs. channel vocoders.

My own listening experience indicates that a serial formant synthesizer appears to model men's voices quite adequately. However, I am puzzled by the fact that no-one has yet synthesized suitable female or child speech with an all-pole model. For many practical situations it is probably adequate to work with an all-pole speech compression system and concentrate on the nastier problem of excitation but I must also confess to a slight unease regarding the suitability of an all-pole model for all human speech.

VII. Comparison of LPC and Channel Vocoders

This is a very complex subject. Rather than make dogmatic statements, let us review some of the history. The recordings originally made by Atal[1] were most impressive; in listening to his LPC simulation synthetic speech by loudspeaker it was often difficult to distinguish between the original and processed utterance. On the other hand, a recent listening experiment by Holmes[6] indicated that listeners preferred his channel vocoder at least as much as his LPC simulations. Thus, depending on one's experiences, data base, subconscious biases etc., vastly different opinions will be formed on relative quality of LPC and channel vocoders. This substantiates our own feeling that terms such as 'listener preference' are not easily subjected to scientific analysis. It seems futile to try to 'prove' that one speech processing system is 'better' than another. What is needed and has not yet been adequately done is a battery of intelligibility testing, including intelligibility in the presence of noise or other interference. Even these tests should not be exploited to compare systems but mainly to satisfy oneself that any given system meets several well accepted rudimentary intelligibility requirements. Given the satisfaction of such requirements, we can face more easily quantifiable questions such as cost, compatability, flexibility, etc. This leaves us with two subjects vis-a-vis LPC vs. Channel Vocoder that we would like to explore further in this paper; namely, a) the coding problem and b) the cost and complexity problem.

a) The Coding Problem

During analysis, the channel vocoder derives approximate samples of the speech spectral magnitude for coding and transmission to the synthesizer. LPC analysis derives the coefficients of an all-pole digital filter. Experience indicates that at least 16 parameters are required to achieve reasonable channel vocoder fidelity while 10 or 12 LPC parameters appear to suffice. What is less understood presently is the number of bits needed to code LPC parameters for narrow band transmission.

Coding has always been a 'black sheep' problem among speech scientists, perhaps because good solutions require experience beyond that of speech processing and more in the realm of communications and network ideas. After many years of trial and error, channel vocoder workers agree that an average of 3-4 bits per spectrum channel and a frame time of 15-25 milliseconds are about right. Coding of spectral channels can never lead to an unstable channel vocoder synthesis filter since the poles of this synthesizer are completely pre-determined by the configuration. Perhaps for this reason, degredation in a channel vocoder is gradual with decreasing bit rate. For LPC, the situation appears to be more volatile. If, for example, the predictor coefficients a_r of equation (1) were to be directly coded for transmission, instability can easily occur unless very fine quantization is used. This follows from the well known fact that direct form digital filters are particularly vulnerable to coefficient errors. For this reason, such coding is not used for LPC. The reflection coefficients[7], k_r which can be derived recursively from the a_r have the excellent property that $k_r < 1$ (for all r) insures stability while $k_r > 1$ (for any r) insures instability. Our own experiments indicate that coding of the k_r for a rate of 4 KBS leads to an LPC system which is effectively always stable. Another coding technique which is presently popular is to code the so-called 'area functions' A_r[8] which are in effect the bilinear transform of the k_r. In particular, one technique uses the log area ratio function L_r;

$$L_r = \log_{10} \frac{A_r}{A_{r-1}} \tag{2}$$

It is obviously a crucial issue as to whether an accepted coding technique leading to a low rate (e.g., 2400 BPS) LPC system can be found; I feel that it is too early now to predict the answer but much activity is taking place on this front and we ought to soon have an answer.

b) Cost and Complexity

Digital signal processing ideas, while making LPC a practical possibility, also improved the implementation methods for channel vocoders. As a result, a certain amount of design thinking about digital channel vocoder implementation has taken place. In addition, we have done simulation of a particular channel vocoder on the fast digital processor[9] (FDP) and are now able to make preliminary comparisons between the computational complexities of channel vocoders and LPC systems. The overall result seems to be that channel vocoders require from 3 to 5 times the computation as LPC. Since this result seems surprising, let us try to explain it.

The major computational activity of a digital channel vocoder is recursive digital filtering. This implies that successive iterations of the digital filtering algorithm take place at the input sampling rate (6000-10000 samples per second) even though the outputs of the band pass filters can be sampled at a much lower rate. In LPC, by contrast, the major analysis computation (correlation) takes place at the frame rate (about 50 Hz). During synthesis, both channel vocoder and the LPC vocal tract model iterate at the sampling rate but the channel vocoder, especially a spectrally flattened one, requires many more multiplications; in our versions, 20 or 24 multiplications are required for LPC synthesis and 196 for channel vocoder synthesis.

VIII. Pitch Problem and Voice-Excitation

Up to now, we have discussed LPC from a purely spectral, or vocal tract point of view, with the preliminary remark that the excitation problem was common to both LPC and channel vocoders. In fact, an opinion expressed by Flanagan[10] at the Stockholm Speech Communications Conference was that the difficulties inherent in the pitch problem overshadow possible differences between various forms of spectrum analysis or their equivalents (e.g., LPC or channel vocoder). This point of view has my sympathy, especially since my own experience has been that pitch extractor performance is quite sensitive to speaker variation, background noise environment type of microphone and (in the case of a remote terminal) the properties of the link between the microphone and the terminal. The severity of the pitch problem has been well recognized by channel vocoder engineers and, in the late 1950's, Schroeder and others at the Bell Telephone Laboratory introduced the concept of a voice-excited vocoder[11]. It was found that distortion of a selected speech band (called the 'base-band') reproduced a good version of the harmonic structure of voiced speech. Thus, a reasonable excitation signal resulted from a spectrally-flattened distorted base-band signal. In practice, during the 1960's it was found that overall rates of 7200-9600 BPS sufficed to transmit all the information from a voice-excited channel vocoder (VEV).

As indicated in Section 5, APC is a different method of bypassing the specific problem of accurate pitch extraction and leads to rates comparable to that of a VEV. To date, no comparison has been made between these two medium rate systems which bypass the pitch problem. It seems to me that two important gaps exist in our studies of LPC, channel vocoders, VEV's and APC's. One is the combination of voice-excitation with LPC analysis and synthesis methods. The other is the development of systems whereby the bit rate needed for the excitation information can vary from either pole of low data rate pitch extraction using pattern recognition techniques to high data rate voice excitation or error signal excitation. The next section deals with some speculative systems (which have not yet been tried by us) on the first of these two subjects.

IX. Spectrally Flattened LPC's using Voice, Pitch or Error Signal Excitation

Let us consider three apparently different methods of speech compression. We have dwelt on channel vocoders and LPC systems; the third is homomorphic vocoding[12]. In all three cases, analysis leading to a good representation of the vocal tract spectrum is the issue. It is the intent of this section to bring some unity into this material by a) proposing a synthesis structure which essentially can be either of these three devices and b) showing that this structure is flexible enough to include voice-excitation or error signal excitation and/or spectrum flattening.

Our proposed synthesizer structure is given in Figure 4 and is seen to be a non-recursive or finite impulse response (FIR) digital filter realized via the fast Fourier transform (FFT). This model is in fact a slight variation on the model used by Oppenheim for his homomorphic vocoder. In his version, Oppenheim postulated that the excitation always consisted of quasi-periodic impulse-like signals caused by either the vocal tract during voicing or noise-like impulses during voicelessness. Thus, he was able to add vocal-tract impulse responses directly. The structure proposed here, although perhaps requiring more computation, allows any form of excitation. Spectrum flattening can be accomplished by dividing each output of the first FFT by its own magnitude. The FFT length should be twice as long as the assumed impulse response length of the vocal tract; thus an FFT size of 256 for a sampling time of 150 seconds resulting in an impulse response length of 19.2 msec. seems appropriate.

Now, given that the chosen impulse response length is long enough for any practical synthesizer, any form of analysis, be it channel vocoding, LPC, homomorphic or anything else, reduces to the problem of finding a good spectral analysis. Attention can be directly focused on the essence of the speech compression problem, namely, to discover a method of representing and transmitting the spectral information with the greatest fidelity and the fewest number of bits.

X. Implementation

It is now generally accepted that implementation of speech processing devices should be done by digital means. At present, the structure of such devices is still an issue. Associated with this issue are a set of as yet unanswered questions:

1. To what extent should speech processing and modems and other duties of a terminal be incorporated into the same piece of digital hardware?
2. How flexible, in terms of bit rate and adaptability to environment, should speech processors be?
3. How much more costly is a programmable digital device as opposed to one with a wired control?
4. What predictions can be made about economy savings via LSI?
5. How much more improvement can we anticipate in speech processing algorithms?

In our opinion, at the present time, reasonable attempts to guess at the answers to the above questions lead to a strong bias in favor of programmable digital devices. At present, Lincoln Laboratory is constructing a small, versatile device which can be used as a full duplex speech processor and probably have enough processing power left over to implement a modem. This device, which we call the Digital Voice Terminal (DVT)[13,14] is controlled by a 1024 register program memory and processes the flow of speech information through a 512 register data memory; the fully overlapped instruction cycle time is 55 nanoseconds. The device is comprised of about 500 packages of 2 nanosecond emitter coupled logic (ECL) circuits, wire-wrapped on 3 conventional (7" x 16") boards plus a fourth board for extra memory and audio filters and peripherals. At present costs, such a device could be profitably marketed at about $25,000. If we postulate a reasonable five year goal of reducing this cost to below $5,000 and perhaps doubling the capability, we can look forward to an eventual device which a) is cheap enough for widespread communications use, b) is very flexible so that new algorithms and, possibly, adaptivity can be easily incorporated and c) can perform other functions, such as modems, in addition to speech processing.

XI. Summary

We have presented our view of the present LPC picture and how it relates to the classical field of speech bandwidth compression. We believe that LPC is an interesting new speech processing technique which should prove useful in speech communications applications. Many problems remain to be worked on, most critically, the excitation problem and the parameter coding problem. Also, further LSI development of high speed digital circuits may be necessary before implementations of LPC and related devices become economic. In conclusion, it can be said that the introduction of LPC ideas along with digital signal processing ideas may lead to a variety of new and improved vocoding algorithms implemented on flexible digital processors for use in speech communications terminals.

This work was sponsored by the Defense Communications Agency. The Department of the Air Force, and the Advanced Projects Agency of the Department of Defense.

REFERENCES:

1. B. S. Atal, S. L. Hanauer, "Speech Analysis by Linear Prediction of the Speech Wave", Journal of the Acoust. Soc. of Am., Vol. 50, No. 2 (Part 2), 1971.

2. J. D. Markel, A. H. Gray, Jr., "Autocorrelation Equations as Applied to Speech Analysis", IEEE Transactions on Audio and Electroacoustics, Vol. AU-21, No. 2, April 1973.

3. Nuggehally S. Jayant, "Digital Coding of Speech Waveforms: PCM, DPCM, and DM Quantizers", Proc. IEEE, Vol. 62, No. 5, May 1974.

4. B. S. Atal and M. R. Schroeder, "Adaptive Predictive Coding of Speech Signals", Bell System Technical Journal, October 1970, pp. 1973-1986.

5. A. J. Goldberg and H. Shaffer, "Low Data Rate Voice Communications using Small Computer", Comm. Systems and Technology Conf., Dallas, TX, April 30-May 1974.

6. B. P. Jordan and L. C. Kelly, "A Comparison of the Speech Quality of a Linear Predictive Coder and a Channel Vocoder", 8th Int. Cong. on Acoustics, London, July 1974.

7. E. M. Hofstetter, "An Introduction to the Mathematics of Linear Predictive Filtering as Applied to Speech Analysis and Synthesis", Lincoln Laboratory Technical Note, July 1973.

8. J. R. Haskew, J. M. Kelly, R. M. Kelly, "Final Report of Project Yoho", Bell Telephone Laboratory, March 1972.

9. B. Gold, I. L. Lebow, R. McHugh and C. M. Rader, "The Fast Digital Processor-a Programmable High Speed Signal Processing Computer", IEEE Trans. on Computers, January 1971.

10. Flanagan -- Private Communication

11. E.E. David Jr., M.R. Schroeder, B.F.Logan and A.J. Presti, "New Applications of Voice Excitation to Vocoders", Proc. of Speech Communication Seminar, Stockholm 1963.

12. A. V. Oppenheim, "Speech Analysis - Synthesis System based on Homomorphic Filtering", J. Acoust. Soc. Am., Vol. 45, 1969, pp. 459-462.

13. A. J. McLaughlin, B. Gold and P. E. Blankenship, "The Digital Voice Terminal", Lincoln Laboratory L-Memo, August 1974.

14. B. Gold, "Parallel and Sequential Trade-Offs in Signal Processing Computers", to be presented at San Diego Conference on Communications, December 1974.

15. Trivox is a hybrid formant vocoder - channel vocoder system being developed by C. P. Smith; published material is not yet available.

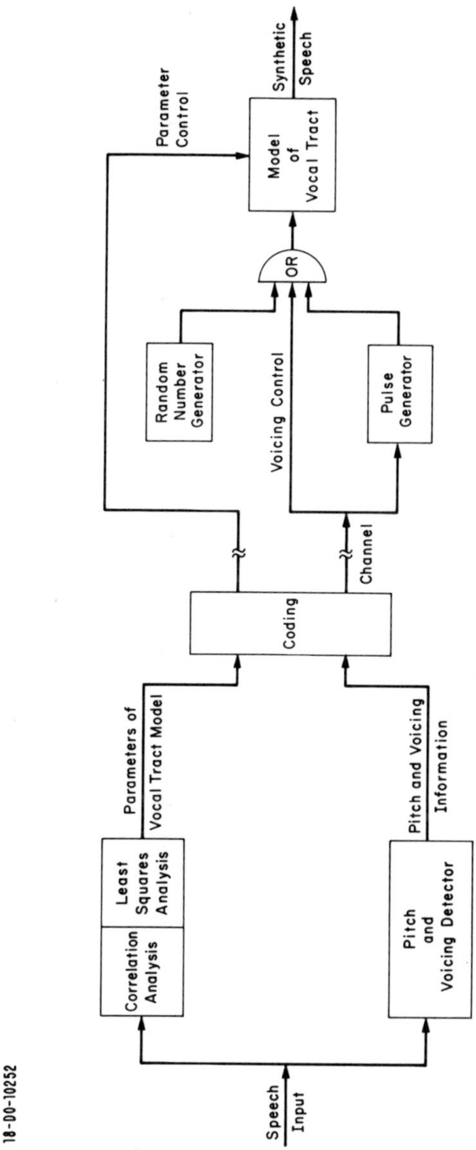

Fig. 1. Linear Predictive Speech Compressor

b 2480 *Volym 1*

$$R = \begin{bmatrix} R_{00} & R_{01} & R_{02} & R_{03} \\ R_{01} & R_{11} & R_{12} & R_{13} \\ R_{02} & R_{12} & R_{22} & R_{23} \\ R_{03} & R_{13} & R_{23} & R_{33} \end{bmatrix}$$

NON-STATIONARY

$$R = \begin{bmatrix} R_0 & R_1 & R_2 & R_3 \\ R_1 & R_0 & R_1 & R_2 \\ R_2 & R_1 & R_0 & R_1 \\ R_3 & R_2 & R_1 & R_0 \end{bmatrix}$$

STATIONARY

TYPES OF CORRELATION MATRICES

Fig. 2. Types of Correlation Matrices

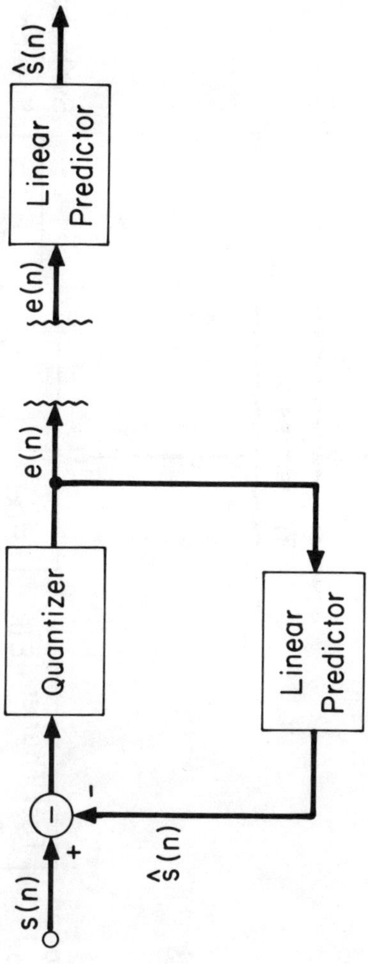

Fig. 3. Linear Prediction

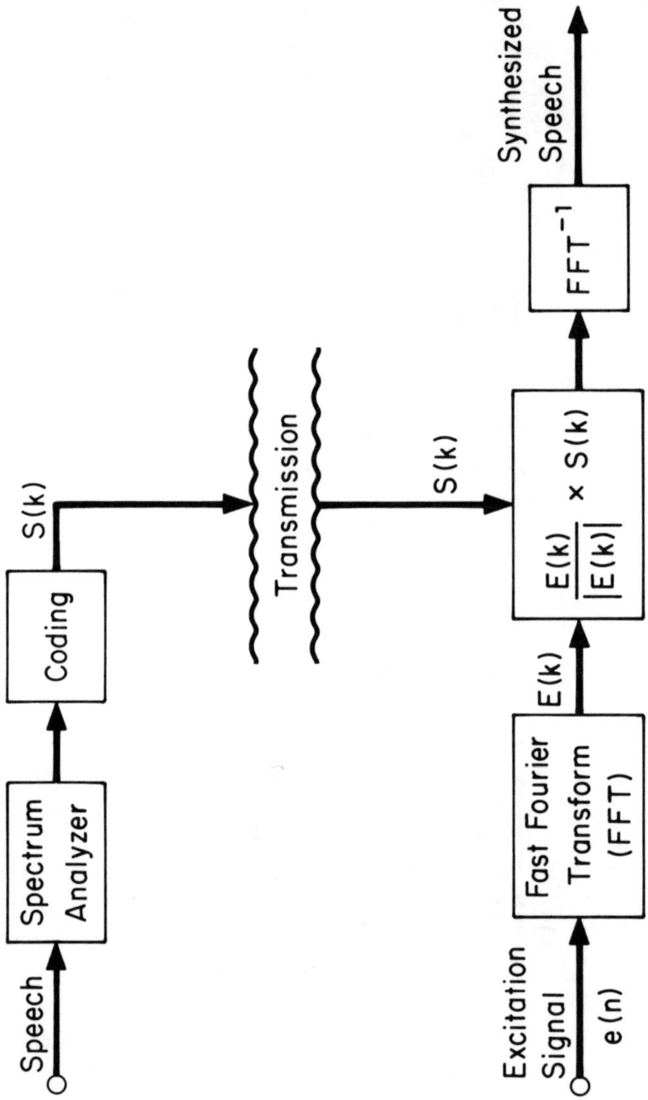

Fig. 4. Conceptual View of a Flexible Speech Bandwidth Compression System

Speech Communication Seminar
Stockholm. Aug. 1–3, 1974

TOWARDS DETERMINING ARTICULATOR POSITIONS FROM THE SPEECH SIGNAL

B. S. Atal
Bell Laboratories, Murray Hill, New Jersey 07974 U.S.A.

Abstract

The relationship between acoustic parameters of speech and positions of different articulators in the vocal tract was investigated - using techniques of linear regression - on a computer-simulated model of the vocal tract. The area function of the vocal tract in the model was specified by seven articulatory variables. It was found that each of these articulatory variables could be estimated accurately as a linear weighted sum of the acoustic parameters derived from the speech output of the model. Several different acoustic representations of speech - such as predictor coefficients, spectrum, cepstrum, formant frequencies, and their bandwidths, or the waveform itself - were used with equal success in determining articulatory variables. In estimating an articulatory variable, knowledge of other articulatory variables was not required. The error in estimating an articulatory variable was found to decrease monotonically with increasing number of acoustic parameters. The applications of this method for studying movement of articulators during speech production, for speech recognition, and for control of articulatory models for speech synthesis are discussed.

Introduction

Information regarding the shape of the vocal tract and articulator movements during speech production is basic to a better understanding of the human speech process. Present methods of obtaining such information are mostly based on x-ray techniques [1,2] which, for obvious reasons, can provide only a limited amount of data. Due to relative inaccessibility of the articulators, direct measurement of articulator positions by optical methods is generally difficult [3]. Hence, there is considerable research interest in developing better methods - for example, based on acoustic measurements - for obtaining the articulatory information. Ideally, one would like to determine the articulator positions directly from the acoustic information in the speech wave. So far, it has generally been believed, that the area function of the vocal tract must be obtained first before deriving the articulatory information from the acoustic data. However, attempts to determine the area function from the speech signal have not been successful [4,5]. The acoustic information in the speech signal cannot, in general, be mapped in a one-to-one manner into an area function without imposing additional constraints of the articulatory mechanism [6]. Other acoustic methods, for example, based on measurement of the lip impedance, also suffer from both theoretical and practical difficulties [7,8,9]. What is the way out of this dilemma? Is it at all possible to obtain the articulatory information from the speech signal?

In this paper, we will attempt to answer these questions by taking a new approach to solve this problem. Rather than trying to find out the area function of the vocal tract, we would attack the problem directly by attempting to determine the relationship between the articulator positions and the

1–742577 *Volym I*

acoustic data. We would present a mathematical framework by which such a relationship can be determined and questions regarding uniqueness of the relationship can be answered.

Considerable work has been done in the past to gain a better understanding of the various factors governing sound transmission in the vocal tract [10,11]. Our knowledge of the acoustic theory of speech production is reasonably complete. Neglecting for the moment the influence of the nasal tract, one can use this theory to determine the acoustic output of the vocal tract from a knowledge of the location and the nature of the excitation and of the area function of the vocal tract at all points between the glottis and the lips. For a fixed source of excitation, the transformation from the area function to the acoustic output is unique, that is, a given area function does not result in two different acoustic outputs. Since the vocal-tract shape is controlled by the positions of different articulators, it is desirable to express the area function of the vocal tract as a function of a number of articulatory variables. If a set of articulatory variables determine the area function completely, it is obvious that the transformation from these variables to the acoustic output of the vocal tract is also unique. Although the transformation from the articulatory to acoustic variables can be considered to be unique, almost nothing is known at present about the uniqueness of the reverse transformation from acoustic to the articulatory variables. If we were in the fortunate position in that the transformation from articulatory to acoustic variables was linear, the problem would have been relatively easy to solve. However, it is not so. It has been suggested that the nonlinearity of this transformation is the principal reason that we cannot obtain the articulatory information from the acoustic. This is not true. For example, a monotonic relationship between two variables may be nonlinear and still be invertible. It is one of the objectives of this paper to investigate the conditions under which a nonlinear relationship between a set of variables is invertible. Such nonlinear but still invertible relationships could be considered "intrinsically linear".

Invertible Nonlinear Transformations

Let us assume that the area function is completely determined by m articulatory variables. Let v_i be a parameter characterizing the acoustic output of the vocal tract. For a fixed source function, it is possible to express v_i as some function f_i of the m articulatory variables $\beta_1,\beta_2,\ldots,\beta_m$ given by

$$v_i = f_i(\beta_1,\beta_2,\ldots,\beta_m). \tag{1}$$

The function f_i includes the different transformations relating the articulatory variables to the area function and the area function to the speech output. The nature of the function f_i depends also upon the particular acoustic parameter v_i under consideration. At this point, an exact knowledge of the function f_i is not necessary. It is sufficient to assume that f_i is a reasonably smooth and well-behaved function so that it can be expressed in a series form as

$$f_i = \sum_{k=1}^{m} a_{ik}\beta_k + \sum_{k=1}^{n} b_{ik}\phi_k(\beta_1,\beta_2,\ldots,\beta_m), \tag{2}$$

where each ϕ_k, k = 1,2,...,n, is a function of the m articulatory variables but is independent of the acoustic parameter v_i. The functions $\phi_1,\phi_2,\ldots,\phi_n$, and the variables $\beta_1,\beta_2,\ldots,\beta_m$ are assumed to be linearly independent in the region of interest in the space of the articulatory variables. As it can be seen, that Eq. (2) is flexible enough to represent a wide range of nonlinear functions, for example, functions which can be represented by a finite Taylor series in the region of interest. Let us now assume that Eq. (2) represents the functions f_i for a number of acoustic parameters - in particular, for $i = 1,2,\ldots,m+n$. It is then possible to rewrite Eq. (2) in the matrix form as

$$\begin{bmatrix} v_1 \\ v_2 \\ \cdot \\ \cdot \\ \cdot \\ \cdot \\ v_M \end{bmatrix} = \begin{bmatrix} a_{11} & a_{12} & \cdot\cdot & a_{1m} & b_{11} & b_{12} & \cdot\cdot & b_{1n} \\ a_{21} & a_{22} & \cdot\cdot & a_{2m} & b_{21} & b_{22} & \cdot\cdot & b_{2n} \\ \cdot & \cdot & \cdots & \cdot & \cdot & \cdot & \cdots & \cdot \\ \cdot & \cdot & \cdots & \cdot & \cdot & \cdot & \cdots & \cdot \\ \cdot & \cdot & \cdots & \cdot & \cdot & \cdot & \cdots & \cdot \\ \cdot & \cdot & \cdots & \cdot & \cdot & \cdot & \cdots & \cdot \\ a_{M1} & a_{M2} & \cdot\cdot & a_{Mm} & b_{M1} & b_{M2} & \cdot\cdot & b_{Mn} \end{bmatrix} \begin{bmatrix} \beta_1 \\ \beta_2 \\ \cdot \\ \cdot \\ \cdot \\ \cdot \\ \phi_n \end{bmatrix} = P \begin{bmatrix} \beta_1 \\ \beta_2 \\ \cdot \\ \cdot \\ \cdot \\ \cdot \\ \phi_n \end{bmatrix}, \qquad (3)$$

where M = m+n. Equation (3) states merely that an acoustic variable can be expressed as a weighted linear sum of the m articulatory variables $\beta_1,\beta_2,\ldots,\beta_m$ and the n functions $\phi_1,\phi_2,\ldots,\phi_n$. Now, if the matrix P is nonsingular, one can invert the relationship and express the articulatory variables in terms of the acoustic variables as shown below:

$$\begin{bmatrix} \beta_1 \\ \beta_2 \\ \cdot \\ \cdot \\ \cdot \\ \cdot \\ \phi_n \end{bmatrix} = P^{-1} \begin{bmatrix} v_1 \\ v_2 \\ \cdot \\ \cdot \\ \cdot \\ \cdot \\ v_M \end{bmatrix}. \qquad (4)$$

It follows from Eq. (4) that

$$\beta_k = \sum_{i=1}^{M} w_i v_i, \quad k = 1,\ldots,m. \qquad (5)$$

Thus, if the articulatory to acoustic transformation could be described by Eq. (3), and the matrix P is nonsingular, then indeed, we can express an articulatory variable as a weighted linear sum of the acoustic variables. It is important to note that the weights w_i on the right side of Eq. (5) are constants for a particular articulatory variable and do not depend on β_k or v_i. The validity of Eq. (5) can be tested by finding out if there are a set of weights w_i, i = 1,2,...,M, such that an articulatory variable can be estimated as a weighted sum of a sufficient number of acoustic variables. The appropriate value of M in Eq. (5) depends upon a number of factors, such as the number of articulatory variables, the nature of the nonlinearities, and, as a practical matter, on the degree of precision necessary for the estimation of the articulatory variables.

Determination of Weights

In order to determine the weights of Eq. (5), one needs a training set containing simultaneous measurements of the articulatory variable under consideration and the corresponding speech output of the vocal tract. Let us define a measure of error between the actual value of the articulatory variable and its estimated value based on Eq. (5). Let $\hat{\beta}$ be the estimated value of the articulatory variable β based on a certain choice of weights w_i, that is,

$$\hat{\beta} = \sum_{i=1}^{M} w_i v_i . \tag{6}$$

The mean-squared error between β and $\hat{\beta}$ is given by

$$E = \langle(\beta-\hat{\beta})^2\rangle_{av} = \langle(\beta - \sum_{i=1}^{M} w_i v_i)^2\rangle_{av}, \tag{7}$$

where $\langle \ \rangle_{av}$ indicates averaging over different values of the articulatory variable β. The weights which minimize E are obtained by setting the derivative of E with respect to each of the weights w_i equal to zero. This results in a set of linear simultaneous equations given by

$$\sum_{i=1}^{M} C_{ji} w_i = r_j, \quad j = 1,2,\ldots,M, \tag{8}$$

where $C_{ji} = \langle v_i v_j\rangle_{av}$, and $r_j = \langle \beta v_j\rangle_{av}$. The correlations C_{ji} and r_j of Eq. (8) are determined from the measured values of the articulatory variable and the corresponding acoustic variables in the training set. The above set of equations are easily solved due to the positive-definite nature of the coefficient matrix. One efficient method of solving such equations is based on the Choleski decomposition [12,13], in which the square matrix of coefficients is first decomposed as a product of two triangular matrices which are transpose of each other. Equation (8) is then rewritten as two separate equations involving triangular matrices only; due to the triangular nature of the coefficient matrix, these equations are solved by recursion. The Choleski decomposition method is particularly suitable for determining the optimum value of M, since the weights and the mean-squared error are obtained for successively increasing values of M. Thus, the solution can be terminated whenever a small enough error is achieved.

Generation of the Training Set

As a first step to test the validity of the above ideas, the training set for determining weights was generated on a computer-simulated model of the vocal tract. The model idealizes the vocal tract as a straight acoustic tube of nonuniform cross-sectional area terminated at the left by the glottis and at the right by the lips. The area function of the vocal tract is specified by seven articulatory variables, namely, the area and location of the constriction formed by the tongue body, the area and location of the tongue-tip constriction, the area of the mouth opening, the lip protrusion, and the length of the vocal tract. The x-ray data [14] suggest that area in the vicinity of the glottis changes relatively little, thus, in the model, the area is set to a constant value of 2 cm^2 up to a distance of 2 cm from the glottis. The section of the vocal tract in the vicinity of the mouth opening is also represented by a uniform tube of length ℓ_m and area A_m. The cross-sectional area of the rest of the vocal tract is represented as a product of two functions, one controlled by the tongue body and the other by the tongue tip. The four variables describing the area controlled by the tongue are:

x_c = the distance of the constriction formed by the tongue body measured from the glottis,

A_c = the area at the tongue-body constriction,

x_t = the distance of the constriction formed by the tongue tip, and

α = a factor by which the area at x_t is reduced due to the tongue-tip constriction.

The vocal-tract area at a distance x from the glottis is expressed in terms of the above four articulatory variables as

$$A(x) = A_b(x)A_t(x), \tag{9}$$

where $$A_b(x) = A_o - (A_o - A_c)\text{Cos}\ \Omega_b(x-x_c), \tag{10}$$

$$A_t(x) = 1 - \alpha/\{1 + \Omega_t(x-x_t)^2\}, \tag{11}$$

and A_o, Ω_b, Ω_t are constants set to 5 cm, 0.3, and 0.1, respectively. An example of the area function based on the above articulatory model is shown in Fig. 1.

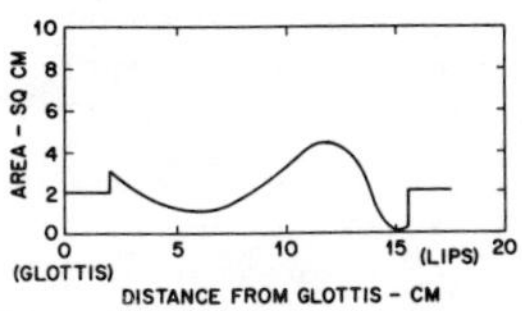

Fig. 1. Typical vocal-tract area function generated by the articulatory model.

In computing the speech output, the area function is quantized in sections each of 1.75 cm in length. The area of each section is assumed to be the geometric mean of the area function included in the section. Three different kinds of losses are taken in account - radiation loss at the mouth, loss due to yielding of the vocal-tract walls, and viscous and heat conduction losses. The radiation load is assumed to be that of a vibrating sphere with the same radius as that of the mouth opening and is represented by a parallel combination of an acoustic resistance and an acoustic mass [15]. The vocal-tract walls are assumed to have a uniform specific impedance consisting of a series combination of a mass of 3 gm/cm^2 and a resistance of 1800 $dyne\text{-}sec/cm^3$.

The training set was generated by varying one or more articulatory variables in the model. The vocal tract was excited at the glottis by a pulse whose spectrum fell at about -12 db/octave. The output speech samples were obtained at a sampling frequency of 10 kHz and analyzed by linear prediction method [16] with 12 predictor coefficients. Additional acoustic parameters needed in Eq. (5) for M larger than 12 were obtained by forming quadratic and cubic functions of the predictor parameters.

Results

In the first test, one articulatory parameter was varied at a time; the remaining articulatory parameters were kept fixed at values typical in speech production. The weights in Eq. (5) were obtained from a training set consisting of the predictor coefficients at 100 different values of an articulatory variable distributed uniformly over the entire permissible range of its variation. A new data set different from the training set was used to test the effectiveness of the weights so determined in estimating the articulatory variable. The error in estimating the articulatory variable was found to be insignificant for all of the seven variables of the model. These results, for the variables x_c, A_c, x_t, α, and A_m, are illustrated in Fig. 2.

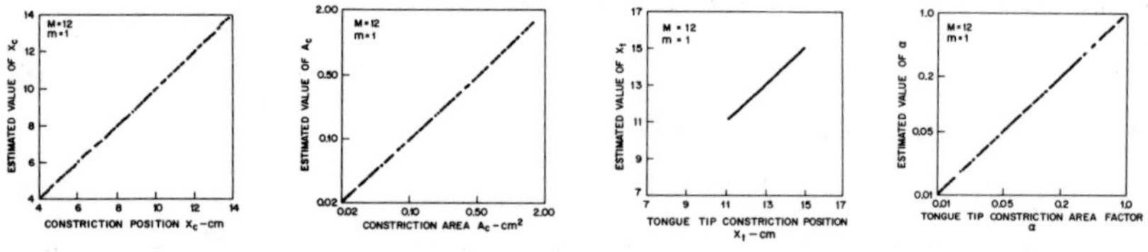

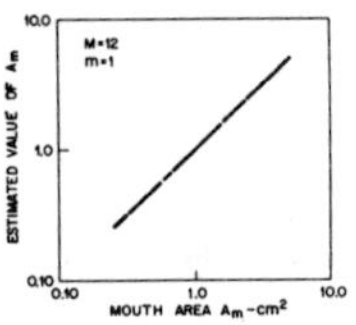

Fig. 2. Comparison between the estimated values of the articulatory variables of the model and their actual values. Only one articulatory parameter was varied at a time. The number of acoustic parameters M was set to 12.

In the figure, the ordinate represents the estimated value of the articulatory variable based on Eq. (5) while the abscissa represents the actual value of the articulatory variable used in the model in computing the predictor coefficients. These results suggest that each articulatory variable, when varied individually, is determined uniquely from the predictor coefficients. Of course, this is not to suggest that each predictor coefficient has a one-to-one relationship with the articulatory variables of the model. In fact, this is not even necessary. One of the strong points of the method presented here is that, in estimating an articulatory variable, it can combine the contributions of a number of acoustic parameters of speech, which individually may not have monotonic relationships with the articulatory variables, to provide a unique answer.

In the second test, four articulatory variables were varied simultaneously - a condition more representative of the normal speech production process. The weights were determined from a training set consisting of the predictor coefficients for 1000 different vocal-tract configurations distributed uniformly over the entire region of interest in the articulatory space. In this case, the error was found to be quite large with M = 12; however, the error decreased monotonically with increasing values of M. The results for the simultaneous variation of the four articulatory variables, x_c, A_c, A_m, and L, are illustrated for M = 100 in Fig. 3. The error in all the four cases is very small - for the location of the main constriction, rms error is 0.3 cm; for the area of the main constriction, the rms error is 8.8%; for the area of the mouth opening, the rms error is 5.8%; and finally for the length of the vocal tract, the rms error is 0.05 cm.

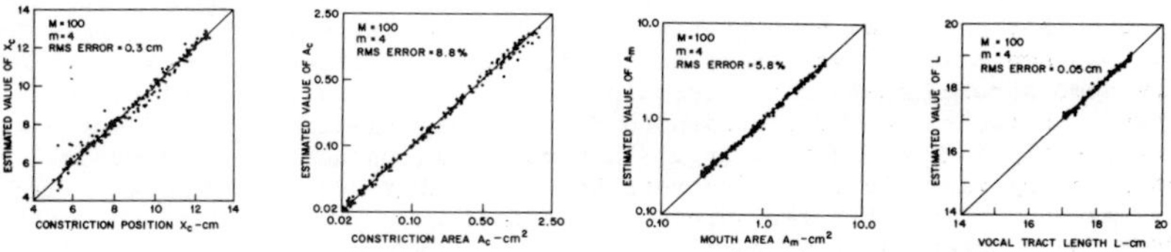

Fig. 3. Comparison between the estimated and the actual values of the articulatory variables. All four articulatory variables were varied simultaneously over their full range. The number of acoustic parameters M was 100.

In another test, an additional constriction at the tongue tip was added to the four previous variables. The number of acoustic variables were increased to 200. Again, error in estimating any one of the five articulatory variables was found to be very small. The result for the location of the tongue-tip constriction is illustrated in Fig. 4. The rms error in predicting the location of the constriction was only 0.18 cm.

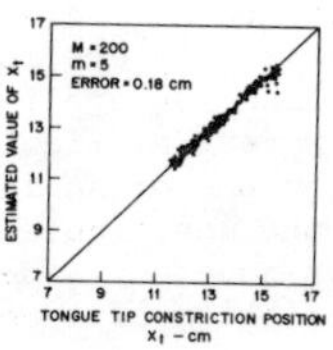

Fig. 4. Comparison between the estimated and actual values of the position of the tongue-tip constriction. Five articulatory variables (see text) were varied simultaneously. The number of acoustic parameters M was 200.

The influence of noise in the acoustic data was also investigated by adding white noise to the speech output of the model. The white noise was added to speech, both in the training and the test sets. No significant differences were observed in the results as compared to the noiseless case for signal-to-noise ratios of approximately 30 dB and above.

These results indicate that, for the model considered in this paper, the articulatory variables can be estimated reasonably accurately from the acoustic data. The method was not found to be sensitive to the choice of any particular acoustic representation of speech provided it was complete. Several different acoustic representations - such as, the predictor coefficients, the spectrum, the cepstrum, the formant frequencies and their bandwidths, the autocorrelation function, or the speech samples themselves - were used with equal success in determining articulatory variables of the model.

Discussion

In this paper, we have presented a method of investigating the relationship between a set of variables using techniques of linear regression. We have demonstrated that, under certain conditions, a nonlinear relationship between variables can be represented as a linear relationship in a space of sufficiently high dimensionality. In particular, we have found that an articulatory variable can be represented reasonably accurately as a linear combination of acoustic variables. This finding is very significant and offers us a potentially attractive method of obtaining articulatory information from the speech signal. What are the possible difficulties in applying this method to real speech? Inherent in the analysis and the results described in this paper is a crucial assumption that we can represent different vocal-tract shapes encountered in speech production by a few articulatory variables. The question - whether such an assumption is true or not - can only be answered by applying the method to a data set obtained directly from the human speech production mechanism. The creation of such a data set requires that we have an independent method of measuring articulatory positions during speech production. Work is in progress to test the method on real speech for various degrees of velar opening. The movement of the velum has been selected for the initial checking because the necessary training set is relatively easy to obtain for the velar opening.

The results, presented in this paper, can be used in many practical applications. The requirement of a training set does pose some problems. However, one needs a relatively small number of samples in the training set which could be generated by using x-ray techniques. On the other hand, for applications, such as control of an articulatory model, it may be sufficient to generate the training set from the articulatory model itself. An articulatory description of speech events may also be more appropriate for applications, such as automatic speech recognition. It is usually very difficult, at the acoustic level, to take advantage of the coarticulation phenomena in the recognition process. In fact, instead of being useful, the coarticulation introduces problems in most automatic speech-recognition schemes. These problems can easily be avoided by using an articulatory description of speech.

Towards determining articulator positions from the speech signals

References

[1] K. L. Moll, "Cineflurographic techniques in speech research," J. Speech Hearing Res. vol. 3, p. 277, 1960.

[2] O. Fujimura, H. Ishida, and S. Kiritani, "Computer-controlled dynamic cineradiography," Annual Bulletin of the Research Institute of Logopedics and Phoniatrics, Univ. of Tokyo, pp. 6-10, 1968.

[3] M. Sawashima and T. Ushijima, "Use of the fiberscope in speech research," Annual Bulletin of the Research Institute of Logopedics and Phoniatrics, Univ. of Tokyo, pp. 25-34, 1971.

[4] B. S. Atal, "Determination of the vocal-tract shape directly from the speech wave," J. Acoust. Soc. Amer. vol. 47(A), p. 65, 1970.

[5] H. Wakita, "Direct estimation of the vocal tract shape by inverse filtering of acoustic speech waveforms," IEEE Trans. Audio and Electroacoustics, Vol. AU-21, pp. 417-427, 1973.

[6] B. S. Atal and J. E. Hartman, "Determination of articulatory parameters from the speech signal," J. Acoust. Soc. Amer. vol. 52(A), p. 182, 1972.

[7] M. R. Schroeder, "Determination of the geometry of the human vocal tract by acoustic measurements," J. Acoust. Soc. Amer. vol. 41, pp. 1002-1010, 1967.

[8] P. Mermelstein, "Determination of the vocal-tract shape from measured formant frequencies," J. Acoust. Soc. Amer. vol. 41, pp. 1283-1294, 1967.

[9] M. M. Sondhi and B. Gopinath, "Determination of vocal-tract shape from impulse response at the lips," J. Acoust. Soc. Amer. vol. 49, pp. 1867-1873, 1971.

[10] G. Fant, Acoustic theory of speech production, The Hague: Mouton, 1970.

[11] J. L. Flanagan, Speech analysis synthesis and perception, New York: Springer-Verlag, 1972.

[12] R. E. D. Bishop, G. M. L. Gladwell, and S. Michaelson, The matrix analysis of vibration, London: Cambridge University Press, p. 265, 1965.

[13] R. S. Martin, G. Peters, and J. H. Wilkinson, "Symmetric decomposition of a positive-definite matrix," Numer. Math. vol. 7, pp. 362-383, 1965.

[14] Reference 10, pp. 107-109.

[15] Reference 11, pp. 36-37.

[16] B. S. Atal and S. L. Hanauer, "Speech analysis and synthesis by linear prediction of the speech wave," J. Acoust. Soc. Amer. vol. 50, pp. 637-655, 1971.

Speech Communication Seminar
Stockholm. Aug. 1–3, 1974

ESTIMATION OF VOCAL TRACT AREA FUNCTIONS BY ADAPTIVE INVERSE FILTERING METHODS AND IDENTIFICATION OF ARTICULATORY MODEL

T. Nakajima, H. Omura, K. Tanaka and S. Ishizaki,
Electrotechnical Laboratory (ETL), 2-6-1 Nagata-cho, Chiyoda-ku,
Tokyo, Japan

Abstract

New methods have been developed to estimate the vocal tract area functions by natural speech wave analysis. First, it is illustrated that the vocal tract area function can be directly estimated from speech wave analysis without extracting formant frequencies, by model experiment analyzing impulse response waves synthesized by simulating a vocal tract. Secondly, methods of impulse response deconvolution from natural speech waves are illustrated, and some experimental examples on natural speech analysis are shown. Further, a method for extracting articulatory parameters from the estimated area function is illustrated. A simple articulatory model, where a mediun cross section of the tongue body is approximated by a fixed radius circle, is proposed. The position of the tongue body is identified from the estimated relative area function using the optimization technique, minimizing the sum of squared error between the vocal tract area function of the model and that of actually measured data. Estimated area functions (in relative values) are thus converted to absolute values by introducing the articulatory model, so information on movements of the jaw and the glottis are extracted, as well as movement of the tongue body.

1. Introduction

Realizing that automatic recognition of the continuous speech of any given person implies first the extraction of only phonemic sound information from the 50,000-100,000 bits per second speech waves and then grouping the information into categories of less than 6-7 bits (about 40 phonemes). An extremely large compaction of the information is thus encountered. The speech analysis method recently developed on the basis of a linear, auto-regressive model[1,2,3] is highly effective in basic idea, by using a model, both simple and valid, where speech is the aggregation of damped sine waves occurring in resonant systems of the articulating organ. Through this procedure, the speech information can be reduced to 2,000-4,000 bits per second, a compaction by about one figure from the original speech waves. To compact still further the 4,000 bits per second information to 6 bit categories, another one figure reduction is necessary by introducing essential and highly effective speech structure characteristics. In this model representation of the pattern structures, use of the region of articulation levels, rather than that of frequency spectrum, may be advantageous, being more intuitive and better corresponding to the phonetics.

2. Estimation of Vocal Tract Area Functions

2.1 Theories and Model Experiments

If the nasal resonance cavity is disregarded, the acoustic organ can be taken as a single tube from lungs to lips[4)5)]. The part from glottis to lips is "smooth" in the change of the cross sectional area, so there is a slight alteration of the uniform acoustic tube. The semi-infinite no-loss uniform tube below the glottis bears the acoustic loss of the vocal tract. From the standpoint of frequency transmission characteristics in the vocal tract, the following description holds true "Resonant frequencies are distributed almost uniformly over the whole frequency region, so the vocal tract does not generally have any frequency transmission characteristics."

The equivalent circuit for a non-uniform acoustic tube of n+1 sections is then given by Kelly's ladder-type network[6], as shown in Fig. 2-1. The tract, at the lips, is connected to an infinite acoustic tube determined by A_1 and r_o; while, beyond section A_{n+1}, it connects to an infinite acoustic tube of the same area (as this A_{n+1}) which causes an acoustic loss.

According to Itakura[1], the partial autocorrelation coefficient k in vocal wave-form (and also parameter κ obtained by ML estimation in Ref. (3)) can be derived equivalently in the self-control system in Fig. 2-2. Neglecting the loss in the vicinity of the lips ($r_o \to -1$), Fig. 2-1 then converts to Fig. 2-3. By comparison between Fig. 2-2 and 2-3, it is seen that the process of deriving parameter κ is a reversal of that circuit for synthesizing speech with the reflection coefficient r in the vocal tract. In consequence, correspondence should be expected between the partial autocorrelation coefficient directly derived from vocal tract impulse responses and the reflection coefficient in the vocal tract[7].

Experiment with synthestic speech: To ascertain the correspondence between partial autocorrelation coefficient and vocal tract reflection coefficient, synthetic speech in the vocal tract with a given area function is analyzed and both the coefficients compared. This experiment is shown sequentially in Fig. 2-4. To be equivalent acoustically to the human vocal tract in its smoothness, it is sufficient for the length of each section to be about 1 cm in the non-uniform acoustic tube. If, in Fig. 2-2 or 2-3, the time delay, the length of each section and the sound velocity are represented by D(sec), ℓ(cm) and c(cm/sec), respectively,

$$D = \frac{2\ell}{c} \qquad (2\text{-}1)\ .$$

When sampling frequency is f(Hz), D=1/f. If sampling frequency is 15 kHz and c=34,000 cm/sec, then ℓ=1.13 cm. For 16 sections, a vocal tract area up to about 18.08 cm from the lips can be given.

Speech synthesis: Synthetic speech is obtained by the procedure shown in Fig. 2-4. In the experiment, the loss in the vicinity of the lips is represented by r_o and the loss distributed in the vocal tract by the reflection coefficients (r_n, $r_{n-1}\cdots$) near a glottis. The sound source equivalent to the vocal cord wave-form is an impulse train prepared in advance, according to a suitable pitch pattern. The -6 dB/oct equalizer is required to correct the superimposition of radiation impedance effect and vocal-cord spectrum, in this case.

Estimation of vocal tract area function: The synthetic speech wave-form obtained is an impulse response in the vocal tract. The κ-parameter, obtained according to the procedure shown in Fig. 2-5, is r_i (i=1, 2, ..., n) and the vocal tract area from lips to throat is A_i (i=1, 2, ..., n+1). If the area at a position in the vocal tract is given, from the relation

$$A_i = \frac{1 - r_i}{1 + r_i} A_{i+1} \quad , \ (i = n, n-1, \cdots, 2, 1) \qquad (2\text{-}2)$$

the relative area function in vocal tract, A_i, can be obtained. Figure 2-6 shows results of the experiment. It is seen that the given vocal tract shape is reproduced almost perfectly.

By trial runs in the experimental system, a given vocal tract shape, regardless of the shape, can be almost perfectly estimated, unless the sharpness of resonances in the vocal tract is considerably high, compared with actual speech (i.e. when the value of A_{n+1} is extremely small, in comparison with the others). In simulating the human vocal tract, the r_o value to express loss in the vicinity of the lips has been given, which is the radiation into a semi-infinite acoutic tube of an area about 97 times as large as that of the opening of the lips. No effect of this, however, is seen upon the accuracy of estimation of the vocal tract area function.

2.2 Estimation of Vocal Tract Area Function by Adaptive Inverse Filtering Methods

A speech wave-form is produced in the process of the convolution of impulse response wave-forms due to radiation impedance, vocal tract and sound-source characteristics. If, based on certain reasonable criteria, vocal cord and radiation impedance characteristics are thus estimated from the speech wave-form, the vocal-tract impulse response wave-form can then be obtained by treatment in the time region, introducing the inverse filtering method.

The problem now is to determine what models are to be introduced for sound source and radiation characteristics. It is desirable for the sound source model to be applicable for both voiced and unvoiced sound. The vocal-cord wave probably consists of a resonant system with freedom degree 2[8]. The frequency characteristic, including sound wave, may be smooth without sharp resonance. It can thus be represented in a low-order, such as two or three, critical-damping digital filter (constrained auto-regressive models). The gross frequency transmission characteristics of a vocal tract is assumed to be flat, so the gross speech spectrum gradient is considered to be based on the glottal wave and radiation characteristics.

Identification of linear models[9] on sound source and radiation characteristics: In the wave-form occurring in secondary-system critical damping driven by white noise, a sample value of the wave-form at time t, x_t, is estimated by a linear combination of the two immediately preceding sample values, i.e. x_{t-1} and x_{t-2}, using the prediction coefficient ε_1: that is,

$$\hat{x}_t = \varepsilon_1 x_{t-1} - \frac{\varepsilon_1^2}{4} x_{t-2}$$

Taking the window length, considered as steady state, to be p times the sample period, and the sum of squared differences between estimated and actual values at time t to be a minimum, the value of ε_1 is determined by the method of least squares. That is,

$$L = \sum_{i=0}^{p-1} (x_{t-i} - \hat{x}_{t-i})^2 = \sum_{i=0}^{p-1} \left(x_{t-i} - \varepsilon_1 x_{t-1-i} + \frac{\varepsilon_1^2}{4} x_{t-2-i} \right)^2$$

The element in the wave-form covariance matrix is

$$C_{jk} = \sum_{i=0}^{p-1} x_{t-j-i} x_{t-k-i}$$

By transformation of $\partial L/\partial \varepsilon_1 = 0$, the cubic algebraical equation is obtained.

$$C_{22}\varepsilon_1^3 - 6C_{21}\varepsilon_1^2 + (4C_{02} + 8C_{11})\varepsilon_1 - 8C_{01} = 0 \qquad (2\text{-}3)$$

ε_1 is given as the real root, satisfying $|\varepsilon_1| < 2$ in this equation.

Similarly to the case of the 2nd order system, in the wave-form occurring in 3rd order critical damping system driven by white noise, a sample value at time t is expressed by linear joining of the immediately preceeding three sample values.

$$\hat{x}_t = \varepsilon_2 x_{t-1} - \frac{1}{3}\varepsilon_2^2 x_{t-2} + \frac{1}{27}\varepsilon_2^3 x_{t-3}$$

where the ε_2 is then given as the real root satisfying $|\varepsilon_2| < 3$ in solution of the following algebraical equation of 5 degrees.

$$C_{33}\varepsilon_2^5 - 15C_{23}\varepsilon_2^4 + (54C_{22} + 36C_{13})\varepsilon_2^3 - (243C_{12} + 27C_{03})\varepsilon_2^2 + (243C_{11} + 162C_{02})\varepsilon_2 - 243C_{01} = 0 \quad (2\text{-}4)$$

The 2nd order critical damping system can represent the smooth slope of overall frequency characteristics, while the 3rd order critical damping system gives further correction of the same kind of frequency characteristics. The process of inverse filtering thus becomes as follows. Correction of the overall frequency slope is first made by 2nd order-system, critical damping inverse filtering. For this corrected wave-form, a covariance matrix (C_{jk}) is then obtained. Then, by the 3rd order-system, a correction is made of the midway bend in frequency characteristics of given speech sounds. Block diagrams for adaptive inverse filters of sound source and radiation characteristic are depicted in Fig. 2-7(a)(b). When 15 kHz sampling frequency is chosen, the simplified 2nd order system is experimentally ensured to be available for the application to a wide variety of speakers' utterances, including nasalized sounds,; it corrects the gross frequency-spectrum bend near 3.75 kHz $(\varepsilon_3 = C_{02}/C_{22})$

Experiments: In analyzing natural speech, the sampling frequency was settled upon as 15 kHz. Then, the length of a section is about 1.1 cm, from Eq.(2-1). The vocal tract length obtained is up to 20 sections, to represent the vocal tract of an adult man. In this way, the vocal tract area function 22 cm inward from the lips can be expressed. The window length and the frame interval, in analysis, then become 20 msec rectangular and 10 msec, respectively, in common with the adaptive inverse filtering and vocal-tract parameter derivation processes. Speech is input from an electret-condenser microphone and the wave-form through a 60-7500 Hz band pass filter is sampled at 15 kHz. The cubic and the 5 degree algebraic equation can be easily solved by numerical calculation (the Newton-Raphson method). The results of analysis of a continuous vowel from an adult man are shown in Fig. 2-8. In the figure, the vocal tract pattern fits the curve of Chebyshev's polynominal of the original pattern, obtained from the reflection coefficient. Fitting is made by the method of least squares in the logarithm region for vocal tract area function, and further this is done to raise the accuracy of position and quantity, in the constriction of a vocal tract, and, further, to keep the area function away from a negative region. This process assures more complete separation of vocal tract characteristics from a speech wave based on the assumption that vocal tract area function is smooth along the longitudinal direction. Examination of the vocal-tract frequency transmission characteristic before and after the fitting shows that the polynomial, for a vowel, is sufficient by up to the 9th term.

Numerals at the left are frame numbers at 10 msec intervals, lips on the left-hand side and throat on the right-hand side. Area values are normalized at maximum. Each section is 11 mm long.

3. Identification of an Articulatory Model Based on Estimation of Vocal-Tract Area Function

3.1 Articulatory model and its identification

The vocal tract pattern, obtained by analysis of natural speech, carries major information on the phoneme among the various kinds of speech information. This pattern is applied for the speech recognition by pattern matching methods. On the other hand extraction of some articulatory parameters, such as lips, tongue etc. from this pattern, is available for solving the co-articulation problem. In the latter case, a certain articulatory model should be introduced, in principle, in order to extract articulatory parameters from the vocal tract area function. It is appropriate that the articulatory model describes the essential properties necessary and sufficient to describe the phonemic information and, at the same time, has a simple structure, with the view of performing identification of a model by using the estimated value of the vocal tract area function. From these viewpoints, Fujimura's cylindrical model[4)] was adopted as the first approximation. This model is for vowels, in which the tongue is approximated by a cylinder of fixed radius, and is considered to change its position in the oral cavity. But there is a possibility of it being developed by simple improvements into a model effective for consonants[10)]. As shown in the cross-sectional view in Fig. 3-1, the present model is constituted in such a way that the palate is represented by the upper half of a circle whose radius is R, and the tongue by a circle whose radius is r. Point A(a,b) on the upper part of the glottis is a fixed point in a voiced sound, but the model also works for a voiceless sound by shifting the a (x-coordinate of A) in accord with an estimated cross-sectional value at the glottis.

The transformation for the vocal tract area function to the median cross-sectional area function has been given by a definite power (2/3 power), irrespective of place.

In case the articulatory point is back from the center, that is, $x \leqq 0$, the front-wall of the pharynx is represented by a segment $\overline{AB}$ connecting point A(a,b) and point B, while, in case the articulatory point is to the front ($x>0$), the front-wall of the pharynx is shifted backward ($\overline{AB'}$) a little, corresponding to the nonlinear characteristic shown in Fig. 3-2. However, the shifting degree of the front-wall from segment $\overline{AB}$ to $\overline{AB'}$ is varied according to the information (value of a) concerning the glottis in vowels and, in case of consonants, the degree becomes less.

The median cross sections at the palate part and the pharynx part of the articulatory model are given by the following equations, respectively, by taking the coordinates (x,y) of the center of the tongue as unknown variables in Fig. 3-1.

$$f_i(x,y)=R-\sin(i\theta)\cdot y+\cos(i\theta)\cdot x-\sqrt{r^2-x^2\sin^2(i\theta)-2\sin(i\theta)\cos(i\theta)xy-\cos^2(i\theta)\cdot y^2}\ ,\quad (i=1,2,\cdots m) \qquad (3\text{-}1)$$

$$f_0(x,y)=R+x+\sqrt{r^2-y^2}-F(x)\ ,\qquad (F(x)=\overline{BB'}\ \text{in Fig. 3-2}) \qquad (3\text{-}2)$$

$$g_j(x,y)=R-\left(1+\frac{jl}{b}\right)\left(a-x+\sqrt{r^2-y^2}+F(x)\right)+a\ ,\quad (j=1,2,\cdots n) \qquad (3\text{-}3)$$

The model identification is carried out without using the values of a certain number of sections of the lip part, among the actual vocal tract area functions. Unknown variables x,y and α are determined so as to minimize the sum of square errors between the area function in the model and the relative cross sectional value multiplied by the unknown multiplier αu_i, $(i=1,2,\ldots.,m+n+1)$. Namely,

$$\min_{x,y,\alpha} L(x,y,\alpha)=\min_{x,y,\alpha}\left[\sum_{i=0}^{m}\left\{f_i(x,y)-\alpha u_{i+n}\right\}^2+\sum_{j=1}^{n}\left\{g_j(x,y)-\alpha u_j\right\}^2\right] \qquad (3\text{-}4)$$

Values x, y, α are given by the solution of simulataneous equations with respect to unknown variables x, y and α;

$$\frac{\partial L(x,y,\alpha)}{\partial x}=0 \quad (3\text{-}5),\qquad \frac{\partial L(x,y,\alpha)}{\partial y}=0 \quad (3\text{-}6),\qquad \frac{\partial L(x,y,\alpha)}{\partial \alpha}=0 \quad (3\text{-}7)$$

Further, the optimization procedure will be reduced to that shown in Fig. 3-3 eventually, since an arbitrary set of x,y gives a unique solution satisfying Eq. (3-7).

3.2 Experiments

The constants of the articulatory model were determined by trial experiments using the data (same as shown in Refs.(12)(13)) of continuous vowels/i, e,a,o,u/ by a man's utterance. First, the glottis position was estimated from the obtained vocal tract area function, then the identification of the articulatory model was performed by data on 16 section (1 section is about 1.1 cm) from the glottis to the palate. The constants were determined as R=4.0(cm) and r=2.7(cm) by varying the constants of the model in various ways and, by judging their fitting degree with the data.

The glottis opening is given by the value of point A(a,b) in the articulatory model. Normal action of the model was ascertained by taking A(a,b)=(-3.6,-4.5) according to experiment for a voiced sound. However, for a voiceless sound, it is necessary to open the glottis wider. Assuming the value at maximum opening in voiceless sounds as A(-2.5,-4.5), the interval value between them is given continuously. The value at the glottis of an estimated vocal tract area function is used for this control. Concerning the initial value of (x,y), it was also found that both a method of starting from (0,0) and a method of starting from the immediately preceding frame value being out convergence in continuous vowels. However, in case of starting from the immediately preceding frame value, no action occurred in the transition from the voiceless sound to the back vowels. The number of iterations required for convergence was about 7 times on an average, when the accuracy in convergence was ε_2=0.2mm and the width of the initial step was 3mm.

The experimental results are shown in Fig. 3-4 and Fig. 3-5 concerning the continuous vowels /i,e,a,o,u/. Figure 3-4 shows the confirmable relation between the model and the estimated median vocal tract cross sectional area function in typical frames of 5 Japanese vowels. From these figures, it is clear that vowel sounds are represented by this articulatory model. The relative vocal tract area function is converted to an absolute one by the simultanious estimation of optimum multiple value α. Therefore, the movements of cross section at the lips and glottis show the movements of lips and glottis, respectively.

In the articulatory model proposed here, the tongue is represented by a circle, so that the jaw movement is not directly extracted. The jaw movement is considered to be important in the development of a dynamic articulatory model, so that it was attempted to estimate the approximate jaw movement from the estimated (x,y) and the opening of the lips[13].

Results of identification experiments of the articulatory model are shown in Fig. 3-5 for continuous vowels /i,e,a,o,u/ of a male speaker. In these figures, (a) - (e), show movements of articulatory parameters explained in Fig. 3-1, respectively.

4. Conclusion

(1) In analysis of vowels from four adult men, four adult women and children (4 and 5 years old), very reasonable vocal tract shapes could be obtained. /b/,/d/ and /g/ sounds are also separable distinctly as changes in the articulatory points.

(2) The sound source wave form obtained helps to differentiate between voiced sound, plossive and silent, in perception of speech and carries the prosodic features.

(3) These speech analysis processes are all included in the adaptive digital filter, so it will be possible to process them in real time with pertinent hardware.

(4) In application to speech recognition, the vocal tract pattern can be used in either pattern matching or feature extraction approach. Concerning the feature extraction, a method for extraction of articulatory parameters by the identification of an articulatory model was proposed.

(5) According to experiments on continuous vowels, most stable results are obtained concerning the articulatory point, opening of lips and the state of the glottis. Compared with these parameters, the smoothness of movements of the tongue in the upward and downward directions is somewhat inferior. There remain some points to be improved in the transformation from these parameters to jaw movements. Treatment considering dynamic characteristic of the jaw would be required to solve this problem, as well as model improvement in static state.
(6) In order to extend the model to the voiceless sound (no-sound), control was performed for the glottis state and the pharynx front-wall in accord with the value of the estimated vocal tract area function. According to the experiments, the opening and closing of the glottal part can be extracted quite definitely, so that the parameter can be effectively utilized for the judgement of the voiced or voiceless sound, as well as an application to pitch extraction in the future.
(7) Owing to the introduction of the articulatory model, each of the extracted parameters have already been normalized quite effectively. Each parameter will be more easily treated by removing various noises by the application of an optimum estimation method using a dynamic articulatory model. The parameters are closely related to the distinctive features in phonemics, so that each articulatory parameter would be connected to the phonemes through the intermediary of distinctive features.

Acknowledgement

The authors wish to express their sincere thanks to Mr.K.Fuchi, Chief of Speech Processing Section, Information Science Division, for his incessant strong encouragment in this study, and to Dr.H.Nishino, Head of Information Science Division, for giving the opportunity to present the paper to the SCS-74.

References

1)F.Itakura, S.Saito: Digital Filtering Technique for Speech Analysis and Synthesis, Proc. 7th ICA 25Cl (1971)
2)B.S.Atal,et al: Speech Analysis and Synthesis by Linear Prediction of the Speech Wave, JASA Vol. 50, No.2 (Part 2) (1971)
3)E.Matsui, T.Nakajima, et al: Speech Analysis by Kalman Filter Theory, Bulletin of the Electrotech. Lab. Vol.36, No.3 (1972)
4)J.Oizumi, O.Fujimura,et al: The Science of Phonetics, Univ. of Tokyo Press
5)G.Fant: Acoustic Theory of Speech Production, Mouton & Co. (1960)
6)J.L.Kelly,et al: Speech Synthesis,Proc.Speech Comm.Semi.in Stockholm(1962)
7)H.Wakita: Estimation of Vocal Tract Shape by Optimal Inverse Filtering and Acoustic Articulatory Conversion Methods,SCKL Mono.No.9(July 1972)
8)K.Ishizaka: What Makes the Vocal Cords Vibrate, Proc. 6th ICA B-1-3 (1968)
9)G.Box,M.Jenkins: Time Series Analysis, Holden-Day (1969)
10)C.Coker, O.Fujimura: Model for Specification of the Vocal-Tract Area Function, JASA, 50, p637~655 (1971)
This paper is based on the following papers.
11)T.Nakajima,et al: Estimation of Vocal Tract Area Function by Adaptive Inverse Filtering Methods, Proc. of Tech. Committee on Speech, A.S. of Japan, S-72-21, Feb. 1973
12)T.Nakajima,et al: Estimation of Vocal Tract Area Functions by Adaptive Inverse Filtering Methods, Bul. Electrotech. Lab., Vol.37,No.4 (1973)
13)T.Nakajima,et al: On the Identification of Articulatory Model based on the Estimation of Vocal-Tract Area Function, Proc. of Tech. Committee on Speech, A.S. of Japan, S-73-30, Jan. 1974.

Estimation of Vocal Tract Area Functions by Adaptive Inverse Filtering Methods and Identification of Articulatory Model

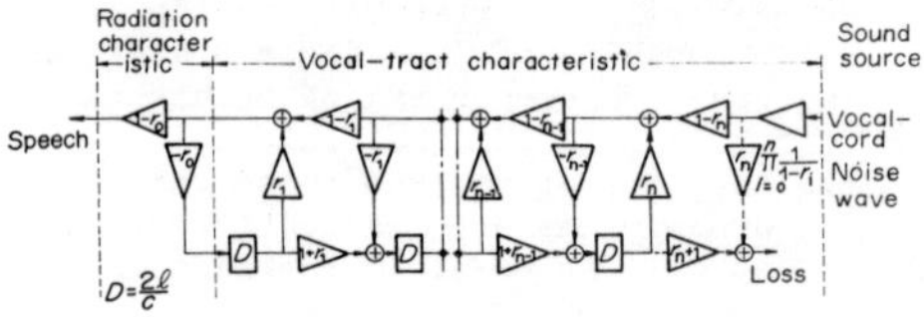

Fig.2-1 Speech production simulation

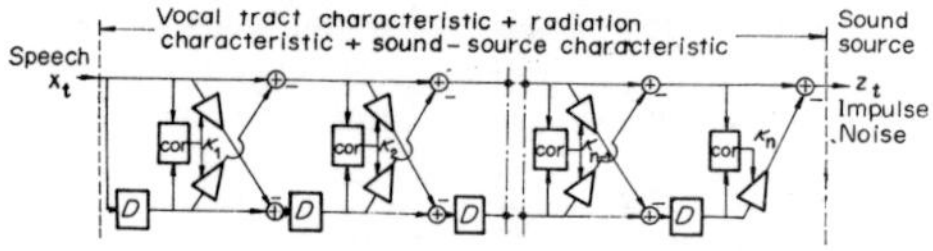

Fig.2-2 Self-control system in the derivation of partial auto-corralation coefficients

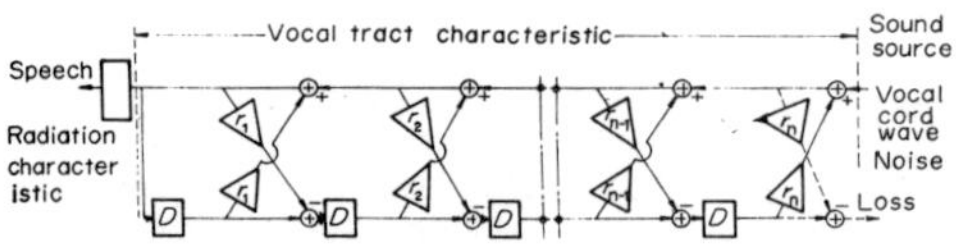

Fig.2-3 Equivalent circuits for Fig.2-1

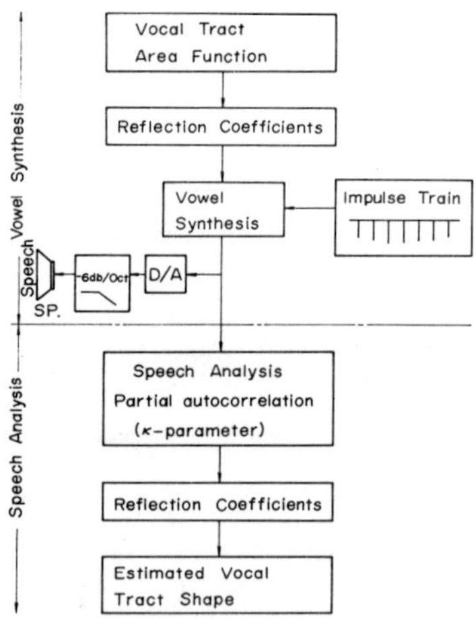

Fig.2-4 Estimation of the vocal tract area function from synthetic speech

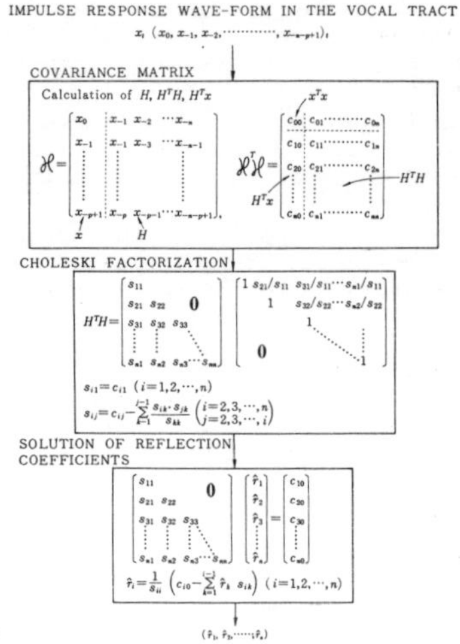

Fig.2-5 Derivation of reflection coefficients from vocal tract impulse response

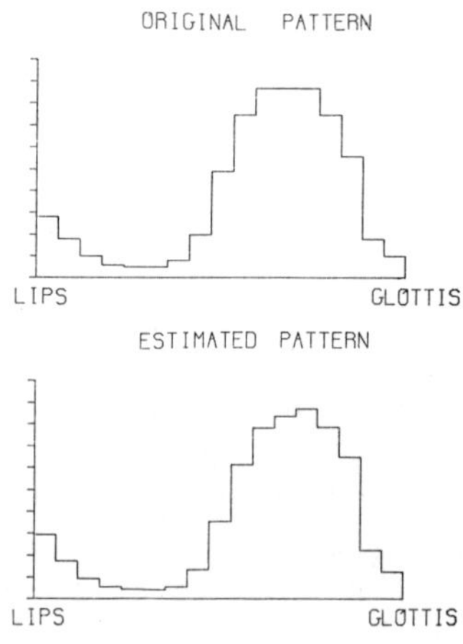

Fig.2-6 Vocal tract shape in speech synthesis and vocal tract shape estimated from synthetic speech. (vowel /i/)

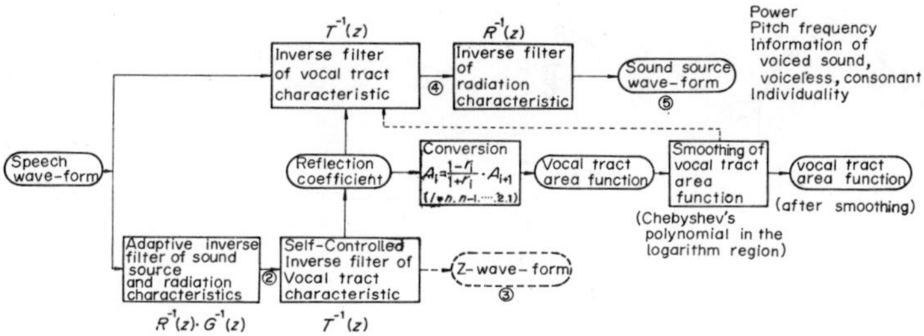

Fig.2-7(a) Derivation of vocal tract area function and sound source

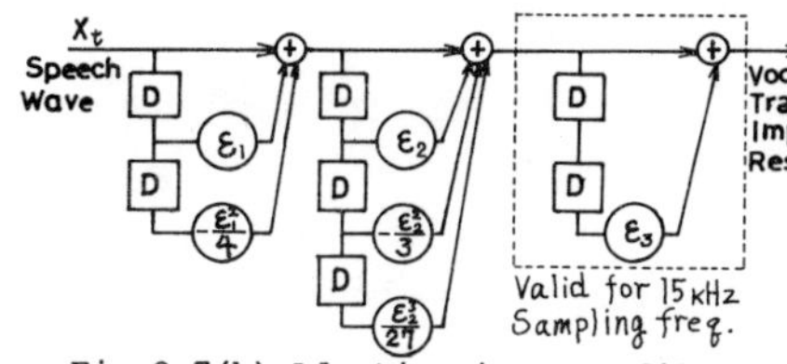

Fig.2-7(b) Adaptive inverse filter shown in figure 2-7(a)

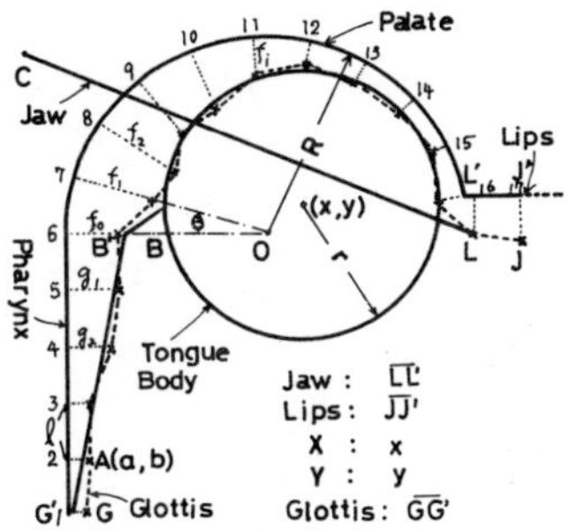

Fig.3-1 Articulatory model

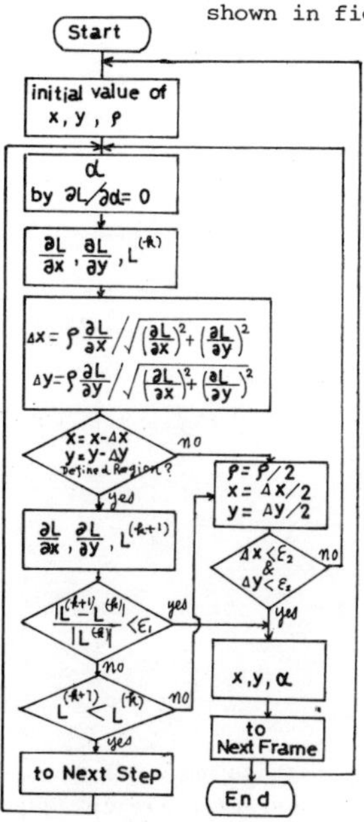

Fig.3-3
Optimization technique for model identification

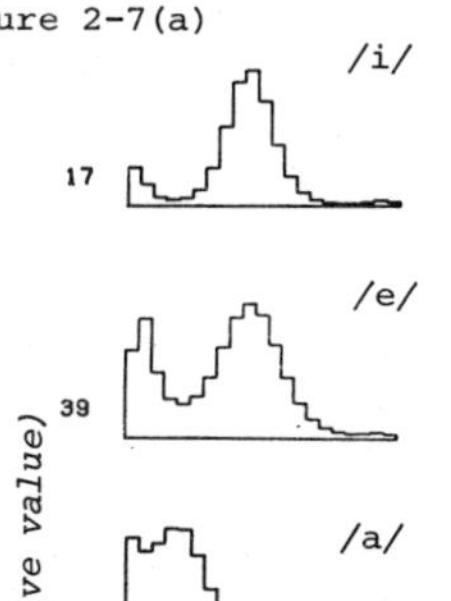

Fig.2-8 Examples of estimated vocal tract area functions (adult man) (1 section: 11 mm)

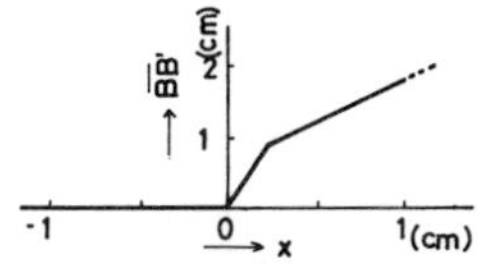

Fig.3-2 Control of pharynx front wall

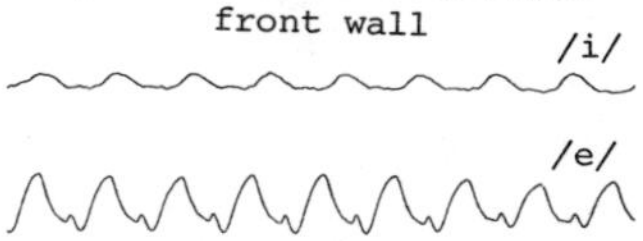

Fig.2-9 Vocal-cord wave which corresponds to the each sound shown in Fig.2-8

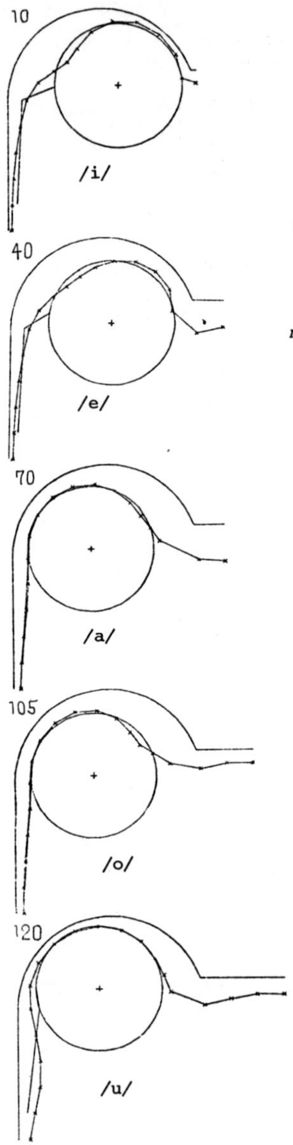

Fig.3-4 Examples of identified models

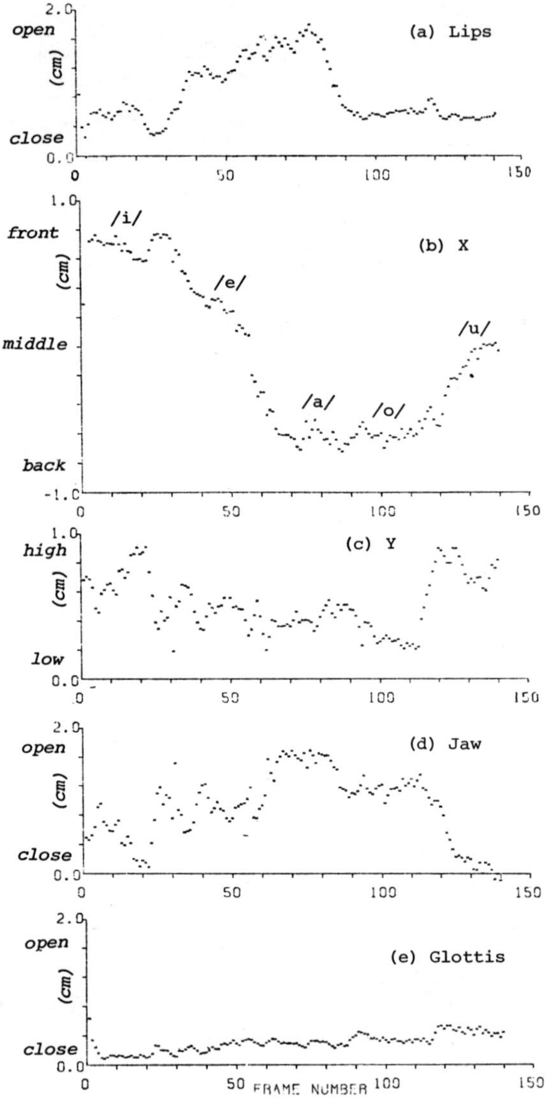

Fig.3-5 Examples of extracted articulatory parameters (/ieaou/)
(window: 20msec,frame: 10msec)

Speech Communication Seminar
Stockholm. Aug. 1–3, 1974

ARTICULATORY TRACKING OF THE ACOUSTIC SPEECH SIGNAL

D. Lloyd Rice, Phonetic Laboratory, Linguistics Department, UCLA, Los Angeles, California 90024

Abstract

This paper describes a research project with the goal of tracking a speech signal with a set of articulatory parameters, representing the controls needed to operate an articulatory speech synthesizer. Several major parts of the system are discussed in detail, with emphasis on problems and proposed alternatives. Some preliminary results are presented, using the system to match isolated vowels of a single speaker. Some speaker dependent characteristics of the system are discussed. The system is expected to be useful for studying the organization of the human vocal tract and may have applications to automatic speech recognition.

Introduction

The Articulatory Tracking system, ARTRAK, is based on ALASS, an automatically controlled speech synthesizer described earlier (1971). Figure 1 shows a basic block diagram of the ALASS system for matching vowel articulations. At the upper left a test vowel is input and a spectrum analysis is performed. The spectrum is stored for later reference by the comparator. Now the tongue control loop is started. Beginning with an arbitrary initial tongue shape, a vowel is produced by the line analog synthesizer. This vowel is then spectrum analyzed and its spectrum is compared with the stored target spectrum. The comparator determines an error value which depends on the degree of difference between the two spectra. This error value is used by the parameter adjustment strategy in determining which way to readjust the synthesizer so as to minimize the difference between the two spectra. The adjustment process iterates until no more improvement can be made in the spectrum match.

A major problem in designing such a system is that of describing a system of constraints on possible tongue movements. In a recent experiment, Harshman et al (1974) analyzed the tongue shapes in the midsagittal plane occurring in the vowels in the words "heed," "hid," "hayed," "head,"

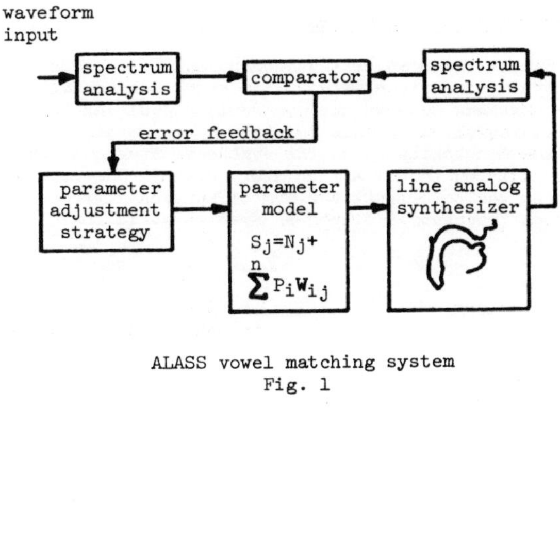

ALASS vowel matching system
Fig. 1

"had," "hod," "hawed," "hoed," "hood," and "who'd" as spoken by 5 American speakers. Using a PARAFAC (1970) factor analysis system, they showed that the movements of the tongue in a vowel can be described in terms of 2 parameters. The 2 tongue shape parameters determined in this experiment have been incorporated in the ARTRAK model. A third parameter has been added which controls only the lip closure and does not affect the shape of the tongue itself.

Tracking continuous speech

The input signal is a speech waveform which is spectrum analyzed via a Markel autocorrelation LPC filter. In the continuous speech tracking system, successive LPC analyses will be performed at fairly small time steps, depending on the difficulties encountered with jumping out of track. This is a trade-off between minimal spectrum analysis vs. efficient operation of the tracking algorithm. The parameter controlled synthesis system produces sample spectra for comparison with the stored target spectrum using a difference-minimization algorithm. The synthesizer parameters are automatically adjusted by the minimization algorithm until the best match is found to the target spectrum and the current synthesis parameter settings are recorded as representative of the input signal at the current time frame. A number of details of this matching process will be discussed at some length shortly.

As the analysis moves on in time along the input signal, a good prediction can be made of the approximate parameter values needed based on the previous settings and their motion. Several variations are possible here, including a second-order filtering process already built in the optimization procedure, which could easily be extended to monitor the tracking process. A more interesting question must be considered here, however. That is that the tracking process must have a fair degree of stiffness, or low pass filtering, to prevent the vowel parameters from being thrown out of lock by rapid changes involved in consonant articulations. The research question here is whether filtering thresholds can be found which will allow the tracker to follow rapid formant transitions while enabling it to hold still or move only slowly during voiceless intervals when little or no formant data is available from the input signal.

Spectrum distance measure

One of the most critical components of the optimization procedure is the spectrum comparison method. An error measure must be taken which captures the distance between the synthetic signal and the stored target spectrum in a meaningful way. This requires, in general, that the error measure decrease monotonically as the synthetic spectrum converges on the target from any position in the articulatory space. The approach used in the original system was to compute the sum of squared differences between synthetic and target frequency-differenced spectra as follows:

$$\varepsilon = \sum_{1}^{N-1}((Tn+1 - Tn)-(Sn+1 - Sn))^2$$

where Tn is the nth point in the target spectrum
Sn is the nth point in the synthetic spectrum.

This was modifed slightly in a later version where the analysis of the synthesizer output was performed at twice the sample rate as that of the natural speech because of aliasing problems in desampling the synthesizer output. The line analog synthesizer must run at a specific sample rate depending on the number of sections used (18 sections in the current model force a basic sample rate of 17776 Hz). However, the basic squared difference error measure was the same as described above. Frequency differencing was done to minimize differences due to overall spectrum slope and maximize formant frequency and bandwidth differences. More recent work has shown that this error measure is inadequate over large distances. That is, if the matching procedure is started in approximately the correct region so that the spectrum is not too different from the desired target, the system is able to make changes in the appropriate direction and correctly match the target. If, on the other hand, the procedure is started with parameter values such that the formant peaks are shifted by more than about 10 times the bandwidth of the peak, this error measure does not decrease properly as the synthetic and target formant frequencies move relative to one another. Other error measures are being considered which will incorporate some direct measure of the distances between formants. This involves, of course, the usual formant tracking problem of determining which peak is which, although there now exist in the literature a number of solutions to this problem which work fairly well based on the smooth spectra of all-pole LPC analysis. Alternatively, a more elaborate search procedure is being considered based on a full spectral range error value for movement on each parameter axis, rather than having to optimize from a single scalar error measure.

Short cut using the Wakita conversion

The present model uses a lengthy computation to determine the frequency spectrum corresponding to a particular set of values of the tongue control parameters. First the parameter weights and values are multiplied and summed across all parameters to obtain deflections from the neutral shape. These deflections are added to the neutral to obtain the sagittal plane cross-dimension values which are converted to area values via an exponential function model. The tube shape thus defined is used in a volume velocity iterative line analog speech synthesizer, driven by a simulated glottal pulse as described below. The acoustic waveform output of the synthesizer is then analysed with a Markel LPC inverse filter to obtain the magnitude spectrum. Wakita (1972) has described a direct transformation from the area function to Markel inverse filter coefficients which could tremendously shorten the computational task. I have not done this yet, until I can explore more fully the characteristics of that model regarding losses at the vocal tract walls. The synthesizer presently uses an area dependent loss model which could not be used with Wakita's transformation. As far as the glottal pulse is concerned, however, the spectrum computed via the Wakita transformation could be corrected by adding to it the log spectrum of the chosen glottal pulse shape. Alternatively, this glottal pulse correction could be subtracted once from the target spectrum which could then be directly compared to the Wakita "tube" spectrum. This possibility will be carefully evaluated because of the large possible saving in computational time.

Glottal pulse model

In the line analog synthesizer model, an attempt is made to produce waveform output with as near as possible natural speech quality. Toward this end, a simulated glottal pulse is used to drive the synthesizer based on a curve found to be most natural in listening experiments by Rosenberg (1971). His glottal pulse curve type "B" was modified by marking a point in time on the falling portion and after this time letting the y value decay exponentially toward zero instead of continuing to zero in a sharp corner as in his model. The decay constant is computed such that there is no discontinuity in the slope at time T_{dx}, the decay onset time (see Figure 2). As the parameter T_{dx} becomes larger, approaching Tfall, the spectrum slope decreases giving relatively more energy at higher frequencies. With the glottal pulse parameters as shown in Figure 2 the glottal volume-velocity spectrum has a roll-off of approximately 13 db per octave.

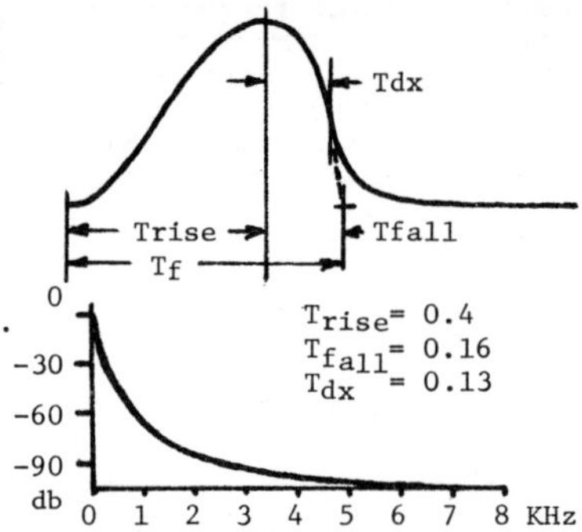

Fig. 2

Some vowel matching results

As an initial test of the PARAFAC derived tongue parameter model, the ALASS tracking system was used to recover the articulatory parameter values needed to match the acoustic signals of several of the vowels of the same set originally used in the PARAFAC analysis. The neutral tract shape used was the mean shape over all vowels for the particular speaker, also as used in the PARAFAC analysis. Figures 3 through 6 illustrate the quite high degree of fit in the mid-sagittal plane for the position of best match in the acoustic domain. This degree of fit is even more interesting, considering that a fairly high error remained in the acoustic domain at the best match position. In one case, F1 was too low by nearly 200 Hz. The discrepancy between a good match in the sagittal plane and a poor match in the acoustic domain can be explained by the fact that the synthesizer contains a fixed mapping of sagittal plane cross-dimension values onto area function values, not tuned to the individual speaker. In fact, such a speaker tuned mapping could now be constructed by relaxing the tongue constraints in the model and finding the actual area function needed to best match the acoustic signal. However, the fact that the tongue did not move to a position of better acoustic match must be explained by the limitation of the constraints imposed by the parameter model. We see a constraint system operating here which imposes fairly tight restrictions on the tongue motion; in none of the four cases tried could the tongue move away to compensate for a systematic error in another part of the system. On the other hand, if the cross-dimension to area function conversion were correct for that speaker, we should expect to see the tongue move to just those positions necessary to attain the target vowels.

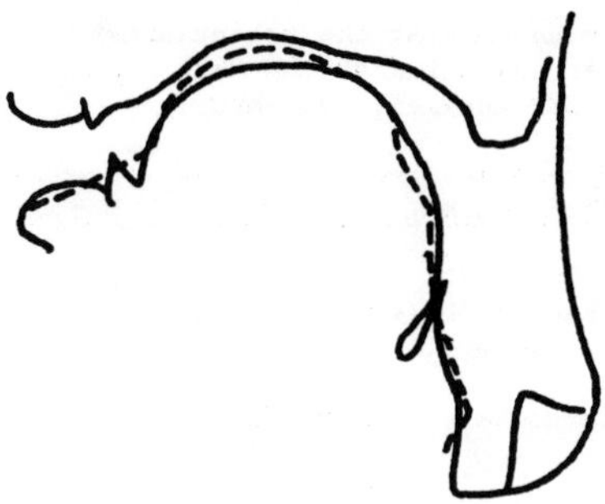

Fig. 3 "heed"

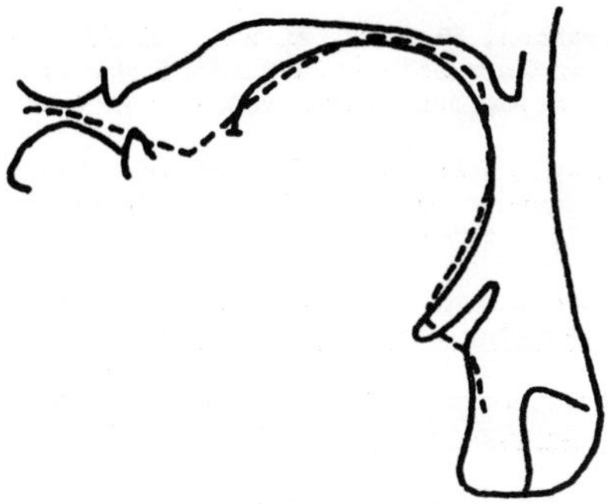

Fig. 4 "who'd"

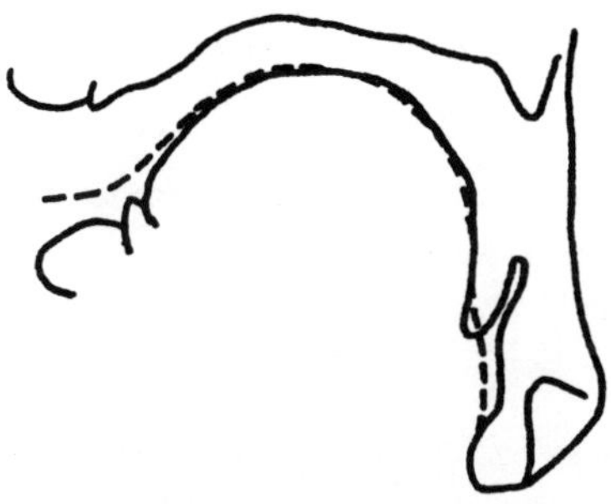

Fig. 5 "head"

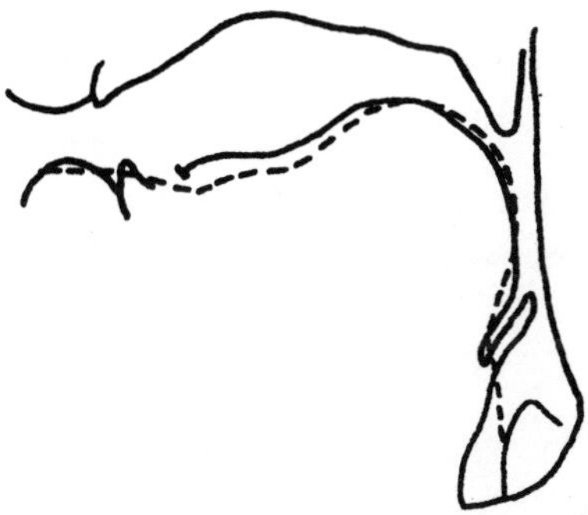

Fig. 6 "hawed"

Solid lines: Tracings from x-rays
Dotted lines: Tongue outline at best ALASS match position

Harshman, Richard. (1970) PARAFAC. Working Papers in Phonetics 16. UCLA. December.

Harshman, Richard, et al. (1973) Factors underlying the articulatory and acoustic structure of vowels. Paper presented at the 86th Meeting of the Acoustical Society of America. Los Angeles. November.

Markel, John, D. (1971) Formant trajectory estimation from a linear least-squares inverse filter formulation. Speech Comm. Research Labs. Monograph 7, October.

Rice, Lloyd. (1971a) A new line analog speech synthesizer for the PDP-12. Working Papers in Phonetics 17. UCLA. January.

Rice, Lloyd. (1971b) Analysis of tongue parameters for vowels. Working Papers in Phonetics 19. UCLA. June.

Rosenberg, Aaron (1971) Effect of glottal pulse shape on the quality of natural vowels. Journ. of the Acoust. Soc. of America. Vol. 49, No.2, 583-590.

Wakita, Hisashi (1972) Estimation of the vocal tract shape by optimal inverse filtering and acoustic/articulatory conversion methods. Speech Comm. Research Labs. Monograph 9. July.

Speech Communication Seminar
Stockholm. Aug. 1–3, 1974

RECENT ADVANCES IN PREDICTIVE CODING - APPLICATIONS TO SPEECH SYNTHESIS

B. S. Atal, Bell Laboratories, Murray Hill, N.J. 07974 U.S.A.
M. R. Schroeder, Drittes Physikalisches Institut, University of Goettingen, F. R. Germany

Abstract

The linear prediction method is known to provide an accurate and efficient description of speech signals and produces synthetic speech of high quality - in spite of several idealizations that underlie the method. For example, spectral zeros are approximated by poles in the linear prediction method. Such an approximation can introduce errors in the reconstructed speech signal. Similarly, for high-pitched voices, the predictor coefficients do not represent accurately the information regarding the spectral envelope of the speech signal. In this paper, these errors are investigated by analyzing synthetic speech of known characteristics. Furthermore, we discuss methods for analysis and synthesis of speech which take account of the spectral zeros and the effects of voice periodicity.

Introduction

Since its introduction, the technique of linear prediction [1-4] has found widespread use for providing an efficient representation of speech signals [5-7]. In general, speech synthesized by the linear prediction method is of high quality and suffers very little degradation in the analysis-synthesis process. Yet, the synthetic speech is not indistinguishable from the natural and, in close listening, a slight difference between the two can be heard. Why? There are several reasons directly related to the various idealizations inherent in the linear prediction model of speech production. In this paper, we will attempt to discuss two important limitations of the linear prediction analysis and describe modifications of the method for avoiding such problems.

In the linear prediction method, the filtering properties of the vocal tract, the radiation at the mouth opening, and the glottal wave are represented by an all-pole filter, typically with 12 poles at a sampling frequency of 10 kHz. The all-pole model of the vocal tract is quite accurate for vowel and vowel-like sounds. However, the model does not provide an accurate representation of the speech signal when there are additional zeros in the transfer function of the vocal tract. These zeros can arise if the nasal tract is coupled to the main vocal tract through the velar opening - as is the case for nasal consonants and nasalized vowels - or if the source of excitation is not at the glottis but is in the interior of the vocal tract. In addition, the zeros can be introduced by the transmission characteristics of the environment where the recordings are made.

The all-pole filter in the linear prediction method represents the properties of the spectral envelope of the speech signal. As is well known, the voiced-speech waveform is nearly periodic. The waveform, consequently, represents the spectral information accurately only at the harmonics. Often, the harmonic spacing is quite large to provide an adequate sampling of the spectral envelope. Under such circumstances, the predictor coefficients do not provide an accurate representation of the spectral envelope for high-pitched voices.

We present, in this paper, a speech analysis method for estimating both poles and zeros of the vocal-tract transfer function. By taking account of the zeros of the transfer function, we hope to eliminate one of the limitations of the linear prediction method in analyzing nasalized sounds. We will also present a method of reducing the interaction between the period length of voiced speech and the predictor coefficients.

Linear Prediction with Spectral Zeros

A spectral zero, unless it is cancelled by a closely-located pole, produces two separate effects in the spectrum, namely, a dip in the spectrum in the neighborhood of the frequency of the zero ("anti-resonance frequency") and an asymptotic 12-dB/octave rise in the spectrum beyond the anti-resonance frequency. In principle, the spectral properties of a zero can be approximated with arbitrary precision by additional poles in the all-pole model [4]. Such an approximation, however, is likely to be inefficient except for highly-damped zeros. Furthermore, it is difficult to produce a local dip in the spectrum by using additional poles without introducing ripples at other frequencies in the spectrum.

In general, we find that the 12-dB/octave rise in the spectrum can be approximated satisfactorily by additional poles. However, significant errors are often introduced in the frequency region in the vicinity of the zero. Two examples, typical of the all-pole approximation of spectrum with a single complex zero at 800 Hz, are shown in Fig. 1.

In linear prediction based on the all-pole model, every speech sample is predicted as a linear combination of the previous p samples of the signal. Let us assume now that there are q zeros in the transfer function in addition to p poles. For a discrete linear filter with p poles and q zeros, the nth sample of its output is expressed as

$$s_n = \sum_{k=1}^{p} a_k s_{n-k} + \sum_{k=0}^{q} b_k \delta_{n-k}, \tag{1}$$

where δ_n is the nth sample of the excitation at the input of the linear filter, the coefficients a_k represent the contribution of the poles, and the coefficients b_k represent the additional contribution of the q zeros. The predicted value of the nth speech sample is then given by

$$\hat{s}_n = \sum_{k=1}^{p} a_k s_{n-k} + \sum_{k=1}^{q} b_k (s_{n-k} - \hat{s}_{n-k}), \tag{2}$$

Thus, the predicted value of a speech sample is represented as a sum of the linear combination of both the past p speech samples and past q prediction-error samples. For comparison, in the all-pole model, the predicted value is equal to the linear combination of only the past p speech samples. The unknown coefficients $a_1,......,a_p;b_1,......,b_q$, of Eq. 2 are found by minimizing the mean-squared prediction prediction error defined as

$$E = \langle (s_n - \hat{s}_n)^2 \rangle, \tag{3}$$

where $\langle\ \rangle$ indicates averaging over the analysis interval. It is to be noted that the mean-squared prediction error is a quadratic function of the unknowns a_k, $k=1,2,...,p$; it is, however, not a quadratic function of the unknowns b_k, $k=1,2,...,q$. Therefore, on setting the various partial derivatives of E with respect to unknown parameters of the error to zero, one obtains a set of simultaneous *nonlinear* equations which must be solved by the use of iterative techniques. The solution of such nonlinear equations in our case is considerably simplified since the coefficients a_k, representing the poles, can be estimated without any knowledge of the coefficients b_k representing the zeros. To prove this result, we multiply both sides of Eq. 1 by s_{n-r}, and perform an average over the index n. We then obtain

$$\langle s_n s_{n-r} \rangle = \sum_{k=1}^{p} a_k \langle s_{n-k} s_{n-r} \rangle + \sum_{k=0}^{q} b_k \langle \delta_{n-k} s_{n-r} \rangle, \tag{4}$$

Since the linear filter is causal (that is, its output is zero before the application of the input), it can be seen that the correlations $\langle \delta_{n-k} s_{n-r} \rangle$ on the right side of Eq. 4 are zero for $r > q$. The set of equations represented in Eq. 4 are linear in p unknowns $a_1,......,a_p$ and can be solved in a straight forward manner. We, thus, have to solve only q nonlinear equations by iterative methods.

Influence of Pitch on the Predictor Coefficients

Voiced speech is periodic and its spectral envelope is defined accurately only at the harmonics of the fundamental frequency. It is then natural to ask if the periodicity of voiced speech has any significant influence on the predictor coefficients. In order to gain a better understanding of such interactions, let us review very briefly the linear prediction method. The all-pole model of linear prediction implies that the nth speech sample can be expressed as

$$s_n = \sum_{k=1}^{p} a_k s_{n-k} + \delta_n, \tag{5}$$

where $a_1, \ldots\ldots, a_p$ are the p predictor coefficients and δ_n is the nth sample of the excitation. The predictor coefficients are obtained by solving a set of linear equations

$$\langle s_n s_{n-i} \rangle = \sum_{k=1}^{p} a_k \langle s_{n-k} s_{n-i} \rangle, \quad i=1,\ldots\ldots,p, \tag{6}$$

for the p unknowns $a_1, \ldots\ldots, a_p$.

On comparing Eqs. 5 and 6, it is easy to see that Eq. 6 will provide a correct solution only if the correlations

$$c_i = \langle \delta_n s_{n-i} \rangle, \quad i=1,\ldots\ldots,p, \tag{7}$$

are zero. The output s_n of the filter can also be expressed as a convolution of the input with the impulse response of the all-pole filter. We can then rewrite Eq. 7 as

$$c_i = \sum_{k=0}^{\infty} h_k \langle \delta_{n-k} s_{n-i} \rangle, \quad i=1,\ldots\ldots,p, \tag{8}$$

where h_k is the kth sample of the impulse response of the all-pole filter. It is obvious from Eq. 8 that, for the solution to be correct, the samples δ_n of the input or, equivalently, of the prediction error be uncorrelated for all delays at which $h_k \neq 0$. However, for voiced speech, the prediction error is periodic and exhibits strong correlation at delays equal to a pitch period and its multiples. Such correlations can introduce errors in the predictor coefficients.

In order to estimate the magnitude of such errors, we synthesized signals consisting of a single formant at different pitch frequencies and analyzed them by the linear prediction method using one complete pitch period for minimizing the prediction error. The frequency and bandwidth of the formant were calculated from the predictor coefficients. The results for the formant frequency are shown in Fig. 2 for three different pitch frequencies. In the figure, F_0 represents the pitch, the abscissa represents the formant frequency used in the synthesis, and the ordinate represents the estimated formant frequency based on the linear prediction analysis. The maximum errors are 11, 30, and 67 Hz at pitch frequencies of 100, 200, and 400 Hz, respectively. Except at $F_0 = 100$ Hz, these errors are above the reported difference limen [8] of 3 to 5% for the formant frequency. The results for the formant bandwidth are shown in Fig. 3. A bandwidth of 50 Hz was used in the synthesis. The bandwidth errors are considerably larger; maximum errors at the three pitch frequencies are 25, 92, and 250 Hz, respectively. Although the difference limens for the formant bandwidths are not known accurately, it appears that the bandwidth errors at $F_0 = 200$ and 400 Hz may be perceptible. Of course, the errors reported here are maximum errors for the worst possible location of the formant frequency in relation to the harmonics. In real speech, these errors will vary considerably depending upon the values of the formant frequency, its bandwidth, and the pitch. They may be perceptually significant particularly for some female and children's voices. Similar results were also obtained for synthetic signals consisting of two or more formants. A typical result, comparing the estimated spectra derived from the predictor coefficients with the actual harmonic spectrum used in the synthesis, is shown in Fig. 4 for $F_0 = 100$ and 200 Hz, respectively. The harmonic spectrum used in the synthesis is shown by symbols '+' at 100 Hz intervals.

The errors due to voice periodicity can be completely avoided if the predictor memory is made large enough to include at least one period of the signal. As a practical matter, this is not a desirable procedure unless the sampling frequency of the signal can be reduced so as to require only a few predictor coefficients. Fortunately, this is possible since the errors due to voice periodicity are perceptually significant only in the first formant region and only when the pitch period is relatively small. This procedure would result in two sets of predictor coefficients - one for the first formant region below about 1000 Hz and the other for the high frequency region above 1000 Hz.

Alternatively, we find from Eq. 8 that the correlations c_i depend directly upon the amplitude of the prediction-error samples. The prediction error is generally very large at the beginning of every pitch period due to the rapid closing of the glottis. A predictor with few coefficients cannot predict such portions of the glottal wave efficiently. Thus, the error due to voice periodicity can be reduced significantly by limiting the interval over which the prediction error is minimized to portions of the pitch period where the prediction error is relatively small.

Illustrative examples of processed speech will be available for listening at the seminar.

References

[1] B. S. Atal and M. R. Schroeder, Predictive coding of speech signals, *Proc. 1967 Conf. on Communication and Processing,* pp. 360-361, November 1967.

[2] B. S. Atal and M. R. Schroeder, Predictive coding of speech signals, *Reports of the 6th International Congress on Acoustics,* Tokyo, vol. II, Paper C-5-4, 1968.

[3] B. S. Atal and M. R. Schroeder, Adaptive predictive coding of speech signals, *Bell Sys. Tech. Jour.* vol. 49, pp. 1973-1986, 1970.

[4] B. S. Atal and S. L. Hanauer, Speech analysis and synthesis by linear prediction, *J. Acoust. Soc. Amer.* vol.50, pp. 637-655, 1971.

[5] F. Itakura and S. Saito, Analysis synthesis telephony based on the maximum likelihood method, *Reports of the 6th International Congress on Acoustics,* Tokyo, vol. II, Paper C-5-5, 1968.

[6] J. I. Makhoul and J. J. Wolf, Spectral analysis of speech by linear prediction, *IEEE Trans. Audio Electroacoustics,* vol. AU-21, pp. 140-148, 1973. See also *Technical Report No. 2304,* Bolt Beranek and Newman, Inc. 1972.

[7] J. D. Markel, A. H. Gray, Jr., and H. Wakita, Linear prediction of speech - theory and practice, *Monograph no. 10,* Speech Communications Research Laboratory, Santa Barbara, California, 1973.

[8] J. L. Flanagan, *Speech analysis synthesis and perception,* New York: Springer-Verlag, 1972. pp. 281.

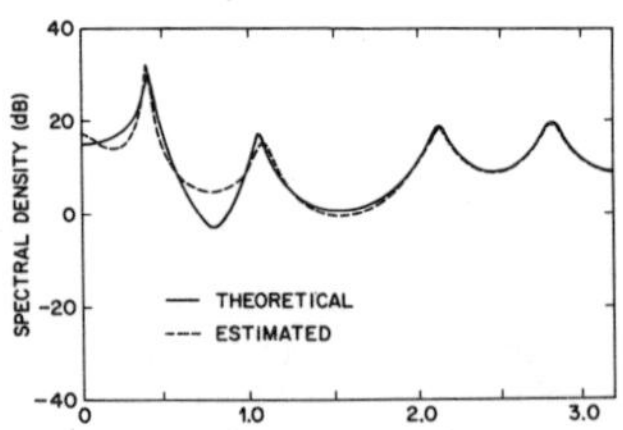

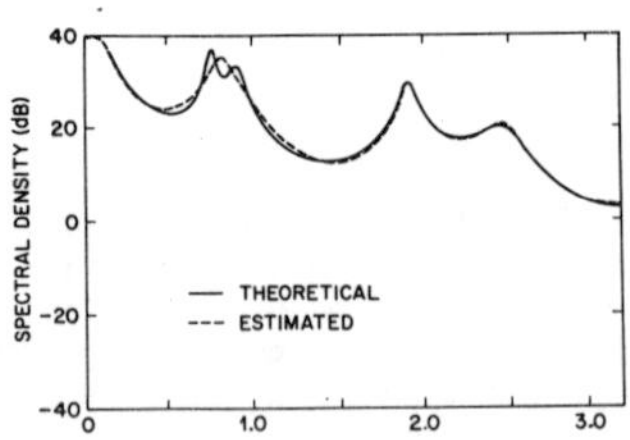

Fig. 1. Two examples of all-pole approximations of spectra consisting of 10 poles and 2 zeros. The solid curve is the theoretical spectrum based on both the poles and the zeros. The dashed curve is the spectrum derived from the linear prediction analysis with 12 poles.

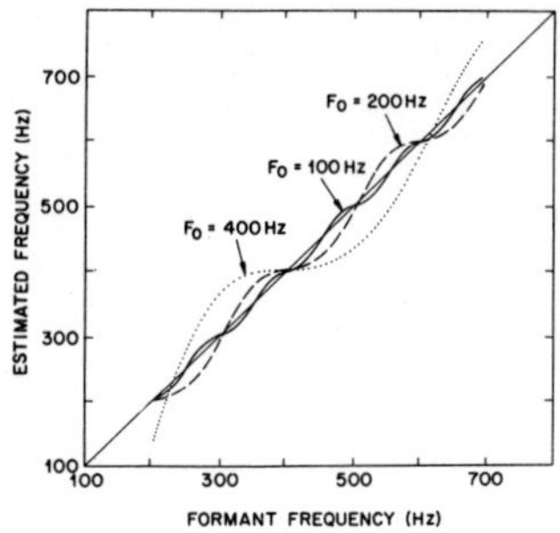

Fig. 2. Comparison of the estimated formant frequency with the actual frequency used in the synthesis for three different pitch frequencies.

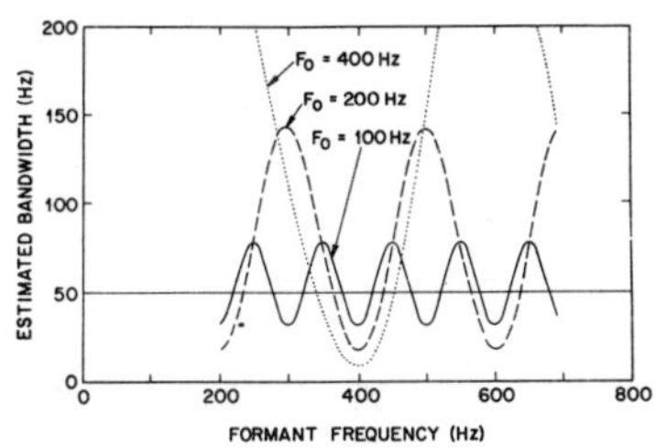

Fig. 3. Plots showing the dependence of the estimated formant bandwidth on the formant frequency and the pitch.

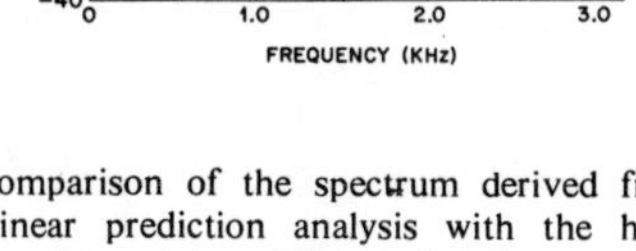

Fig. 4. Comparison of the spectrum derived from the linear prediction analysis with the harmonic spectrum at two different pitch frequencies.

Speech Communication Seminar
Stockholm. Aug. 1–3, 1974

LINEAR ESTIMATION OF SPEECH SIGNALS

L. A. Liporace,
Institute for Defense Analyses,
100 Prospect Avenue, Princeton, N.J., 08540 USA

INTRODUCTION

Since the performance of the linear prediction technique as a speech-analysis tool is contingent upon the degree to which the speech signal is stationary, the speech signal is normally divided into small intervals each of which is assumed to be stationary. The formulation below is aimed at accommodating the nonstationarity more automatically, by allowing the linear-regression filter to be time-varying.

FORMULATION

Denote the digitized speech segment as $x_1, x_2, \ldots, x_N$. The estimate $\hat{x}_n$ of x_n is a time-varying linear regression on the preceding p samples: $\hat{x}_n = c_1(n)x_{n-1} + \ldots + c_p(n)x_{n-p}$, where $c_k(n)$ is a polynomial in n of degree $M - 1$: $c_k(n) = c_{k0} + c_{k1}n + \ldots + c_{k,M-1}n^{M-1}$. Define $e_n = x_n - \hat{x}_n$, $e = (e_1, \ldots, e_N)T$, $\|e\| = (e^Te)^{1/2}$, $r_{jk}(i) = \Sigma_n n^i x_{n-j} x_{n-k}$, $R_0 = (r_{01}(0), \ldots, r_{0p}(0), \ldots, r_{01}(M-1), \ldots, r_{0p}(M-1))^T$, $C = (c_{10}, \ldots, c_{p0}, \ldots, c_{1,M-1}, \ldots, c_{p(m-1)})^T$. Let A_i denote the $p \times p$ matrix whose (j,k)-th element is $r_{jk}(i)$, and let A be the $MP \times MP$ matrix composed of M^2 sub-matrices as follows:

$$A = \begin{bmatrix} A_0, A_1, \ldots, A_{M-1} \\ \vdots \\ A_{M-1}, A_M, \ldots, A_{2(M-1)} \end{bmatrix} .$$

In terms of these quantities, we can express the length-squared of the error vector e as

$$\|e\|^2 = r_{00}(0) - R_0^T A^{-1} R_0 + (AC - R_0)^T A^{-1}(AC - R_0) .$$

Since A is positive-definite, the absolute minimum of $\|e\|^2$ is obtained with the coefficients C satisfying $AC = R_0$.

Thus $\|e\|^2_{min} = r_{00}(0) - R_0^T A^{-1} R_0 = r_{00}(0) - C^T R_0.$

Figure 1 illustrates the improvement in performance obtainable by allowing the linear predictor to be time varying. The curve corresponding to $M = 1$ illustrates the prediction error for standard time-invariant linear prediction; the remaining curves show the prediction error as a function of regression interval for other values of M.

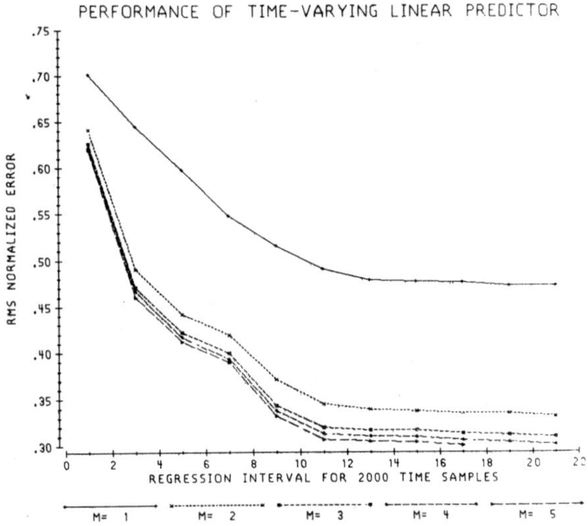

Figure 1

CONCLUSIONS

A theoretical feature of time-varying linear prediction not true of the time-invariant version is the following. For a given time interval, the prediction error can be made arbitrarily small by increasing M. With time-invariant linear prediction the error as a function of the number of predictor coefficients approaches an asymptote.

Synthesized speech generated by means of a time-varying linear predictor is of fair quality for men's, women's and children's voices for analysis intervals of up to 0.5 second with $M = 6$ and $P = 10$. By "fair quality" is meant that the speech was scratchy but perfectly intelligible and the speaker easily identifiable.

Speech Communication Seminar
Stockholm. Aug. 1–3, 1974

LINEAR PREDICTION VS. ANALYSIS-BY-SYNTHESIS

John Makhoul, Bolt Beranek and Newman Inc.
5Ø Moulton Street, Cambridge, Mass. Ø2138, U.S.A.

Abstract

Linear prediction is introduced as a spectral modeling technique in which the signal spectrum is modeled by an all-pole spectrum. The method allows for the modeling of selected portions of a spectrum, for arbitrary spectral shaping in the frequency domain, and for the modeling of continuous as well as discrete spectra (such as filter bank spectra). Linear prediction is compared to traditional analysis-by-synthesis techniques for spectral modeling. It is found that linear prediction offers computational advantages as well as better modeling properties for spectra that have large fluctuations around the spectral envelope. For relatively smooth spectra and for filter bank spectra, analysis-by-synthesis is judged to give better results.

Introduction

Until recently the method of analysis-by-synthesis (AbS) had been the major method for the modeling of speech spectra [1-5]. The introduction of linear prediction (LP) to speech analysis has given us a new method of spectral modeling. This paper outlines the spectral modeling properties of linear prediction and gives applications in the modeling of filter bank spectra, speech recognition and speech compression. Then, a comparison is given between LP analysis and AbS. Further details are given elsewhere [6-7].

Linear Predictive Spectral Modeling

The method of linear prediction was introduced to speech processing basically as a time-domain analysis. Elsewhere [8] we have shown that linear prediction is a correlation type of analysis which can be approached either from the time or frequency domain. Here we shall restrict our attention to the spectral modeling properties of the autocorrelation method of linear prediction.

Given a signal spectrum $P(\omega)$, we desire to model this spectrum by an all-pole spectrum $\hat{P}(\omega)$ given by (assuming a sampling frequency of 1 Hz)

$$\hat{P}(\omega) = \frac{G^2}{\left|1+\sum_{k=1}^{p} a_k e^{-jk\omega}\right|^2}, \tag{1}$$

where the predictor coefficients a_k, $1 \le k \le p$, and the gain factor G are the parameters of the model. The parameters a_k are obtained as a result of the minimization of the spectral error E, which is defined as

$$E = \frac{1}{2\pi} \int_{-\pi}^{\pi} \frac{P(\omega)}{\hat{P}(\omega)} \, d\omega \quad . \tag{2}$$

By setting $\partial E/\partial a_i = \emptyset$, $1 \le i \le p$, there results

$$\sum_{k=1}^{p} a_k R_{|i-k|} = -R_i \quad , \; 1 \le i \le p, \tag{3}$$

where

$$R_k = \frac{1}{2\pi} \int_{-\pi}^{\pi} P(\omega) \cos(k\omega) \, d\omega \tag{4}$$

are the autocorrelation coefficients corresponding to the continuous spectrum $P(\omega)$. By equating the total energy in the signal and model spectra, the gain G is obtained

$$G = R_0 + \sum_{k=1}^{p} a_k R_k \quad . \tag{5}$$

Equations (3-5) completely specify the all-pole model spectrum $\hat{P}(\omega)$.

Above we assumed two things: (a) The signal spectrum is a continuous function of frequency, and (b) the model spectrum spans the same frequency range as the signal spectrum. Below we show how the spectral modeling is performed when the signal spectrum exists at only a discrete set of frequencies, and the matching is performed over a selected portion of the signal spectrum.

Selective Linear Prediction

We wish to match the spectrum $P(\omega)$ in the region $\omega_a \le \omega \le \omega_b$ by an all-pole spectrum given by (1). Call the signal spectrum in that region $P'(\omega)$. In order to compute the parameters of $\hat{P}(\omega)$ we simply map the given region onto the unit circle in the z plane such that ω_a corresponds to an angle of zero, and ω_b corresponds to π, and then follow the procedure outlined earlier with $P'(\omega)$ replacing $P(\omega)$ in (4). If the signal spectrum is discrete then the autocorrelation coefficients are computed from

$$R_k = \frac{1}{N} \sum_{n=0}^{N-1} P(\omega_n) \cos(k\omega_n) \quad . \tag{6}$$

Note that the spectral frequencies ω_n do not have to be equally spaced.

Applications

Here we demonstrate the idea of selective linear prediction as applied to speech recognition and speech compression.

Figure 1 shows a spectrum computed from a 2Ø kHz signal. In order to model the spectral envelope for the whole frequency range from Ø-1Ø kHz, one would probably use anywhere between 24-28 poles for the all-pole model spectrum. A 28-pole fit is shown in Fig. 1.

For speech recognition applications, however, the main region of interest is the Ø-5 kHz region. The spectrum in the 5-1Ø kHz region is of interest mainly for the recognition of fricatives, in which case the total energy in that region might be sufficient. So, instead of modeling the whole spectrum we model only the lower 5 kHz by a lower order all-pole spectrum. We map the Ø-5 kHz region onto the unit circle and follow the procedure outlined earlier. The result for a 14-pole match is shown in Fig. 2. In this manner, not only do we reduce our computations for the poles, but we are also in the advantageous position of having to interpret 14 instead of 28 poles. The total energy in the 5-1Ø kHz region can be easily computed from the spectrum and used for the detection of fricatives.

If instead of simply finding the energy in the 5-1Ø kHz region, one was interested in modeling that region by another lower order all-pole spectrum, then, following the same procedure as before one obtains the desired model spectrum. A 5-pole spectral fit is shown in Fig. 2. The fact that the two spectral fits do not meet at 5 kHz is a direct consequence of this method of matching. Another example is shown in Fig. 3 for the spectrum of a fricative. Here the first half of the spectrum is modeled by a 14-pole spectrum and the second half by a 6-pole spectrum.

Now, the same type of analysis discussed above could have been done in the time domain, but consider what one would have had to do. First, the 2Ø-kHz sampled signal must be sharply filtered at 5 kHz. Second, and very importantly, the signal must be down-sampled to 1Ø kHz by discarding every other sample. Third, a 14-pole LP analysis is performed on the resulting signal. And fourth, in order to obtain the energy in the 5-1Ø kHz region, one subtracts the energy in the 1Ø kHz signal from the energy in the original 2Ø kHz signal. (It is even more complicated if one wants to perform an LP analysis on the 5-1Ø kHz region in the time domain.)

Not only is the time domain analysis more involved and costly, it is also very inflexible. Consider the problem of having to carry the same procedure to match the spectrum in the Ø-3.5 kHz region instead of Ø-5 kHz. In that case, it would be necessary to perform the time-domain down-sampling from 2Ø kHz to 7 kHz: a rather difficult task. The elegance of the method of selective linear prediction lies in the fact that the two

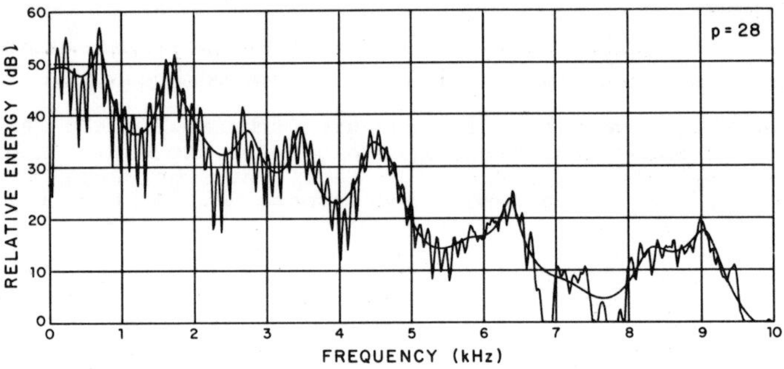

Fig. 1. A 28-pole spectral fit to an FFT-computed spectrum.

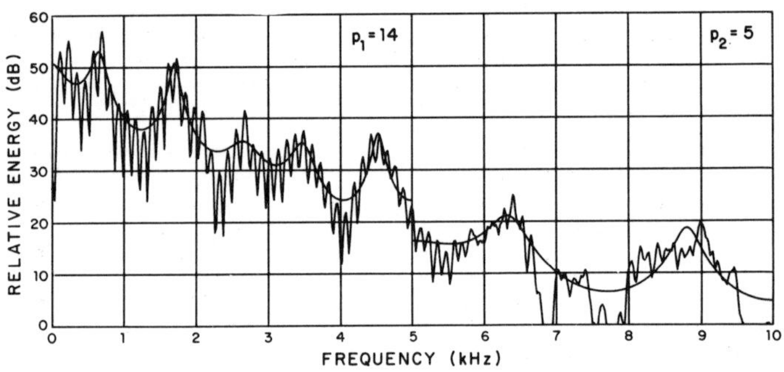

Fig. 2. Application of selective LP to a vowel spectrum.

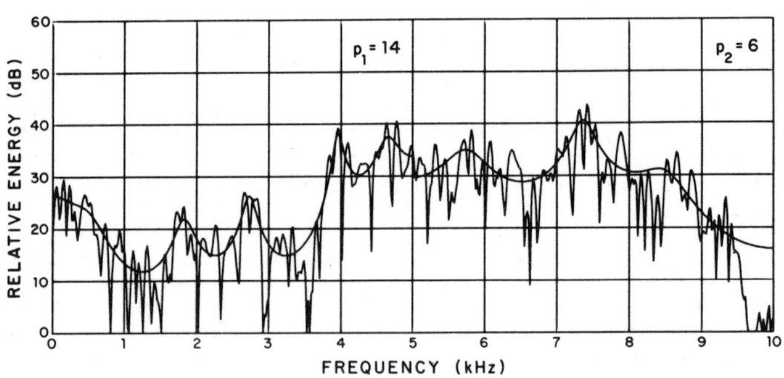

Fig. 3. Application of selective LP to a fricative spectrum.

problems of sharp filtering and down sampling are completely solved by working in the frequency domain.

We are currently applying this property to speech compression systems that employ linear prediction. In this application, it is desirable to be able to test the performance of the system at different sampling rates. We sample the signal at the highest rate desired, and then we simulate the different sampling rates by applying selective linear prediction to the corresponding frequency bands.

Modeling Discrete Spectra

Here we demonstrate the application of LP modeling for filter bank and harmonic spectra. Figure 4A shows a typical 14-pole spectral fit to a vowel spectrum that was obtained from a time signal by a fast Fourier transform (FFT). Figure 4B shows a similar fit to a line spectrum that is typical of filter bank spectra. What we have actually done here is to simulate a filter bank where the filters are linearly spaced up to 1.6 kHz and logarithmically spaced thereafter. Note that the all-pole spectrum for the simulated filter bank is remarkably similar to the one in the top figure, even though the number of spectral points is much less. Another example of this application is shown in Fig. 5 for the spectrum of a fricative.

The dashed curve in Fig. 6A is a 14-pole spectrum. If one applied LP analysis to this spectrum, the all-pole model for p=14 would be identical to the dashed spectrum. The situation is not so favorable for discrete spectra. Let us assume that the dashed spectrum corresponds to the transfer function of a 14-pole filter. If this filter is excited by a periodic train of impulses (unit samples) with fundamental frequency F_0, the spectrum of the output signal will be a discrete line spectrum with spectral values only at the harmonics (multiples of F_0). The line spectrum for F_0=312 Hz is shown in Fig. 6A. Note that the dashed spectrum is an envelope of the harmonic spectrum. The result of applying a 14-pole LP analysis to the harmonic spectrum is shown as the solid curve in Fig. 6A. The discrepancy between the two all-pole spectra is obvious. In general, the types of discrepancies that can occur between the model and original spectra include merging or splitting of pole peaks, and increasing or decreasing of pole frequencies and bandwidths. Pole movements are generally in the direction of the nearest harmonic. As the fundamental frequency decreases, these discrepancies decrease, as shown in Fig. 6B for F_0=156 Hz. The problems existent with higher fundamentals make LP analysis less accurate for the analysis of high pitched voices.

Linear Prediction vs. Analysis-by-Synthesis

The types of analysis discussed above could have all been done using spectral AbS. Below we discuss the relative merits of the two methods.

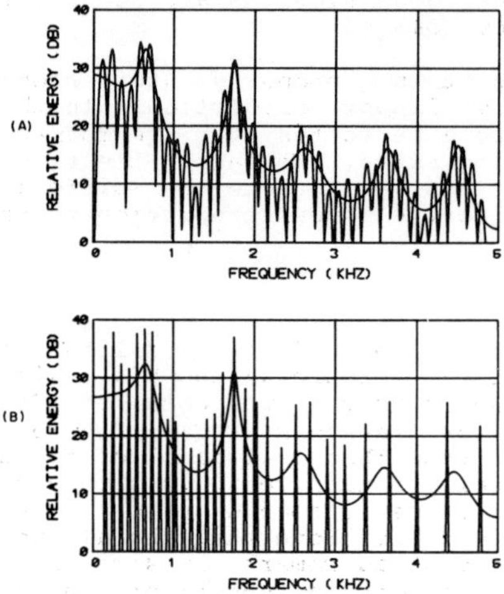

Fig. 4. Application of LP modeling to a filter bank vowel spectrum.

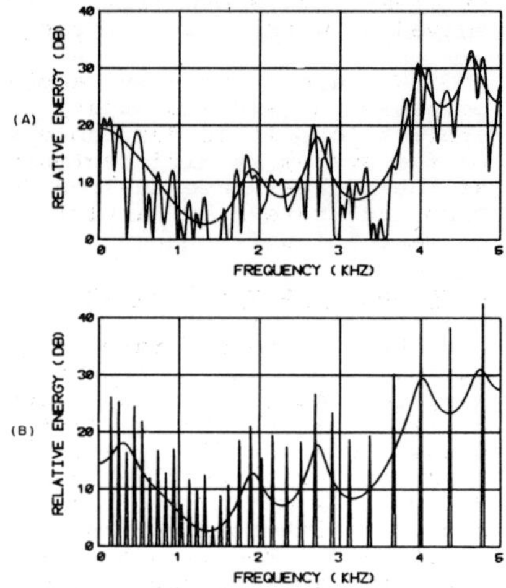

Fig. 5. Application of LP modeling to a filter bank fricative spectrum.

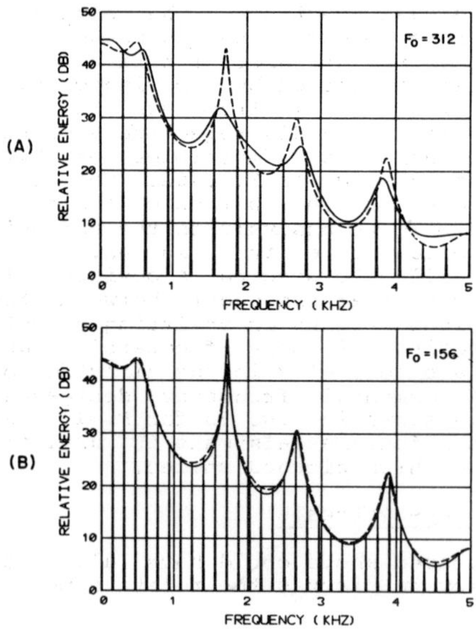

Fig. 6.
Dashed curve: filter all-pole spectrum.
Vertical lines: Harmonic spectrum for
(A) F_o = 312 Hz,
(B) F_o = 156 Hz.
Solid curve: LP model spectrum corresponding to harmonic spectrum.

LINEAR PREDICTION VS. ANALYSIS-BY-SYNTHESIS

The basic difference between LP and AbS is in the definition of the error measure between the signal and model spectra. Equation (2) gives the definition of the error measure in LP. For AbS, the error measure is given (in our notation) by

$$E' = \frac{1}{2\pi} \int_{-\pi}^{\pi} [\log P(\omega) - \log \hat{P}(\omega)]^2 \, d\omega$$

$$= \frac{1}{2\pi} \int_{-\pi}^{\pi} \left[\log \frac{P(\omega)}{\hat{P}(\omega)}\right]^2 d\omega \quad . \tag{7}$$

The two methods have two properties in common: (a) The spectral modeling can be done selectively to any portion of the spectrum, and (b) both error criteria are functions of the ratio of the signal and model spectra, and therefore the matching process should perform uniformly over the frequency range of interest, irrespective of the shaping of the spectral envelope. These desirable properties have been known to apply to AbS for some time, and we see here that they also apply to LP analysis.

One point of departure between the two methods is in the amount of computation necessary to obtain the model parameters. If the model spectrum contains zeros (with or without poles) then the minimization of E in (2) and E' in (7) both lead to nonlinear equations that must be solved iteratively. However, if the model spectrum consists of poles only, as in (1), then LP offers a distinct advantage. We have seen above that for this special (but important) case, the LP parameters are the solution to a set of linear equations (3). In AbS one would still need to perform the nontrivial task of an iterative solution. Another special case of interest for the analysis of glottal pulses is the all-zero case. For this case, a suboptimal LP solution can be obtained by performing LP modeling on the inverse spectrum. However, one must take care to smooth the spectrum first [7]. LP analysis offers another minor computational advantage and that is if the time signal is available then the autocorrelation coefficients for the solution of (3) can be obtained directly from the time domain without the need to compute the spectrum first.

Although computational efficiency is of great concern, it must be weighed against the accuracy of the results and what price one is willing to pay to get the needed accuracy. We shall now discuss the differences between LP and AbS modeling in the manner in which they affect the quality of match between the model and signal spectra. The quality of match is determined (for our puposes) by how well the model spectrum approximates the envelope of the signal spectrum. This matter is completely determined by the definitions of error given in (2) and (7).

We note from (2) that values of $P(\omega)$ that are greater than the corresponding values in $\hat{P}(\omega)$ will contribute to the total error in a more substantial manner than points where $P(\omega)$ is much smaller than $\hat{P}(\omega)$. This means that, after the minimization of error, we expect a better fit of $\hat{P}(\omega)$ to $P(\omega)$ where $P(\omega)>\hat{P}(\omega)$ than where $P(\omega)<\hat{P}(\omega)$. For example, if $P(\omega)$ is the power spectrum of a quasi-periodic signal (such as in Fig. 4A), then the error measure (2) insures that the match of $\hat{P}(\omega)$ to $P(\omega)$ is far superior at the harmonics where the energy is greater, than between the harmonics where there is very little energy. Therefore, we conclude that the LP error measure in (2) results in a model spectrum that is a good estimate of the envelope of the signal spectrum. The situation is not as favorable for AbS. From the error measure in (7) we note that contributions to the total error are equally significant whether $P(\omega)>\hat{P}(\omega)$ or $P(\omega)<\hat{P}(\omega)$. This means that energy at the harmonics and the lack of energy between harmonics contribute equally to the total error. This, of course, will not lead to a good spectral envelope. In general, if the variations of the signal spectrum about the desired spectral envelope are large, then it is expected that LP analysis would give better results than AbS.

The situation is reversed if the signal spectrum is smooth relative to the desired envelope spectrum. First, we point out that if the signal spectrum is a continuous all-pole spectrum, then both methods will yield a model spectrum (with the same number of poles) that is identical to the signal spectrum. However, if the signal spectrum is discrete, then even though its envelope is exactly an all-pole spectrum, we know from above (see Fig. 6) that LP modeling will result in a different all-pole spectrum, with relatively large discrepancies for high fundamentals. For this case, AbS always gives the desired all-pole model, provided the number of harmonics in the spectrum is greater than the number of poles. Also, for modeling of filter bank spectra, such as in Figs. 4B and 5B, AbS is expected to give better results. There is independent evidence [9] that AbS gives a better quality match than LP if the signal spectrum is smooth relative to the desired spectral envelope. However, for many applications the differences in match quality may not warrant the extra computational cost associated with AbS.

Conclusions

Linear prediction offers significant computational advantages over analysis-by-synthesis for the all-pole modeling of speech spectra. In addition, linear prediction gives better match quality for the model spectrum if the signal spectrum exhibits large fluctuations about the desired spectral envelope. Analysis-by-synthesis, on the other hand, is seen to give better results for the modeling of relatively smooth spectra and for filter bank spectra.

LINEAR PREDICTION VS. ANALYSIS-BY-SYNTHESIS

References

[1] Bell, C.G., H. Fujisaki, J.M. Heinz, K.N. Stevens, and A.S. House, "Reduction of Speech Spectra by Analysis-by-Synthesis Techniques," J. Acoust. Soc. Am., vol. 33, No. 12, 1725-1736, Dec. 1961.

[2] Mathews, M.V., J.E. Miller, and E.E. David, "Pitch Synchronous Analysis of Voiced Sounds," J. Acoust. Soc. Am., vol. 33, 179-186, 1961.

[3] Fujimura, O., "Analysis of Nasal Consonants," J. Acoust. Soc. Am., vol. 34, No. 12, 1865-1875, Dec. 1962.

[4] Paul, A.P., A.S. House, and K.N. Stevens, "Automatic Reduction of Vowel Spectra: An Analysis-by-Synthesis Method and its Evaluation," J. Acoust. Soc. Am., vol. 36, No. 2, 3Ø3-3Ø8, Feb. 1964.

[5] Olive, J.P., "Automatic Formant Tracking by a Newton-Raphson Technique," J. Acoust. Soc. Am., vol. 5Ø, 661-67Ø, 1971.

[6] Makhoul, J., "Spectral Analysis of Speech by Linear Prediction," IEEE Trans. Audio and Electroacoustics, vol. AU-21, pp. 14Ø-148, June 1973.

[7] Makhoul, J., "Selective Linear Prediction and Analysis-by Synthesis in Speech Analysis," BBN Report No. 2578, Bolt Beranek and Newman Inc., Cambridge, Mass., April 1974.

[8] Makhoul, J. and J. Wolf, "Linear Prediction and the Spectral Analysis of Speech," BBN Report No. 23Ø4, Bolt Beranek and Newman Inc., Cambridge, Mass., August 1972.

[9] Makhoul, J. and R. Viswanathan, "Quantization Properties of Transmission Parameters in Linear Predictive Systems," BBN Report No. 28ØØ, Bolt Beranek and Newman Inc., Cambridge, Mass., April 1974.

Speech Communication Seminar
Stockholm. Aug. 1–3, 1974

SOME THEORETICAL CONSIDERATIONS FOR LINEAR PREDICTION OF SPEECH AND APPLICATIONS

H. Wakita, Speech Communications Research Laboratory, Inc. (SCRL), Santa Barbara, California 93109, U.S.A., and A. H. Gray, Jr., SCRL and Department of Electrical Engineering and Computer Science, University of California, Santa Barbara, California 93106, U.S.A.

Abstract

The linear prediction method in speech analysis gives us considerable insight into modeling speech production processes. One of the authors previously showed that the linear prediction digital filter is equivalent to a non-uniform acoustic tube model of the vocal tract [1]. This paper describes a more general theoretical background of this aspect of the linear prediction method and shows that the well-known wave equations result when linear prediction digital filtering is extended to the continuous case. From this result, it is expected that some articulatory information can be effectively extracted directly from acoustic speech waveforms.

Introduction

The linear prediction method has become predominant in the area of speech analysis and synthesis in the past few years because of its high efficiency and accuracy. The recent works in this area suggested the possibility of finding some common relationships among various models of the speech production process. In this paper, one such theoretical aspect of the linear prediction method is investigated. The question is: "What differential equation governs the linear prediction digital filtering in speech analysis and synthesis when it is extended to the continuous case?" The following is one answer to this question.

Linear Prediction Digital Filter

A. Linear Prediction Digital Filter

A linear prediction digital filter can be constructed in a recursive manner [1]. The z-transforms of the forward- and the backward-going signals, $E_m^+(z)$ and $E_m^-(z)$ ($z = \exp(j\omega T)$; T is a sampling period), at the input of the m-th stage of the filter (see Fig. 1) can be expressed by a recursive equation,

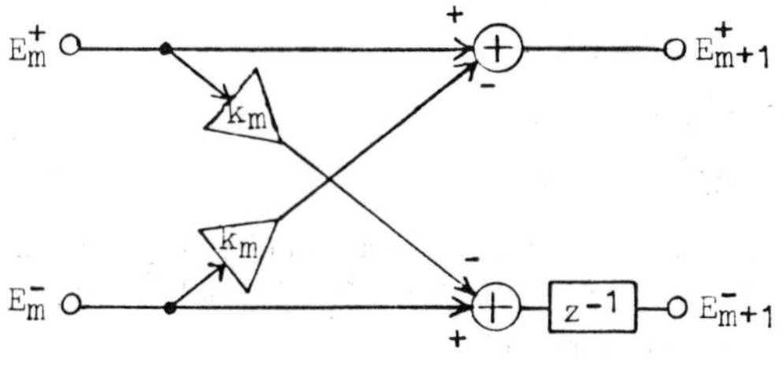

Fig. 1. Linear prediction digital filter.

$$\begin{bmatrix} E^+_{m+1}(z) \\ E^-_{m+1}(z) \end{bmatrix} = \begin{bmatrix} 1 & -k_m \\ -k_m z^{-1} & z^{-1} \end{bmatrix} \begin{bmatrix} E^+_m(z) \\ E^-_m(z) \end{bmatrix} \qquad (1)$$

where k_m is a constant.

B. Introduction of New Variables

If $P_m(z)$ and $U_m(z)$ are defined in terms of a linear combination of $E^+_m(z)$ and $E^-_m(z)$, i.e.,

$$\begin{bmatrix} P_m(z) \\ U_m(z) \end{bmatrix} = G_m(z) \begin{bmatrix} E^+_m(z) \\ E^-_m(z) \end{bmatrix} \qquad (2)$$

where $G_m(z)$ is a 2×2 operational matrix, then

$$\begin{bmatrix} P_{m+1}(z) \\ U_{m+1}(z) \end{bmatrix} = H_m(z) \begin{bmatrix} P_m(z) \\ U_m(z) \end{bmatrix} \qquad (3)$$

where, by the use of (1) and (2),

$$H_m(z) = G_m(z) \begin{bmatrix} 1 & -k_m \\ -k_m z^{-1} & z^{-1} \end{bmatrix} G_m^{-1}(z) \qquad (4)$$

$$\equiv \begin{bmatrix} h^{(m)}_{11}(z) & h^{(m)}_{12}(z) \\ h^{(m)}_{21}(z) & h^{(m)}_{22}(z) \end{bmatrix}. \qquad (5)$$

For simplicity, the system is assumed to be reciprocal and the matrix $H_m(z)$ is assumed to be symmetric. Then, for reciprocity

$$\det H_m(z) = 1 \qquad (6)$$

and for symmetry

$$h^{(m)}_{22}(z) = h^{(m)}_{11}(z). \qquad (7)$$

Under these assumptions, there may be various choices of matrix $G_m(z)$ to satisfy (4). Here, $G_m(z)$ is chosen to be of the form

$$G_m(z) = C_m \begin{bmatrix} Z_m & \beta Z_m \\ 1 & -\beta \end{bmatrix} \qquad (8)$$

By substituting (8) into (4), taking the conditions of (6) and (7) into consideration, Z_{m+1}/Z_m is obtained as

$$\frac{Z_{m+1}}{Z_m} = 1 + \frac{\beta(1+z^{-1})}{1+\beta^2 z^{-1}} \tag{9}$$

In this case, β is to be chosen so as to make Z_{m+1}/Z_m independent of z^{-1}. This results in $\beta = \pm 1$ or $\beta = \pm z$. Here, $\beta = 1$ is chosen (other choices of β give equivalent results). Then,

$$\frac{Z_{m+1}}{Z_m} = \frac{1+k_m}{1-k_m} \tag{10}$$

and

$$\frac{C_{m+1}}{C_m} = \frac{z^{1/2}}{1+k_m} \tag{11}$$

C. Extension into Continuous Case

It is easily obtained from (3) and (5) that the variables $P_m(z)$ and $U_m(z)$ have the following relations:

$$\begin{bmatrix} P_{m+1}(z) \\ P_m(z) \end{bmatrix} = \begin{bmatrix} h_{11}^{(m)}(z)/h_{21}^{(m)}(z) & \det H_m(z)/h_{21}^{(m)}(z) \\ 1/h_{21}^{(m)}(z) & h_{22}^{(m)}(z)/h_{21}^{(m)}(z) \end{bmatrix} \begin{bmatrix} U_{m+1}(z) \\ -U_{m+1}(z) \end{bmatrix} \tag{12}$$

and

$$\begin{bmatrix} U_{m+1}(z) \\ -U_m(z) \end{bmatrix} = \begin{bmatrix} h_{22}^{(m)}(z)/h_{12}^{(m)}(z) & -\det H_m(z)/h_{12}^{(m)}(z) \\ -1/h_{12}^{(m)}(z) & h_{11}^{(m)}(z)/h_{12}^{(m)}(z) \end{bmatrix} \begin{bmatrix} P_{m+1}(z) \\ P_m(z) \end{bmatrix}. \tag{13}$$

Thus, from these relations, plus the use of (6) and (7), the following equations result:

$$P_m(z) - P_{m+1}(z) = -Z_{m+1} \frac{z^{1/4}-z^{-1/4}}{z^{1/4}+z^{-1/4}} [U_m^{(z)} + U_{m+1}(z)] \tag{14}$$

and

$$U_m(z) - U_{m+1}(z) = -\frac{1}{Z_{m+1}} \frac{z^{1/4}-z^{-1/4}}{z^{1/4}+z^{-1/4}} [P_m(z) + P_{m+1}(z)] \tag{15}$$

By the use of the operators and definitions given in the Appendix, the following differential equations result when the time and distance increments approach zero:

$$\frac{\partial p(x,t)}{\partial x} = -\frac{Z(x)}{c} \frac{\partial U(x,t)}{\partial t} \tag{16}$$

$$\frac{\partial u(x,t)}{\partial x} = -\frac{1}{Z(x)c} \frac{\partial p(x,t)}{\partial t} \tag{17}$$

where c is a constant having the unit of velocity. These are well known as wave equations, and thus it is known that the linear prediction digital filtering satisfies discrete wave equations derived from (16) and (17).

D. Boundary Conditions

(1) The boundary condition at the lip end in the linear prediction synthesis filter is $E_1^-(z) = -z^{-1}E_1^+(z)$.

(2) Since the filter is excited by the source corresponding to $E_{M+1}^+(z)$ ($E_{M+1}^-(z) = 0$), it is equivalent to be terminated by the matched impedance at the glottis end so that no reflection occurs between the excitation source and the filter.

E. Discussion

If u(x,t) and p(x,t) are regarded as the volume velocity and the pressure, respectively, and if Z(x) is regarded as $\rho c/S(z)$ (S(x) is an area function), (16) and (17) become wave equations for a non-uniform acoustic tube. Webster's horn equation, thus, directly follows from (16) and (17). Similarly, if u(x,t) and p(x,t) are the current and the voltage, respectively, and Z(x) is a characteristic impedance, (16) and (17) become the wave equations for a distributed transmission line. Thus it can be stated that the linear prediction digital synthesis filter is equivalent to the non-uniform acoustic tube model or the lumped constant transmission line analog model of the vocal tract. The boundary condition at the lip end is realized by connecting a tube of an infinite area or by short-circuiting the vocal tract tube. At the glottis end, a tube of infinite length with cross-sectional area S_{M+1} is connected, i.e., the vocal tract tube is terminated with the characteristic impedance of $\rho c/S_{M+1}$. The constant k_m in (1) is found to be the reflection coefficient in the discrete acoustic tube model as related to cross-sectional areas in (10). More details are discussed elsewhere [1].

Applications

The theoretical aspect of the linear prediction method discussed so far has useful applications to the extraction of some parameters needed in speech research. Some of the applications which have been attempted by the authors are only briefly described here since detailed reports of them have been given elsewhere [1]-[4].

(1) Estimation of the vocal tract shape.

From the equivalence of the linear prediction filter to the acoustic tube model, it is possible to estimate the vocal tract area function by a time domain processing of speech sounds.

(2) Simple conversion between acoustic data and tract shape.

Since the inverse transfer function of the vocal tract is expressed in terms of a polynomial in z^{-1}, formant frequencies and bandwidths are obtained from the roots of the polynomial. Conversely, a polynomial for the inverse transfer function is easily computed from given formant frequencies and bandwidths. Since there is a recursive relation between the coefficients of the polynomial and the reflection coefficients, a discrete acoustic tube shape can easily be derived from a given polynomial for the inverse transfer function, and vice versa.

(3) Estimation of lip impedance poles and zeros.

Lip impedance poles and zeros are known to be another acoustic parameter to obtain the vocal tract area function [5][6]. In order to avoid some of the constraints involved in measuring those poles and zeros, the linear prediction method can be applied to estimate the poles and zeros reasonably well.

(4) Estimation of vocal tract length.

Knowledge of the vocal tract length is necessary to estimate the vocal tract area function. It is also expected to be useful in normalizing some speech parameters to eliminate inter-speaker differences. For given formant frequencies and bandwidths, an infinite number of tube shapes is realizable, each corresponding to a different sampling period. Since the sampling period is related to the tube length in this model, a method for estimating the length has been attempted by the conversion of acoustic data to an area function such that a certain error criterion is minimized.

Appendix

In passing from discrete to continuous case, the following operators and definitions are used. In this case, Taylor series expansion with the remainder term was used.

(1) $$\frac{1}{2}[z^{1/4}+z^{-1/4}]F_m(z) \Leftrightarrow \frac{1}{2}[f(t+\Delta t/2,x_m)+f(t-\Delta t/2,x_m)] = \overline{f(t,x_m)}$$

$$\left(0<\xi<\frac{\Delta t}{2}\right)$$

where

$$z = e^{j\omega 2\Delta t} \text{ and}$$

$$\overline{f(t,x_m)} = f(t,x_m) + \frac{1}{2}\,\frac{1}{2!}\left(\frac{\Delta t}{2}\right)^2[f''(t+\xi,x_m)+f''(t-\xi,x_m]$$

(2) $$\frac{1}{2}[z^{1/4}-z^{-1/4}]F_m(z) \Leftrightarrow \frac{1}{2}[f(t+\Delta t/2,x_m)-f(t-\Delta t/2,x_m)] = \frac{\Delta t}{2}\,\overline{f_t(t,x_m)}$$

where

$$\overline{f\ (t,x_m)} = f'(t,x_m)+\frac{1}{2}\,\frac{1}{3!}\left(\frac{\Delta t}{2}\right)^2[f'''(t+\xi,x_m)+f'''(t-\xi,x_m)]$$

$$\left(0<\xi<\frac{\Delta t}{2}\right)$$

(3) $$\frac{1}{2}[F_m(z)+F_{m+1}(z)] = \frac{1}{2}[f(t,x_m)+f(t,x_m-\Delta x)] \simeq f(t,x_m)$$

4–742577 *Volym I*

(4) $[F_m(z)-F_{m+1}(z)] = f(t,x_m)-f(t,x_m-\Delta x) \simeq \Delta x\ f_x(t,x_m)$

The similar expansion as in (1) and (2) was applied to (3) and (4).

References

[1] H. Wakita, IEEE AU-21 No. 5 pp. 417 (1973) or SCRL Monograph No. 9 (1972).

[2] H. Wakita, JASA Vol. 53 No. 1 pp. 293 (1973).

[3] H. Wakita and A. H. Gray, Jr., JASA Vol. 54 No. 1 pp. 340 (1973).

[4] H. Wakita, Paper submitted to the 87th ASA meeting.

[5] M. R. Schroeder, JASA Vol. 41 No. 4 pp. 1002 (1967).

[6] P. Mermelstein, JASA Vol. 41 No. 5 pp. 1283 (1967).

Speech Communication Seminar
Stockholm. Aug. 1–3, 1974

COMPUTER SUPPORTED GATING OF SPEECH SIGNALS

Anton J. Rozsypal
Department of Linguistics, University of Alberta
Edmonton, Alberta, Canada

Abstract

Temporal gating of speech signals by means of a digital computer presents a flexible, accurate, and timesaving research device in temporal studies of speech. Advantages of digital gating over analog gating techniques are considered. Technical aspects of distortion-free digitization and reconstruction of the analog speech waveform, namely the sampling rate, the number of quantization levels, and the frequency response of the smoothing filter , are briefly mentioned. Potentialities of digital gating are illustrated by describing the features of a gating program currently in use.

Introduction

Temporal gating, also called temporal filtering, is a technique applied in all lines of phonetic research involving segmentation of the speech signal. It helps one to determine acoustic and perceptual boundaries in the speech signal, to subject isolated speech segments to objective or subjective analysis, and to study how deletion, compression, expansion, addition, or replacement of a segment in a speech waveform affects the perception of the altered utterance.

In the past, gating has been accomplished either by manual cutting and splicing of audio tape or by means of various kinds of electronic switching. The recent expansion of computer technology has offered, among others, also a new, powerful research tool in the form of a small laboratory-based digital computer system, which will soon become a necessity also for phonetic research. The present report describes how temporal gating can be successfully accomplished using such a computer.

Digital Signal Processing

Prior to processing by a digital computer the analog speech signal has to be converted into its digital representation. This is achieved in an analog-to-digital converter in two consecutive operations. In the first one, called sampling, the analog speech signal is sampled at a proper sampling rate. In the second step, called quantization, the analog samples are compared with a scale of discrete quantization levels and replaced by a digital value corresponding to the nearest quantization level. These numbers, representing the rounded-off values of the speech waveform sampled at uniform time intervals, are consecutively stored in computer memory.

To recover the original analog waveform, the digital samples are transferred, at the sampling rate, to the digital-to-analog converter where they are transformed into a analog signal of a staircase form. This signal is subsequently smoothed by a low-pass filter, which outputs a signal closely resembling the original speech waveform. The degree of distortion of the recovered analog signal depends on several factors, namely, on the sampling frequency, on the number of quantization levels, and, finally, on the frequency response of the smoothing filter. Quantitative analysis of these factors yields criteria which, if observed, allow us to keep this distortion within acceptable limits.

The optimal sampling frequency depends on the spectral composition of the digitized signal. An insufficient sampling rate results in loss of information about the high-frequency components of the speech signal. By increasing the sampling rate beyond an optimal range the adjoining samples become more and more correlated and consequently redundant. The sampling theorem states that the signal must be sampled at least twice within the period of its highest frequency component. But in a case of sampling at this critical rate the analog signal can be receovered only by using an ideal low-pass filter with a rectangular frequency response. Such a filter is not realizable. Increasing the sampling rate above the critical value increases the frequency gap between the highest speech signal component and the lowest undesired component resulting from the sampling process. By properly selecting the actual sampling rate this gap should be made wide enough to accommodate the skirt of the low-pass filter until it drops about 50 dB. Thus a sampling rate two to three octaves higher than the highest frequency component of the digitized signal can be regarded as sufficient in most applications.

The process of quantization of the samples results in an error signal called quantization noise, which appears as an additive hissing sound in the recovered speech waveform. By dividing the signal amplitude range into a sufficiently large number of quantization intervals this noise can be suppressed below any disturbing level. As a rule of thumb, each bit of the analog-to-digital converter capacity improves the signal-to-quantization noise ratio by 6 dB. For most practical requirements a ten-bit converter should suffice, since then the quantization noise is more than 60 dB below the signal level. A reasonable criterion seems to be to keep the level of the quantization noise several decibels below the level of the other interfering background signals accompanying the speech signal, such as recording room noise, instrumentation hum, or tape hiss.

The conversion rules recommended here apply not only in digital processing of speech, but also in digital processing and generation of analog signals of any kind.

Example of a Gating Program

The gating program described here represents one of the many possible approaches to digital gating. It runs on a small digital computer PDP-12 with 16 k core memory and added analog outputs. The program occupies two 1 k fields of core memory, the remaining 14 k of core capacity are allotted to accommodate the digitized speech waveform. At the highest sampling rate 16 kHz which this program provides the duration of the stored speech utterance is 986 msec.

The speech data can be obtained either by transferring into core the speech material already digitized and stored on digital magnetic tape, or by digitizing a signal from a microphone or, more conveniently, from a master audio tape. If the second option is chosen, the program is advanced into the calibration routine in which the input signal is continuously sampled and displayed on the CRT so that it can be checked for proper level setting. Also, the triggering level and delay of the pre-triggering mechanism is set at this stage. After initiating the sampling routine, owing to the pretriggering feature, the storage of the digitized samples in effect begins a predetermined time interval before the speech waveform exceeds the triggering level.

After the completion of the data acquisition, the digitized signal is displayed and can also be played back over loudspeaker or headphones to check whether the utterance is complete and whether the amplitude of the input signal was properly set. If satisfactory, the digitized recording can be stored on the digital magnetic tape for later processing. The speech utterance is now ready for the actual gating.

Either one or two gating intervals can be utilized in this program, each delimited by two boundary points. Any sample can be selected as a boundary point by setting of console switches and adjusting of potentiometers, using the CRT display as a guide. The boundary points are indicated by greater brightness of the corresponding sample points.

The samples outside the gating intervals can either be deleted or preserved, so that the gating intervals can be played back either as joined together in isolation or in their natural context. In addition, each of the two gating intervals can be either skipped or repeated up to seven times either to compress or to expand the investigated utterance. The sample values of one or both gating intervals can also be replaced by zeros, thus leaving pauses of corresponding duration in the reconstructed waveform. Finally, a pause of variable duration can be inserted following the end point of the first gating interval.

Three playback modes are available. The repeated playback is used for auditory monitoring. Single playback is used for recording the gated speech signal onto audio tape. In this mode the tape recorder is remote controlled by the computer. The third, slowed-down playback mode, is used to produce a graphical record of the gated waveform on an oscillograph with an upper limiting frequency of about 500 Hz. By properly slowing-down the transfer rate between the core and the analog output, the spectrum of the speech signal is compressed so that it matches the limited frequency range of the oscillograph.

Comparison of Digital and Analog Gating Techniques

The digital approach to gating offers many advantages over analog techniques. The major shortcoming of analog gating procedures is that they are too elaborate and thus too time-consuming. In contrast, selection, setting, and resetting of the boundary points in digital gating is fast, simple and convenient. It is aided by immediate visual display and auditory monitoring and by instant switching between alternative playback modes. This flexibility cuts down drastically the pretesting period of the experiment.

In studies published to date the best timing accuracy of gating accomplished using analog techniques is about one millisecond. The digital gating offers temporal resolution better by at least one order of magnitude. The boundary points can be set in any phase of the speech waveform with an accuracy depending only on the sampling rate. Since any sample point of the digitized speech signal can serve as a boundary point, the time resolution is equal to the duration of the sampling interval. For instance, at a sampling rate of 20 kHz the boundary points can be set with an accuracy of 50 microseconds.

An important advantage in digital gating is that no external time calibration is required. As the sampling is done at regular time intervals and the digitized samples are stored at consecutive memory locations, the address of each sample represents its coordinate on the time scale associated with the speech waveform. Accuracy and temporal stability of this scale depends on the design of the clock which generates the sampling interval and the interval at which the samples are transferred from the memory to the analog output.

In analog devices switching transients can hardly be suppressed more than 50-60 dB below the full signal level. On the other hand, no switching transients appear in the output of the digital gate. Perceptible clicks at boundary points are evoked only by stepwise onset, offset, or transition in the gated speech waveform. These clicks are inherent in signal discontinuities and, if desired, can be suppressed by choosing boundary points at signal zero-crossings.

In digital signal processing the distortion of the signal and its signal-to-noise ratio are fully under the programmer's control by proper selection of the sampling frequency, the number of quantization levels, and the frequency characteristic of the smoothing filter. Besides, the digital form of the signal is immune to distortion of any type. Long storage periods or repeated data transfers do not degrade it, which is not the case with signals in analog form.

In some situations it can be advantageous to change the frequency scale of the spectrum of the reconstructed signal. Such frequency scaling can easily be attained on a digital computer by outputting the digital information at any convenient rate, different from the sampling rate.

Recording of testing tapes can be executed under computer control. Even subject testing can proceed under complete computer command provided the full set of stimuli used in the experiment can be accommodated in a mass storage device.

Once the signal waveform is digitized and stored, it can be subjected to many other operations besides gating. Such processing as peak or center clipping, rectification, frequency filtering, analysis of voice pitch or jitter, intensity or duration analysis, and computing of spectral or correlation functions of a variety of types, all can be carried out in digital form.

It has to be admitted that a computer is rather an expensive gate. Besides, it requires qualified programming and maintenance personnel. But once the program is debugged and running smoothly and the experimenter is familiar with the control elements, little time is wasted in non-productive work.

Perhaps the major limitation of digital speech processing is that the capacity of the internal direct access core memory of present-day small computers restricts the duration of speech utterances to be processed to several hundred milliseconds. This problem can be circumvented by using external mass storage devices, but this may result in programs of restricted flexibility.

Speech Communication Seminar
Stockholm. Aug. 1–3, 1974

REDUCTION AND RECONSTITUTION OF SPECTRAL DATA

M. CARTIER and P. GRAILLOT - Département Etudes et Techniques d'Acoustique -
Centre National d'Etudes des Télécommunications - (C.N.E.T.) -
22301 LANNION (France)

Abstract

Spectral data from a channel vocoder are reduced by means of factorial analysis of correspondences. Reduction of vowel data leads to extraction of phonetic features. 3 - 5 factors are needed to reconstitute seven oral vowels. Confusions between synthetic vowels are studied.

Vowels are relatively more sensitive than consonants to a reduction of short-time spectra when projected on general axis. Distinctive features are differently affected by that type of reduction.

Introduction

A minimum number of independant factors may be mathematically extracted using factorial analysis, so that multidimensional data are represented in subspaces with minimum loss of information (in the sense of a given distance). When the initial data are reconstituted and synthesized, a less redundant coding for transmission is obtained. Several applications of factorial analysis have been presented (Kramer and Mathews, 1, Pols et al. 2). A similar method was used by Marano 3 for image-coding. Results obtained with that method applied to speech spectral data are presented. Isolated vowels were analyzed and synthetic sounds were tested : the plane of factors I - II allows a primary classification of the vowels according to two features : grave-acute, compact-diffuse. Compressed speech was then subjected to articulation tests, in order to know the importance of the extracted factors.

The analysis of correspondences

The used statistical method is the analysis of correspondences from Benzecri 4, which differs from the more classic methods of principal components by the following aspects :

- the χ^2 distance is used, therefore we work with relative values (or profiles) and not with absolute values. Exactly, the χ^2 distance is, for the matrix of data.

$$d^2(i,i') = \sum_j \left\{ \left(\frac{f_{ij}}{f_i} - \frac{f_{i'j}}{f_{i'}} \right)^2 / f_j \right\}$$

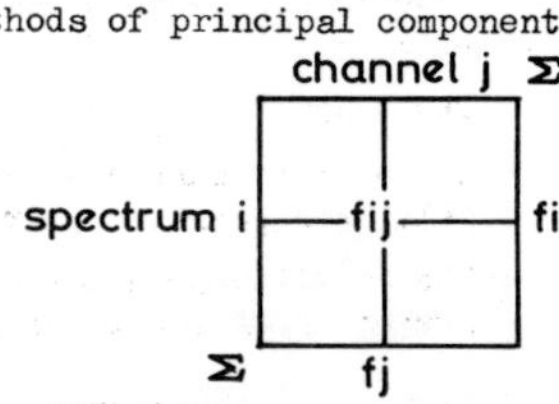

1 H.P. KRAMER, M.V. MATTHEWS : "A linear Coding for Transmitting a Set of correlated Signals" I.R.E. Trans. I.T. 2 p. 41-46 (1956)

2 L.C.W. POLS, L.J.T. VAN DER KAMP, R. PLOMB : "Perceptual and Physical Space of Vowel Sounds - J.A.S.A. 46 - p. 458-467 (1969)

3 P. MARANO : "Application de l'Analyse Factorielle des Correspondances à la Compression des Signaux d'Image" : Ann. Télécom. mai-juin 1972 - p. 163-172

4 J.P. BENZECRI : "L'Analyse des Données" - Dunod (1973).

.../...

- The division by the sum f_i of the spectra implies a normalization and the division by the sum f_j of the channels a preaccentuation.

- The two sets of rows and columns, in this case the channels and the samples of spectra, have a symetric part in the analysis. Therefore both rows and columns can be projected on the same axes.

- The projection of a sample i(a channel j) is homothetic of the centre of gravity of the projections, with the weights f_{ij}, of the channels j(the samples i). Therefore :

$$\begin{cases} Fk(i) = \frac{1}{\sqrt{\lambda k}} \sum_j \left(\frac{fij.\ Gk(j)}{fi} \right) \\ Gk(j) = \frac{1}{\sqrt{\lambda k}} \sum_i \left\{ \frac{fij.\ Fk(i)}{fj} \right\} \end{cases}$$

$F_k(i)$ is the projection of i on the axis k
$G_k(j)$ is the projection of j on the axis k
λ_k is the eigenvalue of this axis

- It is possible to reconstitute the data with k axes from the formula :

$$fij = fi.fj \left\{ 1 + \sum_k \left(\frac{1}{\sqrt{\lambda k}} .\ Fk(i).\ Gk(j) \right) \right\}$$

When we use no factor we have then the hypothesis H_o of statistical independance ($f_{ij} = f_i f_j$). With the axes of the factors, we want to see displayed how our data differ from H_o and in what directions they deviate from independence.

<u>Analysis and reconstitution of vowels</u>

1. A Channel Vocoder is used to analyze and synthesize isolated vowels, to make comparison between original and compressed data easy. A minor drawback consists in the fact that original data are sometimes already distorted. Vocoder used in this study was a 12 channel vocoder (telephone bandwith) with a rate of 2240 bit/s corresponding to a sampling frequency of 40 Hz (16 levels per channel with 3 dB steps, 8 bits for pitch). A speaker uttered 7 oral vowels : a, ɛ, i, y, u, o, ø. The principal axes are calculated from these data.

2. Projections of sounds and channels are superposed on Fig. 1. It can be seen that :

   - The channels are nearly distributed along the circumference of a circle.
   - The extreme channels have negative coordinates on axis II, the middle channels have positive coordinates.
   - The curvilinear abscissa around the circumference corresponds to the channel number (from low to high frequencies).

   Referring to the property of the centre of gravity (the energy of a sound concentrates in the nearest channels), new coordinates of a sound S,

$$\theta = (\vec{OS}, I) - \frac{3\pi}{2} \quad \text{and} \quad x_2 = \vec{OS}.\vec{II}$$

   can be related to graveness and compactness (Fig. 2).

.../...

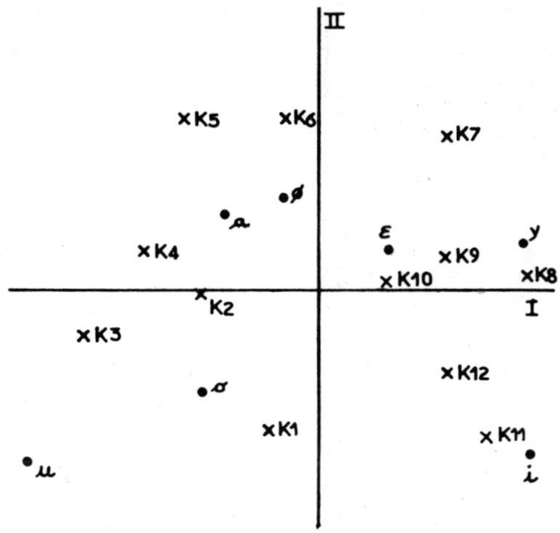

FIG. 1 : Vowels and channels projected on I.II plane

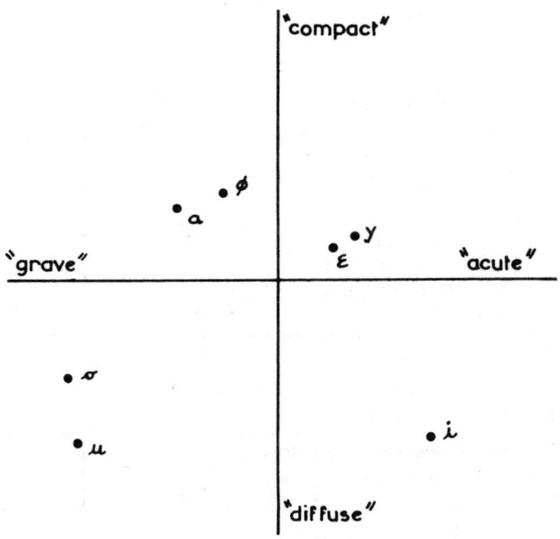

FIG. 2 : Vowels projected on θ-II plane

3. Synthetic vowels reconstituted from projections on the first five three and two axes respectively were tested in a forced choice test (7 answers) ; the four representations (original, 5, 3, 2 factors) of each vowel were heard by 24 listeners 6 times. Excepted for (ø), reconstitution from 3 factors results in a negligeable loss of information. They may be considered as informative as the first two formants. However, 5 factors are needed to make distorsion negligeable for the whole set of sounds (Fig. 3).

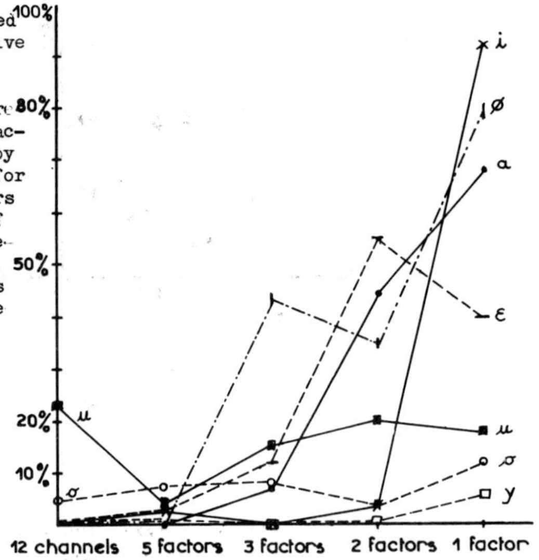

FIG. 3 : % confusion on vowels (7 possible answers)

The confusion matrix has been treated by the same program of analysis of correspondences. Pronounced and heard sounds (rows and colums respectively) are projected on a new I - II plane (Fig. 4). This structure is very close to the usual perceptual structure of vowels (except for ø . That difference between the physical plane and the perceptual plane exists only for (y) This implies that the χ^2 distance is correlated with the perceptual distance, (y) excepted. However, it must be noted that the projections on the first axis of the physical and perceptual spaces are the same.

Another comparison can be made between χ^2 distance and perceptual distance, comparing the percent of confusions and the percent of inertia kept in the subspace (similar to Pols in (7)).

	ORIG	5	3	2	1
Inertia	100	96,8	88,0	74,7	50,8
Confusion	4	3	12	23	44

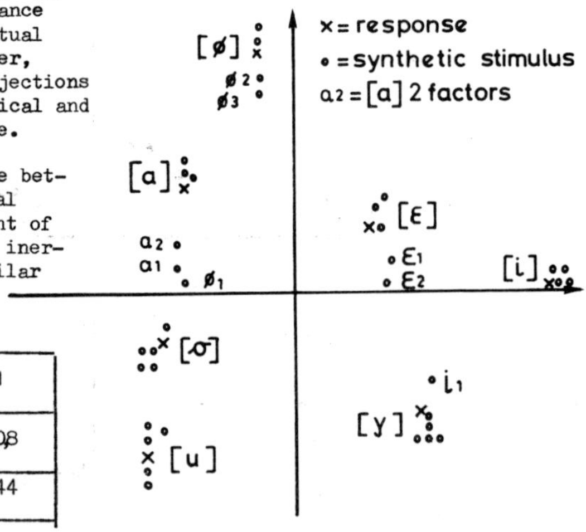

FIG.4: Analysis of the confusion matrix

Perception of initial consonants

The same vocoder (2240 e.b./s ; F_e = 40 Hz ; 250 – 3400 Hz) was used to perform a Diagnostic Rhyme Test (Voiers 5^{e}, french adaptation by Rossi and Peckels 6) : listeners are presented a choice between two words whose only the initial consonants differ. Six distinctive features of consonants are tested separately : voicing, graveness, compactness, sustention, vocality, nasality. One male speaker uttered 216 words (108 pairs) ; the principal axes were determined from the whole set of words. The spectra were projected on 5 dimensions-, 3 dimensions-, and 2 dimensions- subspaces. Six tests were performed : one group (12 persons) listened to original data and data from 5 factors, a second group to the data from 5 factors and 3 factors, a third group to data from 3 factors and 2 factors. Each word was heard twice.

Each step of degradation approximately corresponds to a 1,5 dB loss of signal-to-noise ratio. Detailed results concerning each characteristic of distinctive features are presented on Fig. 5. Graveness and compactness (features 2 and 3) are most disturbed. Especially acute consonants and compact consonants grow more and more disturbed when the number of factors decreases. For instance, "tol" tends towards "pol" with 3 factors : the movement of the 2nd formant is lost (see sonagrams ; more generally the characteristic grave-acute of a vowel is transferred to the consonant by flattening of spectra.

Voicing and sustension are not disturbed by reduction ; that is evident since pitch, energy and center of gravity are preserved using only one or two factors.

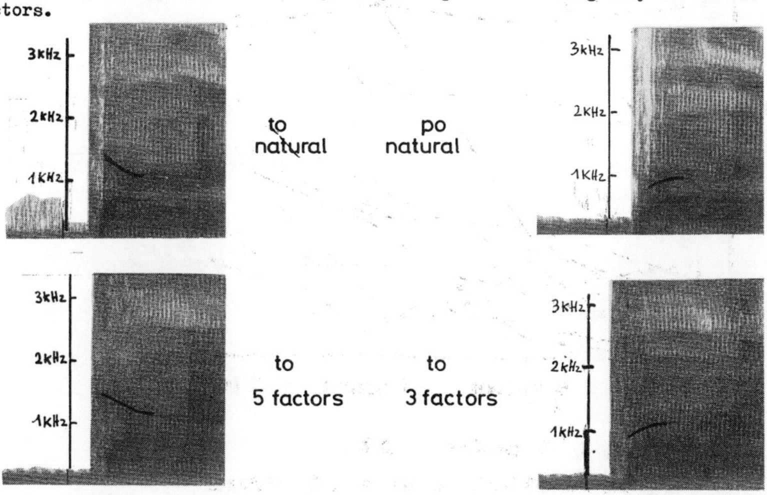

5 W.D. VOIERS et al :"Research on diagnostic evaluation of speech intelligibity AFCRL 72 0694 – TRACOR Inc. 1973

6 J.P. PECKELS, M. ROSSI : "Le test de diagnostic par paires minimales" – Revue d'Acoustique – n° 27 – p. 245 – 262 (1973).

.../...

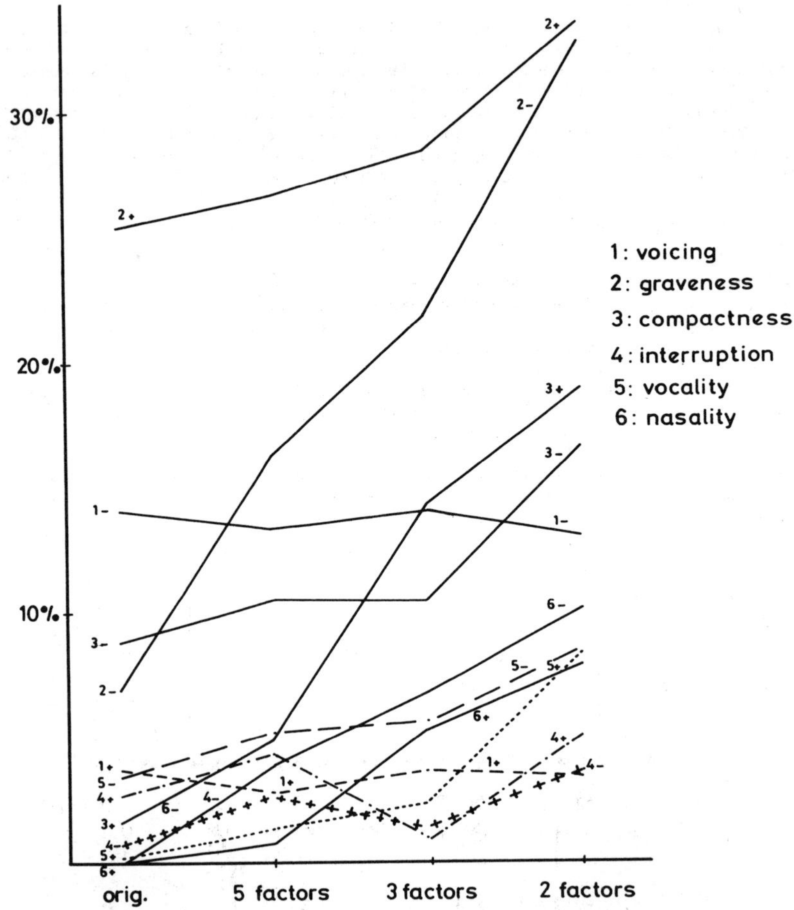

FIG. 5 : % confusion DRT

original : 2400 bit/s filtered 300 - 3400 Hz
one male speaker. axis adapted to speaker

Articulation tests using non-sense syllables

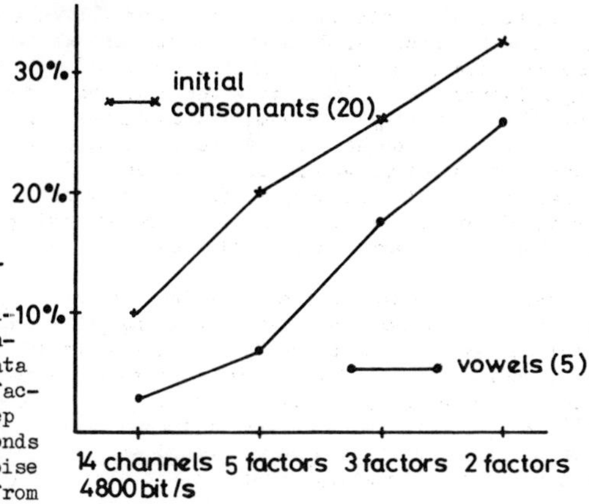

FIG. 7 : % confusion (non-sense CVC) ; general axis, 2 male and 2 female speakers

Tests using logatoms were performed on data reduced from a 14-channel Vocoder with an initial rate of 4800 bit/s ; channels were sampled at 75 Hz. Data reconstitued from 5, 3 and 2 factors are listened to. Each step of degradation nearly corresponds to a 3 dB loss of signal-to-noise ratio ; these results differ from DRT : initial data as well as the test itself are different :

- the original quality is better,
- the axes were determined from data uttered by 4 speakers,
- since axes are not adapted to vowels are relatively more sensitive than consonants, (see Fig. 7)

Analysis of the matrix of confusions between initial consonants reveals that five classes are stable even when 2 factors only are kept : unvoiced fricatives and affricatives, (dʒ), plosives, (ℓ) and nasals, voiced fricatives and (R) (j) (k). (Fig. 8).

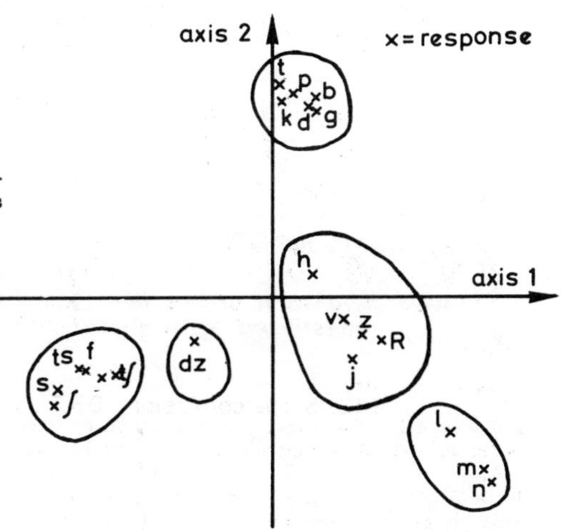

FIG.8:Analysis of the confusion matrix

Conclusions

Reduction of vowels using adapted axes allows a primary classification based on the first two factors. Reduction using general axes results in a relatively greater sensitivity of vowels, while classes of consonants remain quite stable keeping 2 factors only. Estimating the provided parameters is possible by listening to reconstituted data. Those results can be compared to Pols' results 7. Another way of reduction consists in reducing several consecutive, instead of isolated short-time spectra. An example is given on Fig. 9, where the evolution of the first factor (45% of variance) is seen to correspond with segmentation ; three different sets of axes may be used and switched according to the value of the first factor (beginning, center, end of syllable).

Local axes adapted to the sort-time spectrum (8) should provide a greater reduction of spectra using simpler processings than pattern-matching. The advantage of the local axes is indicated by the example of (ø). The reconstitution of this vowel is medium for the first three factors ; the reason is that (ø) is well explained by axes 4 and 5. A classification can be made which results in several classes (ø) being included in one of these classes. Determining a set of axes for each class will result in a more precise and saving coding (in our example, axes 4 and 5 will be immediately found for the class of (ø)).

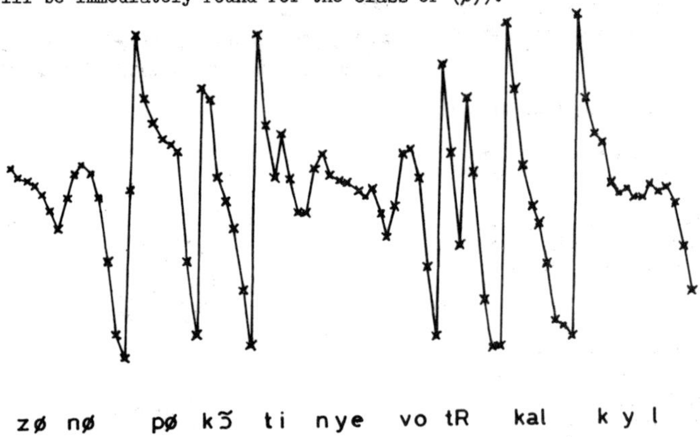

FIG. 9 : Evolution of the first factor, the samples are constitued with three consecutive spectra

7 L.C.W. POLS : "Analysis and Synthesis of Speech Using a broad-band spectral representation" - Symposium on Speech Perception - Leningrad (Août 1973)

8 P. GRAILLOT : "Compression et reconstitution de données issues du Vocoder" - Analyse et Synthèse de la Parole - Rapport C.N.E.T./C.R.L. - Vol. I - (1972-1973) - p. 61-70.

Speech Communication Seminar
Stockholm. Aug. 1–3, 1974

RELATIONS BETWEEN SOME OF THE PARAMETERS OF VOWEL SOUNDS

L.P.C. Jansen, Acoustics Division, C.S.I.R., P.O. Box 395, Pretoria, 0001, South Africa

Abstract

The existence of a relation between some of the parameters of vowel sounds is proved. The relation is expressed in the form of regression equations, whereby one parameter can be predicted fairly accurately from a knowledge of the others. The exact form of the relation varies from one speaker to another, but remains constant for a particular speaker. This was proven through two sets of recordings made with a time interval of 18 months between them. The relation is independent of the type of vowel, the loudness level or the pitch level.

Introduction

Previous research by the author (1) proved that the ratio of the amplitudes of the first and second formants (A_1/A_2) can, under certain circumstances, be used to distinguish between speakers.

Measurements were made of the amplitudes of the first twelve glottal cycles of the diphthong HOY, for a number of utterances of a few different speakers. The result showed that this particular relation between these two parameters can be of value for the purpose mentioned, and also proved that a simple relation between some vowel parameters exists and can be different for different speakers. This result, as well as other undocumented observations, aroused a strong suspicion that there might exist a kind of general relation between some of the parameters of vowel sounds.

It was also thought at the time that such a relation may differ from speaker to speaker, making it useful for the purpose of speaker identification. This fact has since been proven by the author (2).

The relations between some of the vowel parameters are expressed in the form of regression equations, whereby any one parameter can be expressed in the form of a function of certain other parameters. This means that one parameter can be predicted from a knowledge of the others.

This paper is abstracted from the research described in the second part of reference (1), which is repeated as the first part of reference (2).

Basic theory of relations in the form of regression equations

A first degree regression equation with independent variables

$x_1, x_2, x_3, \ldots$ can be written in the form

$$y = b_0 + b_1x_1 + b_2x_2 + b_3x_3 + \ldots\ldots$$

Here b_0, b_1, b_2, b_3, ... are constants and y is the dependent variable. The x_1, x_2, x_3, ... and y respectively correspond to values of different vowel parameters. In this way one of the vowel parameters (corresponding to y) is expressed as a function of the others. For any set of x-values, a value for y can be calculated and therefore predicted. The difference between the measured value and the predicted value of the dependent variable y is called a residue. The values of the regression constants b_0, b_1, b_2, b_3, ... are calculated in such a way that the sum of the squares of the complete set of residues is a minimum. If the dependent variable y can be expressed as a function of the independent variables, then the variance of the residues will be much smaller than the variance of the measured values of y. The ratio between the latter variance and the former may be used in an F-test to determine whether the dependent variable can be predicted from the independent variables, in other words, whether there is a relation between the parameters or not. If the calculated F-value is much greater than the appropriate critical F-value, then some relation definitely exists. This theory may be found in many textbooks on statistics e.g. Li (3).

If the relation between the parameters is not linear, then it can be advantageous to use a second degree regression equation, of the form

$$y = b_o + b_1x_1 + b_2x_1^2 + b_3x_2 + b_4x_2^2 + b_5x_1x_2 + \ldots\ldots$$

In this form the regression equation can compensate to a certain extent for non-linearity.

One important condition for regression equations is that the error variance of any of the parameters should remain fairly constant over the whole range of values, for the units used. In order to comply with this requirement all frequency and amplitude values were converted to logarithmic units prior to fitting it to a regression equation.

Another requirement for regression equations is that there must be a reasonable amount of variation in all the parameters concerned. This variation should be large compared to the error variance for any parameter.

The recordings and the method of analysis

Recordings of the voices of 6 speakers were made in an anechoic chamber. The text consisted of six isolated monosyllabic words incorporating vowels with a wide range of first and second formant frequencies. The subjects were requested to read the text in six different ways, consisting of three loudness levels (soft, normal and loud), each at two pitch levels (low and high). The subjects could choose their own levels according to these rules. The variations were introduced to comply with the requirements mentioned in the previous paragraph.

Pitch synchronous Fourier analyses were made by computer of single glottal cycles at a time. Two analyses were made from each word of text, one near the beginning of the vowel and one near the end. This resulted in a maximum of 72 sets of parameter values for each speaker. Due to technical difficulties it was not always possible to obtain all 72 sets.

The following parameters were measured:

1. the amplitudes of the fundamental frequency component and its second harmonic (A_0 and A_0'),
2. the amplitudes of the first two formants (A_1 and A_2),
3. the frequencies of the first two formants (F_1 and F_2), and
4. the fundamental frequency F_0 (vibration frequency of the vocal folds).

All amplitudes were measured as root mean square values over the full glottal cycle, and were expressed in absolute sound pressure level (dB with respect to 10^{-12} watt/m^2).

The first results for one speaker

At first only one speaker's voice was used and only one glottal pulse per word was analysed. In three instances the first two formants could not be distinguished sufficiently well to make proper measurements, so only 33 complete data sets were available. These were used to make a preliminary investigation about the existence of relations between some of the vowel parameters.

To start with, the data for the individual words were used separately and a large number of first degree regression equations were calculated for this speaker. The amplitudes A_0', A_0 or A_1 were used in turn as the dependent variable and two or more of the remaining variables (excluding F_1 and F_2) were used as the independent variables. Many of these equations were of no use, the calculated F-value being smaller than the appropriate critical F-value. Some equations were very good, however, indicating that the dependent variable can be predicted from the independent variables. A typical example is an equation that was calculated with A_0 as the dependent variable and F_0 and A_2 as the independent variables. This equation has a calculated F-value of 303,8 with a critical F-value of 9,6 at a 5 % level of significance. The multiple correlation coefficient was 0,996. A number of other equations were of similar quality, proving that for certain words there is definitely a relation of some kind between certain of the vowel parameters.

These results proved the existence of relations under certain conditions, but a more general relation was required, combining the sets of parameter values for all six words. Various first degree equations were calculated with F_1 and F_2 now included amongst the independent variables, and using all the available data sets for this speaker.

The results were promising, but not good enough to prove firmly the existence of a general relation between the vowel parameters. For instance, in one case A_0 was expressed as a function of only three parameters F_o, F_1 and A_o. This resulted in a good equation with a calculated F-value of 19,9 and a critical F-value of 2,95. The problem was that the standard deviation of the residues was 2,75 dB, with values of 3 and 4 dB being common. This is much greater than the probable errors in the measurements. This indicates that these independent variables can in fact be used to predict the dependent variable, but that the regression equation used is not of an optimum form to prove the existence of a general relation.

The results with second degree regression equations

The next step was therefore to use a second degree regression equation, which would be able to accommodate a possible non-linearity in the basic relation between the vowel parameters. An equation of this type was calculated in the form

$$A_0 = f(F_0, F_1, F_2, A_0', A_1, A_2)$$

and this gave a much better fit of the data. The calculated F-value was 18,7 with a critical value of 4,5 at a 5 % level of significance. The standard deviation of the residues was only 1,49 dB. This was good, but it involved an equation with 28 constants, while only 33 complete sets of data were available. This means that only 5 degrees of freedom remained for the equation. Even though none of the residues were greater than 1 dB, the small number of degrees of freedom caused the standard deviation of the residues to be quite large. It was therefore decided to try to reduce the number of constants without reducing the significance of the equation. The method used consisted of eliminating the least important independent variables, as described by for instance Li (3), Vol II, p. 105.

This method worked very well and soon a very good equation was obtained, with only 17 constants. The calculated F-value was 30,5 which greatly exceeds the critical F-value of 2,3. The multiple correlation coefficient was 0,969 and the standard deviation of the residues was 1,23 dB, which is very good. It is of the order of experimental errors.

Various other equations were also calculated and the number of constants reduced as above. The choice of the basic dependent variable seemed to be relatively unimportant. Equations with A_0, A_1 or A_2 were about as good as with A_0, described above.

The fact that such a good regression equation as given above could be obtained, proved that some relation does actually exist between the parameters of vowel sounds. The standard deviation of 1,23 dB for the residues of the equation mentioned above should be compared with the standard deviation of 4,41 for all the original values of A_0. The smallest value measured for A_0 was 49,8 dB sound pressure level and the largest was 65,8 dB. The calculated or predicted values were 49,3 and 65,1 dB respectively for these two cases. A better fit of the data can hardly be expected, because of experimental errors. If some definite relation between the vowels did not exist, these results would have been impossible.

All of the equations calculated up to this stage were valid only for the data used, that is, only for this one speaker. Whether similar equations could be obtained for the other speakers still remained a question. The only way in which an answer to this question could be obtained, was to analyse the recordings of the other speakers' voices in the same way.

Full analyses were then made of all the other speakers' voices, resulting in from 49 to 72 complete sets of data for each of the 6 speakers. (Two glottal pulses per word were analysed.)

Through careful investigation it was found that some of the independent variables could be deleted for all 6 speakers, and finally an equation was found which had the same form for all speakers and in which only the values of the constants differed. This was also a second degree equation of the form

$$A_0 = f\,(F_0, F_1, F_2, A_0', A_1, A_2)$$

The relevant results for these equations are given in table 1. Each equation has 21 constants (20 coefficients).

Table 1. The relevant statistics for a general regression equation, for all the speakers. The critical F-values are given for a 5 % level of significance.

Speaker number	Number of data sets	Multiple correlation coefficient	Standard deviation of residues (dB)	Calculated F-value	Critical F-value
1	70	0,936	1,34	24,9	1,8
2	55	0,951	1,16	25,5	1,9
3	49	0,969	1,07	37,8	2,0
4	72	0,970	1,42	56,7	1,8
5	70	0,978	1,01	76,2	1,8
6	50	0,978	1,50	53,6	2,0

Discussion of the results

It is seen from table 1 that all the equations are highly significant. This means that for all 6 speakers the value of the parameter A_0 can be predicted from a knowledge of the other parameters. The constants used in the equation are, of course, different for each speaker.

An estimate of the standard deviation of the residues due to measurement errors, amounts to 1,03 dB for a first degree equation with the same variables, and about 1,3 dB for this second degree equation. It is seen from table 1 that in many cases the final value is smaller than this. This indicates firstly that the accuracy of the measurements was sometimes better than originally estimated, and secondly that the relation between the vowel parameters remains virtually constant for all of the 36 utterances for each speaker. The decision about which particular parameter to use as the dependent variable (usually one of the amplitudes) is of secondary importance. The above results were for A_0 but subsequent results have shown that A_1 is even slightly more predictable with such regression equations.

It is almost certain that if the form of the regression equations were chosen correctly, to correspond with the actual method of vowel production, superior results would be obtained. No attempt has yet been made by the author to do this.

Final and very positive proof of the existence and stability of relations between some vowel parameters comes from the fact that such regression equations as mentioned above could be used for speaker identification. Two sets of recordings of speakers' voices were made with an interval of 18 months between them and both were analysed according to the same method. Regression equations were calculated from the first set of recordings and the parameter values from the second set fitted to these. It was found that if the speakers for the two sets are the same, then there is very little difference between the measured and predicted values of the dependent variable. If the speakers are not the same, the difference is much greater on average. The full results are described in reference (2). This proved both the existence and the individuality of relations between some of the parameters of vowel sounds.

In order to achieve results as good as these, it is of course very important to take great care with the measurements of the parameters. Each recording was accompanied by a special signal to make absolute amplitude measurements possible. The selection of the formants was done with great care and various methods were used to check the accuracy and consistency of each stage of the analysis. The full set of parameter values as obtained by the author can be made available on request.

It should be obvious to the reader that the relation between the parameters of vowel sounds is of a very general nature. It was established with a variety of vowel types, representing great variations in the frequencies of the first and second formants. The fundamental frequency and the amplitudes also varied over quite a range. Indications are that the same relation would hold for vowels of different languages and that it is coupled to the physical process of speech production.

References

1. Jansen L.P.C., Objective speaker identification by analysis of spoken vowels. Unpublished D.Sc. thesis (1969).

2. Jansen L.P.C., Speaker identification by means of some relations between the parameters of vowel sounds. Progress report about research in connection with speaker identification (1973).

   The above two reports may be obtained from the author.

3. Li J.C.R., Statistical Inference, Vol I and II. Edward Brothers (1964).

Speech Communication Seminar
Stockholm. Aug. 1–3, 1974

EXPERIMENTS WITH A VARIABLE-FRAME-RATE CODING SCHEME APPLIED TO FORMANT SYNTHESIZER CONTROL SIGNALS

E. McLarnon, J. N. Holmes and M. W. Judd
Joint Speech Research Unit
Eastcote Road, Ruislip, Middlesex, U.K.

Abstract

A variable frame-rate coding scheme has been applied to the parameters of a parallel formant synthesizer. The operation of the scheme is discussed and some preliminary results presented. Synthesizer control parameters obtained at 5500 bits/s have been coded at 1200 bits/s with very little degradation in speech quality.

Introduction

In formant vocoders the spectral envelope of the input speech signal is represented by a small set of formant parameters. Because these parameters represent vocal-tract resonances they are mostly slowly varying and are normally derived in frames, at a typical rate of 50–100 per second, in the analysis section of the vocoder. Each frame represents a segment of the input speech signal during which the parameters are assumed to be reasonably constant.

For the experiments reported in this paper the formant data used was derived from visual study of spectrograms and speech waveforms, and was used to control a parallel formant synthesizer.[1] The data was represented by 100 frame/s with 11 parameters/frame and 5 bits/parameter. The overall digit rate was therefore 5500 bits/s. The 11 parameters were:-

F_N, A_N	Frequency and amplitude of the main nasal formant
F_1, F_2, F_3	Frequencies of the first 3 vocal-tract formants
A_1, A_2, A_3	Amplitudes of the first 3 vocal-tract formants
A_{HF}	Amplitude of a fixed high frequency formant
F_o	Fundamental voicing frequency
S	A multi-level "degree of voicing" parameter which allows for mixed excitation.

All formant frequencies were linearly related to the quantized parameter values, whereas F_o and the amplitudes were quantized in logarithmic intervals, except for the lowest amplitude level which switched the formant generators off.

For this type of speech representation to form the basis of an efficient low-bit-rate vocoder system it is necessary for the initial bit-rate of 5500 bits/s to be reduced to some lower value, say, 1200 bits/s. If the bit-rate is reduced by simply lowering the frame rate then time blurring will occur and some important articulatory features, such as stop-consonant bursts and certain rapid formant transitions, will not be preserved in the synthesized speech. Alternatively, if the number of bits per frame is reduced significantly then the quality of the synthesized speech will suffer accordingly. Holmes has considered the problem of lowering the bit-rate for formant-based and similar vocoders, and has proposed a variable-frame-rate coding scheme.[2] This coding scheme exploits the fact that the vocoder control parameters mostly change slowly with time, with occasional more rapid variations. When rapid variations do occur they tend to affect most parameters simultaneously, and little available channel capacity is therefore lost by transmitting a complete frame of data at such times. This paper describes the detailed operation of such a scheme when applied to formant data.

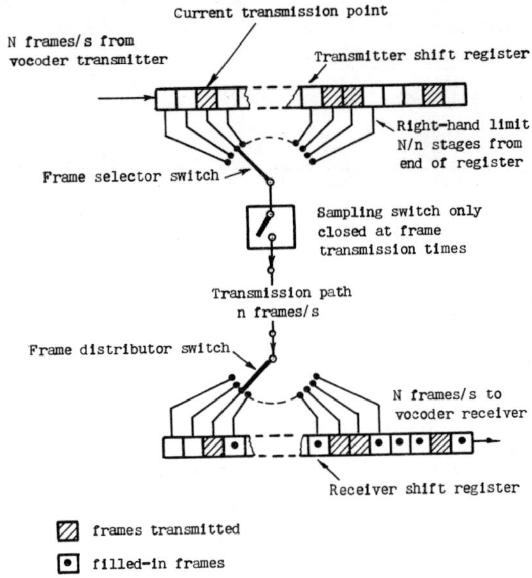

Fig 1 Arrangement of shift registers

Coding Scheme

The operation of the coding scheme may be explained with the aid of fig 1. Two similar shift registers are used to store frames of synthesizer control data, one in the transmitter and one in the receiver. Each stage of each register holds a complete frame of data. At the transmitter, frames input to the coding scheme are fed into the left-hand end of the transmit register at N frames/s, and at the receiver frames to control the synthesizer are taken from the right-hand end of the receive register at the same rate. At some lower rate, n frames/s, frames are selected from those travelling through the transmit register, and are transmitted together with bits to indicate from which register stages they were taken. As soon as a new frame is received, it is loaded at the stage indicated by the extra bits. Any stages between the one just filled and that holding the previous transmitted frame are then filled in, either by repetition of the previous frame or by linear interpolation between the previous and just transmitted frames. The fill-in method to be used is indicated by a further bit that is transmitted with each frame. The arrangement of shift registers just described produces an overall signal delay equal to the time taken for the signals to pass through one shift register.

Most of our experiments have used the following method of selecting frames for transmission from the transmit register. At each transmit time the frames in the register are tested sequentially, starting at the leftmost end, for suitability for transmission. For each frame tested the coding transmitter generates the fill-in frames that would be produced at the receiver if that frame were transmitted. This is done using both methods of fill-in. Based on the difference between input and generated frames three error scores are calculated for each type of fill-in. These error scores reflect the likely perceptual effect that the coding operation is having on the input data, and form the basis on which the decision whether to transmit is made. The method of calculating these error scores will be discussed in the next section.

The three error scores are compared with three error thresholds - one for each type of error score. If, for the frame under consideration, no error score is exceeded for at least one method of fill-in, then that frame is selected for transmission and the maximum error score for each fill-in method determined. Before transmission the parameters in the frame are quantized, and extra data specifying position in the transmit register and the type of fill-in to be used are added to the frame. The type of fill-in chosen is that which gives the lower maximum error score.

If one or more error thresholds are exceeded for both types of fill-in then the coding device continues testing each frame in succession until low enough error scores are found. As each frame is tested the potential point of transmission moves towards the right-hand end of the register. At this right-hand end a limiting condition arises because the transmitted frame moves N/n stages along the register in the interval between frame transmissions. The transmission point must, therefore, be chosen at least N/n stages clear of the right-hand end of the register for interpolation to be possible, irrespective of error scores. This limiting at the right-hand end of the transmit register can cause serious errors in the reconstructed parameters when frames in stages beyond the limit need to be transmitted to preserve important parameter variations.

To reduce the probability of limiting and to make best use of this method of frame selection it is important that the error thresholds are set correctly. If these thresholds are too high then too many frames will be selected from the left-hand end of the register. Similarly, if they are too low then too many frames will be selected from the right-hand end of the register. In either case the performance of the system will be similar to that of a simple system with constant frame rate, n frames/s. To reduce the occurrence of these conditions the thresholds are made to vary along the register so that the transmission point tends towards the centre, but still has a reasonable degree of spread as the signal properties vary. The occurrence of limiting conditions can be further reduced by making the thresholds slowly adapt if the selection point shows a bias towards either end of the register.

Even with these refinements an obvious limitation of this selection method is that it takes no account of the information in later frames in the register when choosing the current frame. If a period of rapid parameter change is stored in the register, such that more than the permitted number of frames would need to be transmitted to satisfy the error criteria, it is obviously better to transmit only the most important frames than to allow the serious errors which might result from right-hand limiting. For this reason a second selection procedure was considered.

In the second selection method the coding device, after selection of the present frame to be transmitted, also determines the frames that are likely to be transmitted in the future. From this calculation it is possible to assess the likelihood of future occurrence of the limiting condition. If a future limiting condition is probable then the criterion of acceptability of the current frame is relaxed to reduce this probability. This second method of selection requires considerably more calculations than the first and probably would not be considered for a practical hardware implementation of the coding scheme.

Calculation of Error Scores

When testing whether a frame needs to be transmitted the coding transmitter generates the output frames that would be produced if that frame were transmitted. In generating these frames quantization effects that will occur on transmission are taken into account. Although, for economy of transmitted bits, the quantization of the transmitted parameters will be fairly coarse, the interpolated parameters can be more finely quantized, since there is no restriction imposed by an overall bit rate on the number of bits per frame allowable at the synthesizer control stage. By comparing input and generated frames "error measures" are calculated for all parameters except fundamental voicing frequency (errors in this parameter were found to be negligible over typical frame intervals). An error measure is defined by the following formula:-

$$E_{mp} = D_p(P-P') \times (\mathrm{Max}(A_p, A_p')+K-L) \times W_p.$$

where E_{mp} is the error measure of parameter p in frame m.

$D_p(P-P')$ is a function of the difference between the input parameter, P, and the generated parameter, P'.

A_p is the amplitude associated with parameter p. For a formant, x, if $P = F_x$ or A_x then $A_p = A_x$. For parameter S, A_p is the greatest of A_N, A_1, A_2, A_3 and A_{HF}.

A_p' is the generated parameter equivalent of A_p.

$\mathrm{Max}(A_p, A_p')$ is the greatest of A_p, A_p' and (L-K).

W_p is a weight depending on the estimated subjective importance of parameter p.

L is whichever is the greater of K and the maximum value of A_1 in the previous 100 frames. This term normalizes the amplitudes with respect to the overall speech level.

K is a constant controlling the extent to which formant amplitude affects the error measure.

In choosing the terms included in the formula for calculating error measures we have tried to take account of the probable perceptual differences between input and generated parameters in the following ways.

We have weighted the error in each parameter by a correspponding amplitude parameter $Max(A_p,A_p')$. This weighting assumes that errors in low amplitude formants will be less significant than errors in high amplitude formants. We have used $Max(A_p,A_p')$ rather than A_p, since errors are likely to be more significant if A_p' is greater than A_p. The particular form of this amplitude weighting term is determined by the fact that the amplitude parameter scales are logarithmic over a 50 dB range, with an "off" condition below the -50 dB level. Errors are given a zero weight if the corresponding formant is switched off or if its level is more than K below the local maximum of A_1. For the experiments so far K has corresponded to 40 dB, but a smaller value may be desirable.

The function $D_p(P-P')$ is implemented in a look-up table which allows greater weight to be attached to large difference errors. A small number of large errors degrades the speech quality more than a large number of small errors. In the initial experiments the look-up table has been made symmetrical about its mid-point, so that positive errors in parameters are given equal importance with negative errors. It is, however, planned to try assymmetrical tables for the amplitude parameters, because one would expect short-duration peaks of amplitude to be subjectively more significant than short-duration dips.

At present the W_p weight is set to unity for each parameter, since we have not yet conducted tests to find how its value should vary from parameter to parameter.

The error measures calculated for the frame being tested can be variously interpreted to give a number of error scores, from which we have selected three to use in our present study.

First, we chose the sum of the generated error measures taken over all fill-in frames and all parameters. We have found that when this error score is large for vowels and other relatively steady-state sounds then the quality of speech synthesized from the generated data is appreciably poorer than that synthesized from the input data. This error score is used, therefore, to indicate frames that need to be transmitted primarily to maintain good quality in slowly-changing sounds.

The second error score used is the maximum total error in any frame summed over all parameters. This score is large when interpolation has occurred through stop-consonant bursts or rapid parameter transitions, and is therefore used to indicate frames that need to be transmitted to preserve such features in the speech.

The third error score we use is the maximum sum of the errors in any single parameter taken over all fill-in frames. This score will be large in the case where one parameter is changing significantly while the other parameters are relatively constant. Its value therefore, indicates frames that need to be transmitted to preserve important variations in a single parameter.

Experiments with a variable-frame-rate coding scheme applied to formant synthesizer control signals

Results

A number of experiments have been conducted using a computer simulation of the scheme described above. A 16-stage register with N at 100 frames/s (160 ms delay) and n at 25 frames/s was chosen for the experiments. The bit-rate reduction and total delay implied by this combination were thought to correspond to realistic practical requirements for an efficient two-way communication system. The formant data used were obtained at 5500 bits/s in the form already described in the introduction. The quality of the speech synthesized from this data at 5500 bits/s was very close to that of the natural speech.

In the first experiment a series of preliminary runs was first performed using different values of error thresholds. Based on the results obtained rules were derived for controlling the thresholds such that the transmission point was allowed to move across the full range of the register as the signal properties changed. These rules were used in the later experiments. No account was taken of likely future transmission points in selecting each frame. The transmitted parameters were not quantized more coarsely than the input parameters - all were described with five bits. The resulting overall transmission rate of 1500 bits/s was made up as follows:-

parameter data	55 bits/frame
address data	4 bits/frame
fill-in data	1 bit/frame
Total	60 bits/frame
frame rate	25 frames/s

Speech synthesized from the coded data was found to be only just detectably different from that synthesized using the original 5500 bits/s input data.

The second experiment repeated the conditions of the first with the addition that the transmitted parameters were further quantized as follows:-

F_1, F_2, F_0	5 bits
A_N, A_1, A_2, F_3, A_3	4 bits
F_N, A_{HF}	3 bits
S	2 bits

An overall transmission rate of 1200 bits/s was made up as follows:-

parameter data	43 bits/frame
address data	4 bits/frame
fill-in data	1 bit/frame
Total	48 bits/frame
frame rate	25 frames/s

Reconstructed parameters used the same quantization of five bits as the input parameters. This accuracy allows the synthesizer parameters to change sufficiently smoothly during slowly changing sounds for single level changes from frame to frame to be barely perceptible. In this experiment the speech synthesized from the coded data was found to be very slightly poorer than that synthesized in Experiment 1.

Fig 2 shows a comparison of input and reconstructed parameters from part of the data used in the Experiment 2. The phrase described is "Two in the bush". The trace TF indicates the transmitted frames and the type of fill-in. If the value of TF is positive then the interpolating fill-in has been used. A negative value indicates that repeated fill-in has been used. For parameter S the maximum positive value present represents fully voiced excitation, while zero represents totally voiceless excitation. Intermediate levels indicate that mixed excitation is required.

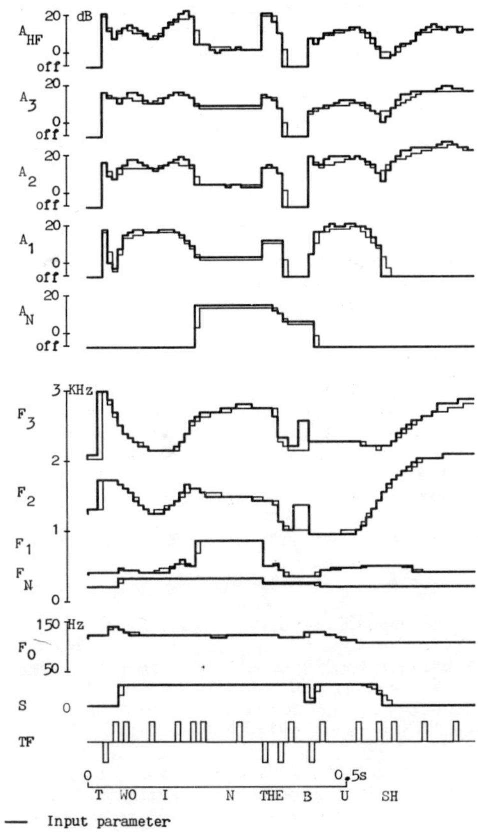

Fig 2 Coding of Synthesizer Parameters

Fig 2 illustrates the ability of the scheme to deal with rapid transitions, in particular the variations in A_1 during the stop burst of [t]. These variations would not have been preserved in a simple coding scheme transmitting every fourth input frame. From the plot of TF we can see that a high local frame rate is required to preserve stop-consonant bursts while reasonably steady-state sounds can be transmitted at a low average frame rate.

Many of the errors in the reconstructed parameters are not perceptually important since the corresponding amplitude parameter is either zero or at a low value. The large errors in F_2 and F_3 during the [b] stop gap, when F_2 and F_3 return to their rest positions, are thus permitted since these formants are switched off during this period.

Fig 2 also illustrates the advantage of having two fill-in methods despite the minor disadvantage that it requires one extra bit per frame. As can be seen the repeated fill-in proves useful in dealing with certain sudden parameter variations such as occur at the end of both [t] and [b] stop gaps. If interpolation fill-in had been used at these points then two frames would have been transmitted in each case. The extra transmitted frame for interpolation fill-in could have caused subsequent limiting at the right-hand end of the transmit register. By using repeated fill-in we have reduced the probability of this limiting occurring at such points of relatively high local frame rate.

In addition to the previous experiments, tests have been made in which the error thresholds were adjusted such that the transmitted frame was always taken from the left-most stage of the transmit register. Thus every fourth input frame was transmitted and the coding scheme thereby made degenerate. Parameters were quantized to the 5 bits of the original data. An overall transmission rate of 1400 bits/s was made up as follows:-

parameter data	55 bits/frame
fill-in data	1 bit/frame
Total	56 bits/frame
frame rate	25 frames/s

As expected speech synthesized from this data was found to be noticeably poorer than that synthesized from the data coded using the full capabilities of a variable-frame-rate scheme in Experiment 1.

Conclusions

Although the coding scheme used in the experiments described in this paper has been tested on only a small amount of formant data, the results so far obtained have been encouraging. As expected, the frame selection procedures have permitted high local frame rates when rapidly changing formant control parameters have been present in the input, whilst maintaining the low average rate needed for efficient transmission. The quality of the speech synthesized from data coded to 1500 and 1200 bits/s was comparable to that synthesized directly from the original 5500 bits/s input data. Some listeners even preferred the quality of the speech synthesized from the lower bit-rate data.

We are now preparing more control-signal data to test the coding scheme further. We hope to find improved distributions for the parameter bits available in each transmitted frame, and for the weights W_p in the error-measure formula. In addition we want to find out how the quality of the synthesized speech degrades as the frame rate is further reduced to produce transmission rates below 1000 bits/s.

In the simulations reported in this paper we have taken account of many of the limitations (such as overall transmit/receive delay) that would exist if the coding scheme were applied to a real-time communication link. On the basis of the results obtained so far we therefore believe that the scheme outlined could be used to increase the transmission efficiency of practical formant-based vocoder systems, or of other types of vocoder whose control signals possess similar characteristics. For non-real-time applications, such as voice storage in computers, an even greater economy might be achieved by using longer shift registers.

References

1. HOLMES, J N: 'The Influence of Glottal Waveform on the Naturalness of Speech from a Parallel Formant Synthesizer'.
IEEE Transactions on Audio and Electroacoustics, June 1973, 21, No 3, pp 298–305

2. HOLMES, J N: 'A Variable-Frame-Rate Coding Scheme for Speech Analysis-Synthesis Systems'. Electronics Letters, in press.

Speech Communication Seminar
Stockholm. Aug. 1–3, 1974

EFFICIENCY AND LIMITATIONS OF LINEAR TRANSFORMATIONS IN DIGITAL SPEECH TRANSMISSION

D. Längle and E. Paulus, Institut für Datenverarbeitung, Technical University of Munich, West Germany

Abstract

In order to approach the limitations of linear transformations in block quantisation of speech signals, bounds for the bitrate have been established, which apply to the digital transmission of the coefficients of the Karhunen-Loève-expansion (KLE) of complete pitch periods. Pitch-synchronous block quantisation has been chosen because it is known from previous investigations /4,5/ to be superior to conventional block quantisation. It is shown that pitch-synchronous KLE may help not only to reduce redundant information but may as well eliminate some irrelevant information. The results are summarized by rate distortion functions which indicate the minimum bitrate necessary to transmit one instantaneous impulse response of the vocal tract per pitch period at a certain mean square quantisation error, provided that consecutive pitch periods are treated independently of one another and that the full frequency range of the speech signal is to be maintained.

Introduction

Digital coding of analog signals usually provides data for an approximate reproduction of samples which have been taken at a constant sampling rate. The distortion of the reproduction depends on the available number of bits/sample, however, a favourable relation between bitrate and distortion may be achieved by carefully tuning the coding scheme to the statistics of the signal source. Efficient source coding may involve a linear transformation such that m consecutive samples x_i are combined into a vector

$$X' = (x_1, x_2, \dots x_m)$$

which is expanded into a series in terms of a set of m orthonormal base vectors $A_1, A_2, \dots A_m$. Thus the sequence of samples is broken up into a sequence of vectors X, and for each vector m coefficients

$$p_i = A_i'X \quad i = 1, 2, \dots m$$

can be encoded instead of the original samples. Reproduction will lead to approximations $u_i \approx p_i$ of these coefficients, and finally an approximation

$$Z = \sum_{i=1}^{m} u_i A_i \quad \text{for} \quad X = \sum_{i=1}^{m} p_i A_i$$

can be obtained.

In order to achieve ultimate coding efficiency, the variances σ_i^2 of the

6–742577 *Volym I*

coefficients are required to differ as much as possible /2/. This requirement is met by the coefficients of the well known Karhunen-Loève-expansion /1/. Therefore, this expansion is of special interest whenever theoretical bounds either for the distortion (mean square error) or for the bit rate are to be explored.

The main characteristic of the KLE is a special set of orthonormal base vectors which is composed of the eigenvectors of the covariance matrix

$$S = E\ (XX').$$

(For convenience an expected value $E(x_i)=0$ is assumed for any sample x_i). The eigenvectors A_1, ... A_m are ordered into a sequence such that a monotonous decrease of the corresponding eigenvalues is achieved:

$$\lambda_1 \geqslant \lambda_2 \geqslant \lambda_3 \ldots \geqslant \lambda_m.$$

The variances of the expansion coefficients are

$$\sigma_i^2 = \lambda_i \qquad i = 1, 2, \ldots m$$

and, as has been mentioned before, are as different from one another as possible. This is also the reason for the well known fact that the convergence rate of the KLE cannot be exceeded by any other series expansion. This means that termination of the expansion after r<m terms in case of the KLE yields the smallest possible mean square error:

$$d = E\ (|X - \sum_{i=1}^{r} p_i A_i|^2) = \sum_{i=r+1}^{m} \lambda_i.$$

The favourable properties of the KLE are essentially due to the fact that the expansion coefficients are linearly uncorrelated, and that linear correlations among the original samples are converted into deviations between the variances σ_i^2. The deviations are the more pronounced the more the original samples are linearly correlated.

Application of the KLE to speech signals

In most previous applications of the KLE to speech signals /2,3/ the vector X was considered to represent a segment from a stationary stochastic sequence of samples. However, it has been shown /4,5/ that the efficiency of the KLE in digital coding of voiced speech can be considerably increased if a stationary stochastic sequence of complete pitch periods rather than of single samples is assumed. The increase is due to the fact that correlations between samples within a pitch period are much more pronounced than correlations between samples within an arbitrarily selected segment of the speech wave. In order to exploit these very high correlations, it seems necessary to submit complete pitch periods to the KLE. However, since the fundamental frequency may vary with time, there will be periods of different durations while the KLE apparently requires segments of a constant duration. The difficulty can be avoided by encoding a segment of constant duration from each pitch period. It has been shown that the speech wave within the remainder of the pitch period can be predicted rather easily from the samples within the encoded segment provided that the duration of this segment is sufficiently large /4/. Thus, digital coding of the expansion coefficients of a selected segment can provide sufficient data for the reproduction of the complete period. Several durations of the selected segment have been investigated and a choice of 4 ms has been found to be quite reasonable for male voices. At a sampling rate of 20 kHz this duration covers m = 80 samples which constitute the vector X.

In order to perform the KLE, the eigenvectors of the covariance matrix of the samples within the selected segment are required. It has been shown /5/ that a reasonably reliable estimate of the covariance matrix can be obtained from 25 s to 30 s of voiced speech. Additionally, the speaker dependence of the estimate has been shown to be quite moderate. Thus, an estimate based on utterances of a particular speaker applies fairly well to utterances of other speakers. There have been several reasons to base the estimate of the covariance matrix on a certain approximation to the speech wave rather than on the speech wave itself. In the following only the main reason with respect to coding efficiency will be reviewed. It is common practice to assume the speech wave to represent the response of the vocal tract to a periodic sequence of excitation pulses which stem from the oscillation of the vocal cords. The response to a single excitation pulse decays rather quickly and may be considered an instantaneous impulse response that reflects the combined effects of the waveform of the excitation pulse and of the instantaneous shape of the vocal tract. During a single pitch period the speech wave can be approximated by the most recent impulse response, and moderate deviations from this approximation will be due to a few superposed previous impulse responses. However, such deviations reflect the fundamental frequency rather than the shape of the vocal tract and may be considered irrelevant since the fundamental frequency does not represent a distinctive feature for phoneme discrimination, at least if a language such as English or German is considered. Therefore, digital coding of a single period should provide data for an accurate reconstruction of the instantaneous impulse response, while the deviations from this approximation may be treated less carefully. To this aim the base vectors should be matched to the statistics of the impulse response, which means that the proper base vectors are the eigenvectors of the covariance matrix of the sampled impulse response. Thus, estimation of the covariance matrix has been based on several thousand instantaneous impulse responses which were extracted from recorded samples of voiced speech and have been normalized to a constant level of the excitation pulses. Details about the extraction procedure have been reported in /5/.

Efficient coding of the expansion coefficients

Limitations of coding efficiency can be represented by the minimum bitrate that is necessary to transmit the selected segments at a prespecified signal-to-noise-ratio

$$\mathrm{SNR} = 10 \log \frac{E\,(X'X)}{E\{|X - \sum_{i=1}^{m} u_i A_i|^2\}} \ \mathrm{dB}$$

As can be seen from the definition of the SNR, the "noise" or "distortion" is represented by the mean square quantisation error. In case of normally distributed expansion coefficients p_i, it is known /6/ that coding is most efficient if all the expansion coefficients yield equal contributions to the total distortion provided that no single contribution D exceeds the variance of the respective coefficient. If the variance of a coefficient is too small to meet the requirement, the coefficient must be encoded by zero bits, which mean that it is omitted from the expansion. In case of the KLE, the omission of coefficients with small variances leads to a termination of the expansion after r<m terms, where the integer r depends on the prespecified distortion or rather on the contribution D of a single coefficient:

$$\begin{aligned} \sigma_i^2 &= \lambda_i > D \quad \text{if} \quad i \leq r \\ \sigma_i^2 &= \lambda_i \leq D \quad \text{if} \quad i > r . \end{aligned} \tag{1}$$

Thus the total distortion

$$E\{|X - \sum_{i=1}^{r} u_i A_i|^2\} = r \cdot D + \sum_{i=r+1}^{m} \lambda_i$$

is composed of equal contributions of r remaining coefficients and additionally of the mean square error that is due to the omission of m - r coefficients. In order to achieve this distortion the r remaining coefficients must be transmitted at a bitrate greater than

$$R = \frac{1}{2} \sum_{i=1}^{r} \text{ld} \frac{\lambda_i}{D} \text{ bit / pitch period.} \tag{2}$$

The bound is known from rate distortion theory and will indeed be somewhat lower since the assumption of normally distributed expansion coefficients represents the "worst case".

The interrelation between the minimum bitrate R and the SNR can be summarized by a rate distortion function. Considering $E(X'X) = \sum_{i=1}^{m} \lambda_i$, and hence

$$\text{SNR} = 10 \log \frac{\sum_{i=1}^{m} \lambda_i}{r \cdot D + \sum_{i=r+1}^{m} \lambda_i} , \tag{3}$$

an estimate of the rate distortion function can be computed from the eigenvalues of the estimated covariance matrix by evaluating r,R, and SNR for various specifications of D. Fig.1 presents the results for several different durations of the selected segment. The resulting rate distortion functions apply to the transmission of one instantaneous impulse response per pitch period. For a given duration of the selected segment, the corresponding rate distortion function indicates the maximum SNR that can be achieved at a given number of bits per pitch period. It should be kept in mind that the indicated SNR does apply only to the selected segment and not to the entire pitch period. Assuming a fixed segment duration and a prediction of the remainder of each period as proposed in /4/, for any bitrate an SNR that applies to the entire pitch period can be computed. For a segment duration of 4 ms, fig. 1 again presents the results for various durations of the entire pitch periods.

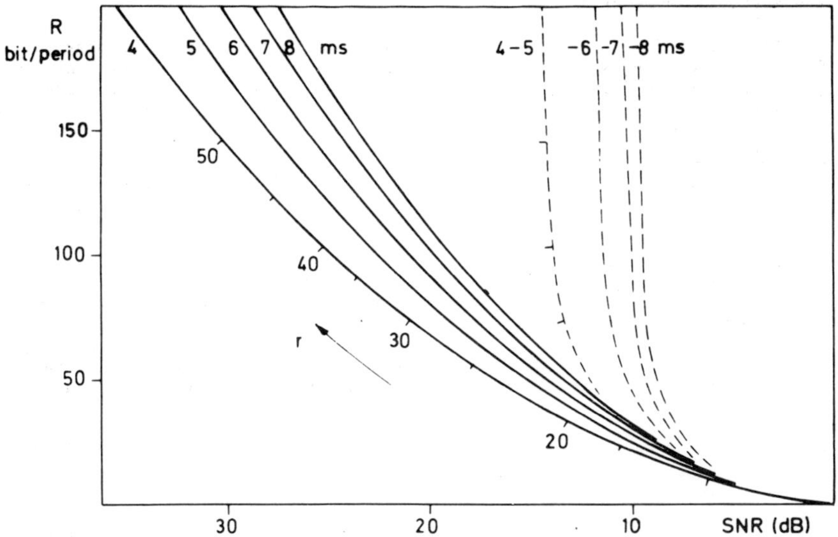

Fig. 1 Rate distortion functions for selected segments, and bitrate versus maximum SNR for entire pitch periods (dotted lines).

Assuming a bitrate of about 75 bit/period, the rate distortion function indicates that the SNR for selected segments of 4 ms cannot exceed an upper bound of approximately 21 dB. However, for the same bitrate it also follows from fig.1 that the maximum SNR which can be achieved for entire pitch periods of 8 ms is bounded below 10 dB. For pitch periods of 5 ms, 6 ms and 7 ms the respective bounds are approximately 13 dB, 11 dB and 10 dB. Accordingly, there will be an upper bound to the average SNR between 21 dB and 10 dB if the fundamental frequency is assumed to vary between 250 cps and 125 cps. At a mean fundamental frequency of e.g. 180 cps, this bound would apply to a bitrate of about 13.5 kbit/s. In order to obtain an accurate estimate of the bound, it would be necessary to refer to the probability density function of the fundamental frequency. Of course, such a bound is not really ultimate since segments of equal duration have been considered together with a special method for the prediction of the remainder of each period.

In order to achieve an ultimate bound the selected segments must be extended to the durations of the entire pitch periods. This means that separate sets of base vectors must be applied to pitch periods of different durations. In this case the rate distortion functions presented in fig.1 would apply to entire pitch periods. Returning to the example of a bitrate of 75 bit/period or 13.5 kbit/s respectively, upper bounds for the SNR ranging from 21 dB to about 16 dB are indicated by the rate distortion functions for the various durations ranging from 4 ms to 8 ms. Thus, the ultimate bound for the average SNR will be somewhere between 16 dB and 21 dB when the fundamental frequency again is assumed to vary between 125 cps and 250 cps. An accurate estimate of the ultimate bound could be based on the probability density function of the fundamental frequency.

The reported results have been determined under the assumption that the full frequency range of the speech signal is to be maintained. A present investigation is performed in order to obtain corresponding results for speech signals that are limited to the standard telephone frequency band.

Acknowledgement

This work was supported by the "Bundesministerium für Forschung und Technologie" of the BRD.

References

/1/ K. FUKUNAGA and W. L. G. KOONTZ: Representation of Random Processes Using the Finite Karhunen-Loève-Expansion. Information and Control 16 (1970), 85 - 101.

/2/ S. J. CAMPANELLA and G. S. ROBINSON: A comparison of Orthogonal Transformations for Digital Speech Processing. IEEE Trans. Commun. Techn. COM-19 (1971), 1045 - 1050.

/3/ P. NOLL: Redundanzreduzierende Sprachcodierung - Eine vergleichende Betrachtung verschiedener Verfahren. In: Signalverarbeitung, W. SCHÜSSLER Ed., Erlangen 1973, 354 - 361.

/4/ E. PAULUS and D. LÄNGLE: Die Anwendung der Karhunen-Loève-Entwicklung für die digitale Sprachanalyse und -synthese. In: Signalverarbeitung, W. SCHÜSSLER Ed., Erlangen 1973, 362 - 369.

/5/ D. LÄNGLE and E. PAULUS: Estimation of Correlation Characteristics Applying to Pitch-Synchronous Karhunen-Loève-Expansion of Speech Signals. Paper B4, Proc. 1974 Int. Zürich Seminar on Digital Communications, Zürich, Switzerland 1974.

/6/ J. J. Y. HUANG and P. M. SCHULTHEISS: Block quantization of Correlated Gaussian Random Variables. IEEE Trans. Commun. Syst. CS 11 (1963), 289 - 296.

Speech Communication Seminar
Stockholm. Aug. 1–3, 1974

INTELLIGIBILITY OF SPEECH RESYNTHESIZED BY USING A DIMENSIONAL SPECTRAL REPRESENTATION

Louis C.W. Pols, Institute for Perception TNO, Soesterberg
The Netherlands

Abstract

An on-line analysis and synthesis system is described based on a dimensional spectral representation of speech. CVC intelligibility raises from 25.2% to 83.7% using 2- to 17-dimensional spectral information for the resynthesis. The quality of the synthesized speech is surprisingly good given that only gross spectral features are used. The system has many applications in speech research, since easy control of many parameters is possible.

Introduction

The spectral representation I am referring to is based on an analysis with a parallel set of 14 one-third octave filters between 400 Hz and 8000 Hz, and 3 filters of 90 Hz bandwidth below that region. The output of these 17 filters, after logarithmic amplification and envelope peak detection, are sampled every 10 msec.
Advantages of this spectral analysis system are:

- it makes real-time analysis possible
- no complicated circuitry has to be built, most filters are right from the shelf,
- the bandwidths of the filters used compare reasonably with the frequency resolution of the inner ear,
- this spectral representation is straightforward, objective, and is at least as efficient as a formant representation (Pols et al., 1973; v.Nierop et al., 1973).

The system is a <u>dimensional</u> spectral representation since each bandfilter spectrum is described as a point in a 17-dimensional space, having coordinate values equal to the levels in the 17 filters. A set of 10-msec speech samples comprises a collection of points in this space. Any arbitrary amplitude spectrum has a position in this space. However, according to limitations of the speech producing mechanism, speech spectra will only partly fill this space. For this reason a considerable dimensional reduction appears to be possible. A straightforward procedure for this dimensional reduction is the principal-components analysis applied on the variance-covariance matrix of the level-normalized spectra (Klein et al., 1970). Successive new directions (eigenvectors) are derived, explaining as much of the variance (eigenvalues) as possible. These new directions, being linear combinations of the original dimensions, can be seen as spectral features. Fig. 1 gives the first eigenvector or factor for 270 CVC words (14,111 10-msec samples) explaining 55.1% of the total variance. We see that this factor compares low and high frequency energy in the spectrum. Mainly for that reason this factor happens to be a very efficient discriminator between sonorant and non-sonorant sounds. The factor is used for that purpose together with the zerocrossings count. The independence of this first factor from the speech material chosen can be seen from the dashed curve in Fig. 1, which gives the first eigenvector for a larger piece of spoken text (31,922 10-msec samples).

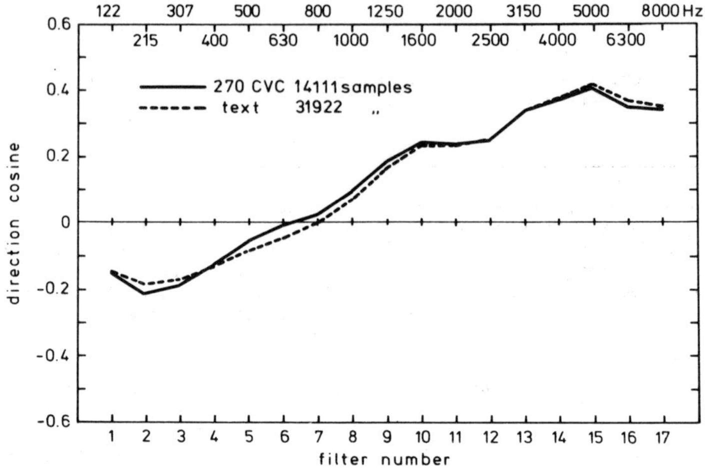

Fig. 1. The first eigenvector of the variance-covariance matrix of the level-normalized bandfilter spectra of all 10-msec samples from two sets of speech utterances.

Table I gives, as an example, the basic data of an analysis of the word |fat|. In the sixth column label "1" indicates a non-sonorant speech sample, and number "2" indicates a sonorant. This labeling is derived from the number of zerocrossings (column 3) and the coordinate value (column 5) of that speech sample along the first dimension, which eigenvector was given in Fig.1. All 14,111 samples of the 270 CVC words (all 15 Dutch vowels combined with all possible 18 initial consonants, see Pols (1972)) are classified in those two groups. Figs.2 and 3 give the first three eigenvectors for those two subsets of speech samples. These two eigenvector bases are used for an m-dimensional representation of all speech samples.

Resynthesis

The good results achieved with the dimensional representation of speech spectra in speech analysis, perception and recognition (Pols et al., 1973; v. Nierop et al., 1973; Pols et al, 1969; Pols, 1971; Pols, 1972) gave us the confidence that a resynthesis would also be possible. The m-dimensional spectral representation ($m \leqslant 17$) can be used to reconstitute a 17-dimensional spectrum, using the variable information in the first m dimensions together with the average spectral information in the remaining dimensions (Pols, 1973). Successive 10-msec 17-dimensional spectra are made audible again with a channel vocoder-type synthesizer. The ordinary way to do this is to modulate the outputs of a parallel set of filters, excited from a pitch-modulated, constant average power pulse-generator, or a noise source (Flanagan, 1972). We preferred a computer-controlled filter excitation.

The principle is that 17 digital-to-analog converters generate pitch-synchronous pulses with a variable amplitude. By integrators the pulses are shaped to sawtooth-like periodic signals, which excite the filters. The am-

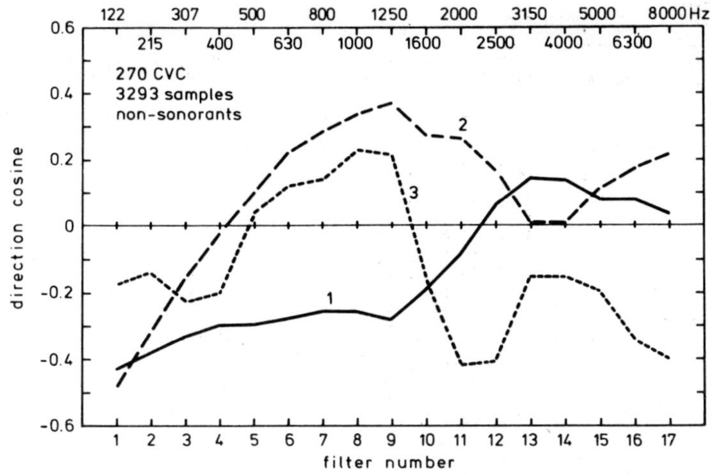

Fig. 2. First three eigenvectors of the group "1" speech samples (non-sonorants).

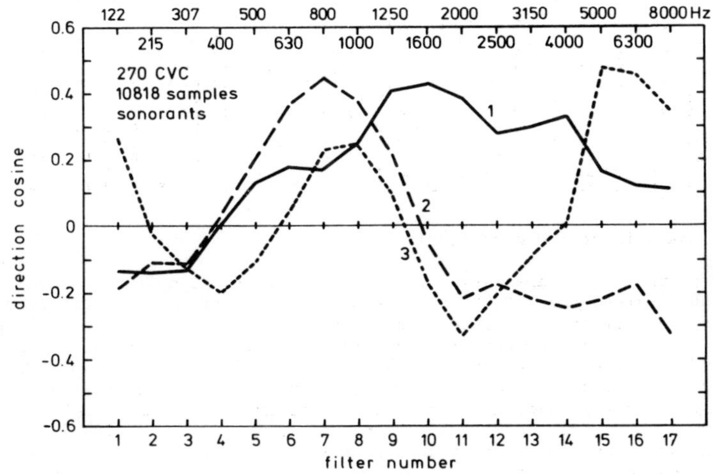

Fig. 3. First three eigenvectors of the group "2" speech samples (sonorants).

SAMPLE NUMBER	OVERALL LEVEL IN dB	NR. OF ZEROCR.	F_o	DIM	"1"=NON-SONORANT "2"=SONORANT	8000	6300	5000	4000	3150	2500	2000	1600	1200	1000	800	630	500	400	317	215	122 Hz	DISTANCE
1	2	3	4	5	6	7	8	9	10	11	12	13	14	15	16	17	18	19	20	21	22	23	24
1	28	26	0	19	1	13	19	20	21	19	14	14	15	12	7	8	5	6	7	2	11	15	71
2	29	33	0	10	1	15	19	24	25	21	18	20	17	14	11	4	6	10	6	4	4	4	18
3	31	42	0	11	1	19	23	25	25	21	18	16	16	12	8	6	10	8	2	4	0	2	15
4	32	35	0	18	1	20	23	24	24	21	21	16	10	12	11	11	10	8	6	7	9	12	15
5	30	33	0	14	1	21	18	23	21	18	19	19	14	14	7	7	4	10	8	2	7	11	14
6	32	42	0	13	1	24	23	22	23	21	22	18	16	11	11	7	5	6	7	0	3	7	15
7	31	42	0	11	1	23	22	23	26	20	19	16	14	10	11	9	6	7	6	0	3	6	7
8	32	44	0	12	1	23	22	24	28	23	16	19	17	15	9	9	8	4	7	10	0	5	13
9	33	42	0	14	1	21	21	22	24	25	20	18	19	16	13	9	7	11	10	10	7	0	13
10	32	40	0	11	1	23	22	25	23	19	19	20	18	18	14	11	11	10	6	2	1	0	13
11	33	44	0	13	1	23	20	25	24	22	20	24	20	13	11	7	9	11	7	7	4	1	11
12	33	48	0	16	1	24	23	23	24	20	22	21	15	13	15	9	9	10	13	13	0	4	13
13	35	44	0	13	1	27	28	27	22	22	24	19	16	17	12	11	16	15	13	7	0	0	15
14	31	45	0	12	1	25	23	25	22	21	17	20	16	14	10	10	15	16	18	10	0	0	16
15	32	36	0	14	1	27	25	27	22	20	16	18	15	15	9	9	17	21	16	10	5	0	9
16	34	39	0	20	1	25	23	25	23	22	16	17	18	16	7	14	17	20	18	10	5	6	11
17	34	40	0	10	1	27	26	25	24	24	24	25	17	18	13	11	8	18	17	7	4	0	19
18	40	39	0	17	1	25	27	31	28	25	24	28	24	22	16	16	11	20	19	7	6	0	18
19	35	30	0	12	1	22	24	30	27	23	26	25	24	21	21	16	14	16	18	15	9	7	28
20	35	25	0	30	1	21	26	25	20	21	22	22	20	18	13	19	15	17	16	22	24	36	36
21	59	3	134	98	2	4	14	14	21	29	28	22	22	34	43	44	46	46	44	42	37	44	83
22	62	4	133	102	2	7	17	15	23	26	23	20	26	36	46	47	52	52	47	43	42	45	13
23	63	7	133	99	2	9	13	15	28	32	29	23	27	36	51	48	54	53	45	40	45	42	13
24	64	6	133	90	2	12	20	23	33	33	29	25	29	40	52	52	55	50	42	39	45	42	12
25	65	6	122	89	2	12	23	24	34	32	27	24	29	40	51	55	56	48	42	39	45	40	6
26	65	9	112	95	2	13	20	21	31	30	24	23	27	38	50	57	58	49	43	41	43	39	9
27	64	8	113	90	2	22	25	23	29	30	23	21	26	37	50	56	59	50	42	42	42	38	12
28	63	7	115	85	2	20	25	28	36	31	24	17	24	32	47	54	58	51	41	42	42	37	12
29	61	5	115	82	2	22	31	31	36	30	23	15	18	25	41	50	56	53	42	41	41	37	15
30	57	6	115	87	2	16	28	25	30	25	18	11	14	18	33	44	50	51	45	41	40	33	11
31	40	6	115	85	2	6	16	18	6	10	0	0	4	3	21	30	42	42	42	31	33	31	30
32	30	5	115	83	2	0	1	0	0	0	0	0	0	0	4	18	33	31	32	28	31	21	23
32	132 MSEC																						
33	36	27	0	19	1	27	30	29	20	15	17	17	18	16	20	18	14	10	13	15	0	8	78
34	36	54	0	23	1	32	34	35	23	12	9	8	10	5	8	6	8	8	8	7	1	8	30
35	36	53	0	20	1	29	34	36	23	15	12	14	7	4	9	6	10	15	5	2	0	6	13
36	33	46	0	18	1	22	28	33	23	21	14	10	10	5	9	9	10	14	6	3	8	7	21
37	35	46	0	20	1	21	29	34	27	17	10	11	10	6	7	13	12	14	11	5	0	0	17
38	34	35	0	23	1	16	23	31	27	16	7	11	12	10	6	9	10	21	18	3	0	0	15
39	30	34	0	21	1	12	23	27	23	15	11	13	12	9	7	9	10	18	16	6	2	8	20
40	29	33	0	27	1	8	17	23	22	12	9	6	9	14	6	11	8	12	15	10	5	3	15
41	29	25	0	31	1	8	11	23	17	11	8	5	6	13	10	10	9	15	12	2	5	6	13
42	29	18	0	35	1	6	12	22	20	10	3	4	6	5	5	15	10	13	5	0	6	10	15
43	26	11	0	36	1	4	10	16	18	6	4	3	5	0	3	8	7	12	3	5	3	9	11
44	27	1	0	50	2	0	1	12	12	0	0	3	7	3	4	5	10	9	8	7	4	12	18
END																							

Table I. Analysis of the word |fat|.

plitudes of the pulses are varied in such a way that the output of each filter has the desired level for that speech sample. After adding the filter outputs, on-line resynthesized speech is derived. For unvoiced sounds the digital to-analog converters generate clocked noisy pulses. For a simplified block diagram of the synthesizer, see Fig. 4. The timing is visualized in Fig. 5. New information is updated every 10 msec, the pulses are generated pitch synchronously, or noisy. According to this asynchronysm three digital buffers (registers A, B and C, see Fig. 4) are needed. Not drawn in Fig. 4 is the time delay which can be introduced between registers B_k and C_k and between "switch$_k$" and "gate$_k$" in order to correct for the different onset times of the filters with different bandwidths. Fig. 5 also shows that, every 10 msec, the computer during only a short period (1-2 msec) has to send information in digital form to the peripheral apparatus, which has its own timing. This means

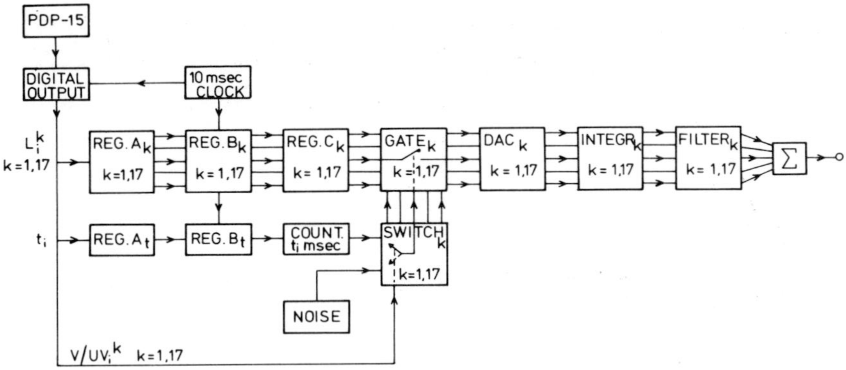

Fig. 4. Block diagram of the synthesis system.

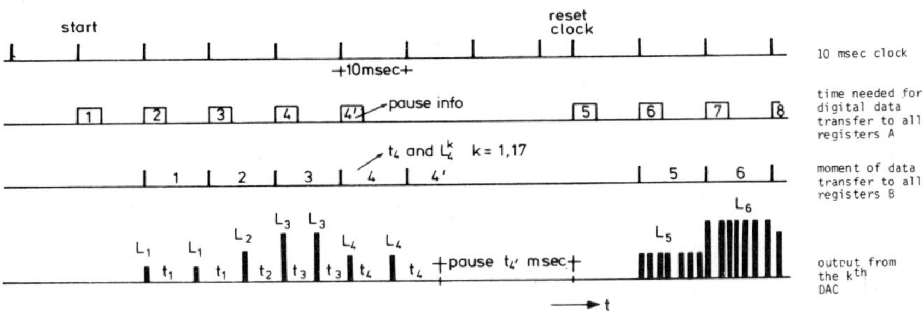

Fig. 5. Timing in the synthesis system. This example gives the timing for an artificial speech sound consisting of 4 voiced samples, followed by a pause, and then some unvoiced 10-msec samples.

that on-line synthesis is possible with a background-foreground or a time-sharing system.

Experiments

The programmable speech synthesizer itself is not yet fully operational, so only preliminary results from some pilot experiments can be given. One of the restrictions is that up to now only voiced sounds could be synthesized.

An intelligibility test was done with 120 CVC words. These mono-syllabic words were composed by combining all 15 Dutch vowels with the 7 initial consonants m, n, l, r, w, j, absent. As final consonants the same set was used together with ŋ . The 15 vowels in isolation also belonged to the list. About half of the words were meaningful. Twenty normal hearing subjects listened, after some training, once to a randomized list in which all words occurred

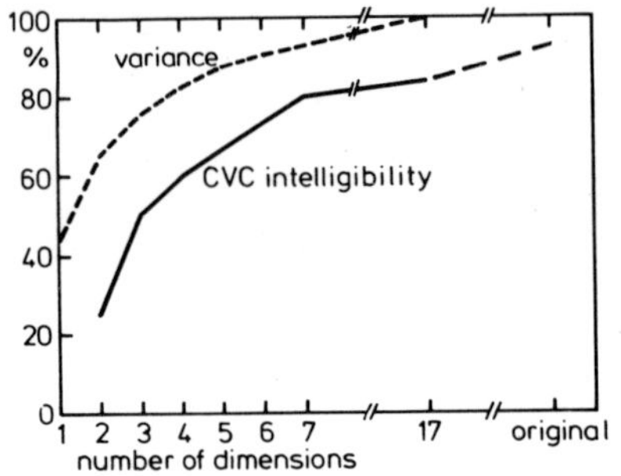

Fig. 6. CVC intelligibility score as a function of the number of dimensions used for resynthesis. The dashed curve gives the amount of explained variance.

RESPONSE

STIMULUS	u	ɔ	o	ɑ	a	ɛ	œ	ϕ	I	e	y	i	other
u	156	0	7	0	0	0	8	1	1	3	42	30	4
ɔ	101	72	12	13	0	4	5	6	2	5	8	4	0
o	38	11	138	5	5	0	1	8	1	11	4	1	9
ɑ	4	123	29	65	2	1	3	0	0	1	0	0	4
a	0	27	56	18	98	1	3	2	0	4	0	0	23
ɛ	2	7	10	6	2	52	79	2	60	5	1	2	4
œ	2	11	6	9	4	17	78	3	67	15	9	9	2
ϕ	1	0	2	0	4	1	5	69	10	125	3	3	9
I	1	1	0	1	0	5	26	1	119	11	13	52	2
e	1	0	0	0	1	2	3	22	17	167	4	13	2
y	0	0	0	0	0	1	5	0	17	25	60	124	0
i	5	0	0	0	0	0	6	4	16	15	32	152	2

Table II. Vowel confusion matrix added over 29 subjects. The subjects identified the monosyllabic words, as resynthesized by using a 2-dimensional spectral representation, the response category "other" stands for diphthongs and no response.

under 5 conditions. These conditions had to do with the amount of dimensional spectral information used for resynthesis. All original 17 dimensions were used in the first condition, in the other four conditions 7, 4, 3 or 2 dimensions were used. As expected, the CVC intelligibility increased with the number of dimensions used, see Fig. 6. There was not much difference between a synthesis using 7 (92,9% of the variance explained) and 17 dimensions. There is a good correlation between intelligibility score and amount of explained variance. The scores will be higher if the subjects are trained separately for each condition. The intelligibility of the original utterances is also given in Fig. 6.

In another experiment we tested with the same 20 listeners the effect of constant pitch and constant overall level on the CVC intelligibility. The naturalness of course diminished but, relative to the natural pitch and level

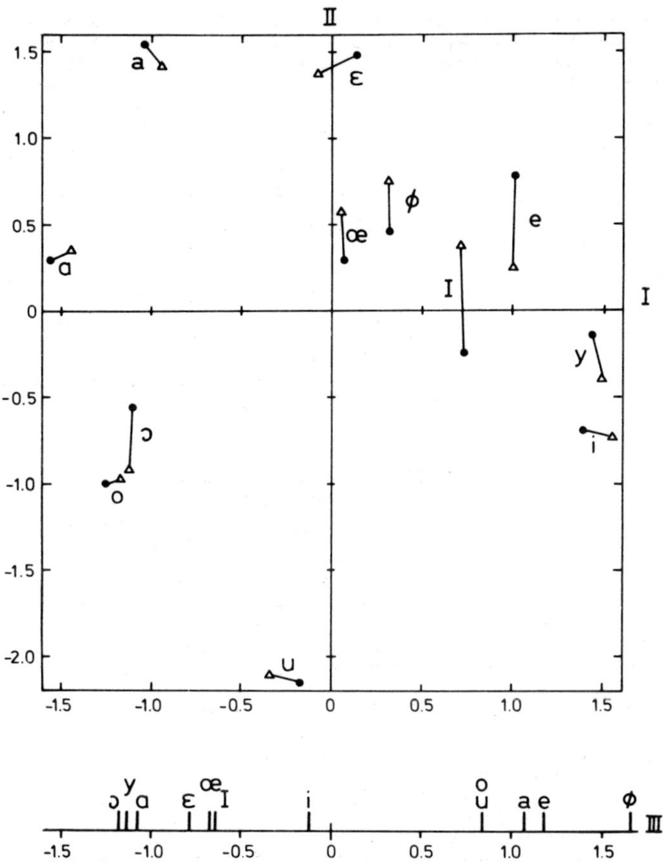

Fig. 7. A canonical matching of the 3-dimensional perceptual and physical vowel representation, see text.

condition, there was hardly any loss in intelligibility. The words were generated using all 17-dimensional spectral information.

In a third pilot experiment we directed our attention to vowel confusions. 29 Subjects listened to a complete list of the same 120 words synthesized under 5 different conditions of spectral information (17, 7, 4, 3 and 2 dimensions). Only the condition in which the words were synthesized using the 2 dimensions gave enough vowel confusions to make a further analysis possible. The confusion matrix, added over all subjects (see Table II), was very asymmetric and had response bias. Applying the procedure proposed by Wagenaar (1968), we corrected for this response bias which resulted in a similarity (half) matrix. This matrix was used as input for a Kruskal (1964) multidimensional scaling program. The 4-dimensional solution had 1,6% stress, in 3 dimensions the stress was 2,0%, and in 2 dimensions 10.8%. This suggests that the perceptual vowel representation derived from the identification experiment was at least 3-dimensional. This seems to be in contradiction with the fact that the words were synthesized using two physical dimensions. However, actually a third parameter was present, that of the duration of the vowel sounds. This becomes also clear if one tries to correlate the 3-dimensional perceptual solution (2.0% stress) with the 3-dimensional spectral representation of the 12 average vowel sounds, applying a canonical matching procedure (Pols et al., 1969).

Fig. 7 gives both matched configurations in the I-II plane. A high correlation along these two dimensions exists (.955 and .954), suggesting that the information in the two physical dimensions used to resynthesize the words indeed are interpreted also as perceptual attributes by the subjects. The third perceptual dimension (see lower part of Fig. 7) correlates not at all with the third physical dimension (r =.177), but gives a good representation of the durational differences between the vowel sounds. Long and short vowels are well separated, with the vowel |i| somewhere in the middle, which is reasonable. The only outsider is the long vowel |y| .

Discussion

The foregoing experiments illustrate some of the possibilities of this synthesis system. In general, the interesting features of this system are:

- the synthesis is computer-controlled and easily programmable, without putting heavy load on central-processor time, since all timing is controlled by the peripheral synthesizer itself;
- if data from the 10-msec samples can be read in fast enough from disk, long utterances in any order can be synthesized in real time;
- the quality of the resynthesized speech, using all 17 dimensions, is good enough for many applications. The parameters necessary for synthesis can be achieved with a straightforward analysis system without human interpretation.
- easy control of many parameters in the resynthesized speech utterances is possible, controllable parameters are:
  - . pitch contour, by changing column 4, see Table I
  - . overall intensity contour, by changing column 2
  - . spectral quality of (parts of) the utterance, by changing columns 7 to 23;
  - . speeding up or slowing down (part of) the utterance without spectral distortion, by repeating or deleting samples, or, even more sophisticated, by varying the 10 msec clock, see Fig. 5;
  - . changing and introducing or deleting pauses between and within words;
  - . using m dimensions, $m \leq 17$;
  - . parts of one utterance can easily be changed with parts of other utterances.
- if enough data are gathered to get insight in the dynamic structure of speech, expressed in terms of this dimensional representation, also synthesis-by-rule will be possible.

References

Flanagan, J.L. (1972), *Speech Analysis Synthesis and Perception*, Springer Verlag, Berlin, 2nd Edition.

Klein, W., Plomp, R., and Pols, L.C.W. (1970), "Vowel Spectra, Vowel Spaces, and Vowel Identification", J. Acoust. Soc. Amer. *48*, 999-1009.

Kruskal, J.B. (1964), "Nonmetric Multidimensional Scaling; A Numerical Method", Psychometrika *29*, 115-129.

Nierop, D.J.P.J. van, Pols, L.C.W., and Plomp, R. (1973), "Frequency Analysis of Dutch Vowels from 25 Female Speakers", Acustica *29*, 110-118.

Pols, L.C.W. (1971), "Real-Time Recognition of Spoken Words", IEEE Trans. Comput. C-*20*, 972-978.

Pols, L.C.W. (1974), "Analysis and Synthesis of Speech Using a Broad-Band Spectral Representation", Proc. of the Leningrad Symp. on Auditory Analysis and Perception of Speech, Academic Press, (in press).

Pols, L.C.W., Kamp, L.J.Th. van der, and Plomp, R. (1969), "Perceptual and Physical Space of Vowel Sounds", J. Acoust. Soc. Amer. *46*, 458-467.

Pols, L.C.W., Tromp, H.R.C., and Plomp, R. (1973), " Frequency Analysis of Dutch Vowels from 50 Male Speakers", J. Acoust. Soc. Amer. *53*, 1093-1101.

Speech Communication Seminar
Stockholm. Aug. 1–3, 1974

ANALYSIS-CONVERSION-SYNTHESIS SYSTEM FOR IMPROVING NATURALNESS AND INTELLIGIBILITY OF SPEECH AT HIGH-PRESSURE HELIUM GAS MIXTURE

Hisayoshi SUZUKI, Gen OOYAMA and Ken'iti KIDO
Res. Inst. of Elect. Comm., Tohoku University, Sendai, JAPAN

Abstract

This paper presents a novel technique for improving naturalness and intelligibility of helium speech using a time domain analysis of speech signal based on linear prediction, time domain design of digital recursive filter, and conversion of impulse response of speech production system. The helium speech "unscrambler" introduced in this paper shifts downward linearly the formant frequencies of helium speech without shifting the fundamental frequency. This unscrambler has been implemented by a program of general purpose computer. Experiments on vowels of synthesized helium speech in the case of conversion ratio $\beta=0.5$ show that the system works so satisfactorily that the errors in the formant frequencies are less than 2%, where error is defined as percent difference between the desired value of formant frequency and the actually obtained value.

Introduction

When speech is produced in a high pressure Helium-Oxygen atmosphere, a unique type of speech distortion is encountered. This kind of distorted speech is called "helium speech". Although information about the distortion may not be completely obtained, the following factors can be taken into account for making a helium speech unscrambler, a device to improve naturalness and intelligibility of helium speech [1].

1° the linear vowel formant frequency shift
2° the nonlinearity in formant frequency shift
3° formant band widths are not substantially affected by pressure
4° speaker's fundamental frequency is relatively unaffected by helium
5° the disparity in overall sound pressure level (SPL) between voiced and unvoiced sounds
6° the relative loss of high frequency energy
7° the poor signal-to-noise ratio common in the underwater environment where helium speech is produced

Of these, the most prominent factors are 1° & 4°.

The helium speech unscrambler described in this paper primarily takes into account of 1°, 3°, and 4°.

Transfer Functions and Impulse Response of Speech Production System

When a time varying vocal tract shape is excited, speech is produced. Time series $\{h(nT)\}$ (where n=0, 1, 2,..., and

T=sampling interval) is assumed to represent the sampled values of impulse response h(t) of speech production system which includes the characteristics of vocal tract, glottal flow and radiation. Transfer function H(z) is defined as a z-transform of {h(nT)}:

$$H(z) = 1 + h(T)z^{-1} + h(2T)z^{-2} + \cdots + h(kT) + \cdots. \quad (1)$$

Let us consider a system whose transfer function is represented by a ratio of polynomials with real coefficients:

$$H(z) = \frac{1 - b_1 z^{-1} - b_2 z^{-2} - \cdots - a_q z^{-q}}{1 - a_1 z^{-1} - a_2 z^{-2} - \cdots - a_p z^{-p}} \quad (2)$$

H(z) represents a recursive digital filter with p poles and q zeros. Voiced speech is produced by applying a sequence of impulses, spaced at the pitch periods, to the digital filter. Voiceless speech is produced by applying a sequence of white noise samples, spaced T seconds apart, to the filter. Within a short interval of time (10-25msec) the human vocal tract is assumed to be fixed in shape, and accordingly, the parameters a_i and b_i are time invariant. Such a time interval is called a "frame". Parameters a_i and b_i in the transfer function H(z) can be estimated framewise from speech signals by a technique of time domain speech analysis taking account of zeros as well as poles [2]. For simplicity, however, we have restricted our attention to the system represented by an all pole type digital filter:

$$H(z) = \frac{1}{1 - a_1 z^{-1} - a_2 z^{-2} - \cdots - a_p z^{-p}} \quad (3)$$

In this case, the coefficients a_i can be obtained by various methods in linear prediction analysis [3]. A reasonably acceptable method of them is to solve an autocorrelation normal equation:

$$a_1 R_{|i-1|} + a_2 R_{|i-2|} + \cdots + a_p R_{|i-p'|} = R_i, \; i=1, 2, \cdots, p' \quad (4)$$

where R_i is autocorrelation of signal S_n, and (5)

$$S_n = S(nT) = \begin{cases} \text{sample of windowed signal, } n=0, 1, 2, \cdots, N-1 \\ 0, \text{ otherwise} \end{cases} \quad (6)$$

We have used sampling frequency 20KHz (T=0.05msec), Hamming window with 30msec width (N=600) and the number of poles p=12 for processing the helium speech at this stage.

In order to estimate the impulse response h(kT) from speech signal we use a relationship between h(kT) and system parameter a_i which is estimated directly from speech signal by eq. s (4), (5) and (6). By equating eq. s (1) and (3), we get:

$$\frac{1}{1 - a_1 z^{-1} - a_2 z^{-2} - \cdots - a_p z^{-p}} = \sum_{h=0}^{\infty} h_k z^{-k} \quad (7)$$

where $h_k = h(kT)$, $k=0, 1, 2, \cdots$

From eq. (7), a relationship between h_k and a_i is given by:

$$h_k = a_1 h_{k-1} + a_2 h_{k-2} + \cdots + a_k h_0, \; k=0, 1, 2, \cdots \quad (8)$$

where $a_i=0$, for $i < 0$, $i \geqq p+1$, and $h_0=1$

Thus, impulse response series $\{h_i\}$ of the speech production system can be estimated from given speech signal. The important thing we have utilized for making the helium speech unscrambler is that we can synthesize a digital filter whose impulse response is equal to a given time series. If we make the digital filter whose impulse response is equal to the h'_i which is another series of sampled values of impulse response $h(t)$ with sampling interval $T'(\neq T)$, and if we operate the filter with the sampling interval T, all the frequency characteristics of the filter is shifted by the factor $\beta=T'/T$ along the frequency scale. Theoretically, there is no problem on the stability of the filter as far as the both time series are made from an impulse response $h(t)$. In practice, however, we can know not the impulse response $h(t)$ but the sampled values $h(kT)$. Therefore we should use some interpolation technique in order to get $h'_k(=h(kT'))$ and pay some attention for the stability of synthesized filter. There are three methods to get a digital filter whose impulse response is equal to a given time series. The first is to construct a non-recursive filter, that is, to calculate a convolution between imput signal and impulse response $\{h'_i\}$. The second is to construct an all pole type recursive filter:

$$H'(z)=\frac{1}{1-a_1z^{-1}-a_2z^{-2}-\cdots-a_{p'}z^{-p'}} \qquad (9)$$

where coefficients a_i, $i=1, 2, \cdots, p'$ are given by solving a set of linear equations:

$$a'_1h'_{k-1}+a'_2h_{k-2}+\cdots+a'_kh'_0=h'_k,\ k=1, 2, \cdots, p' \qquad (10)$$

we call this type of filter construction *direct method*. The third is to construct an all pole type recursive filter whose coefficients are calculated by the same way as calculating a_i from speech signal, in which the total-squared error between a given impulse response and its predicted value is minimized. a'_i $(i=1, 2, \cdots, p')$ is obtained by solving an autocorrelation normal equation:

$$a'_1V_{|i-1|}+a'_2V_{|i-2|}+\cdots+a'_{p'}V_{|i-p'|}=V_i,\ i=1, 2, \cdots, p' \qquad (11)$$

where V_i is autocorrelation of impulse response series $\{h'_i\}$. Eq. (11) forms p' equations with p' unknowns to be solved for the coefficients a'_i.

Derivation of impulse response of synthesis filter, $\{h'_i\}$

Impulse response $\{h(kT)\}$ estimated from input signal is stretched along the time scale by the factor β to make another impulse response $\{h'(kT)\}$. Fig. 1 illustrates the correspondence between those impulse responses in the case of $\beta=2/3$. Points marked ∘ and · on the curves show the sampled values of impulse response $h(t)$ and $h'(t)$ respectively. The impulse response $h'(kT)$ is derived from $h(kT')$ in such a manner that $h'(kT)$ marked · is equal to the value $h(kT')$ on the curve for $h(t)$, where $T'/T=\beta$.

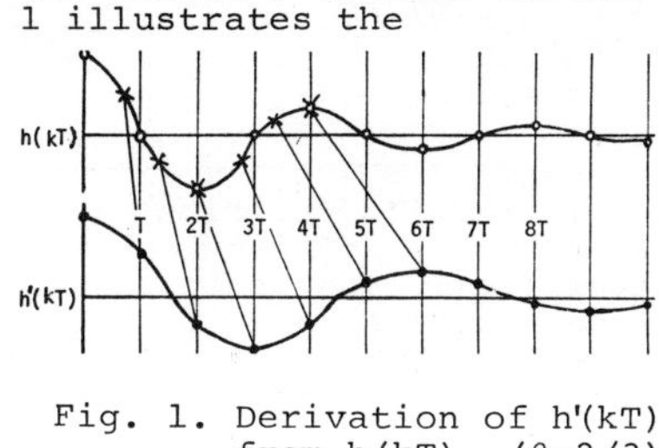

Fig. 1. Derivation of h'(kT) from h(kT). (β=2/3)

In order to get the values $h(kT')$, we need an interpolation from sampled values. Two methods of interpolation have been examined in this study. The one is to use sampling function and the other, linear interpolation.

1. Interpolation by sampling function: Because the $h(t)$ is reasonably assumed to be band limited within 1/2T Hz, $h(t)$ can be represented by sampling function:

$$h(t) = \sum_{k=-\infty}^{\infty} h_k \frac{\sin\,(\pi/T)(t-kT)}{(\pi/T)(t-kT)} \tag{12}$$

Using this equation, we can get a relationship between two series of sampled values as follows:

$$\begin{aligned} h'_m &= h(mT') = h(m\beta T) \\ &= \sum_{k=-\infty}^{\infty} h_k \frac{\sin\pi(m\beta-k)}{\pi(m\beta-k)} = \sum_{k=0}^{L} h_k \frac{\sin\pi(m\beta-k)}{\pi(m\beta-k)} \end{aligned} \tag{13}$$

The conditions that $h_k=0$ for $k < 0$, and $h_k \to 0$ for $k > L$ are applied here. From a point of view of shortening the computing time, L should be as small as good approximation is obtained.

2. Linear interpolation: An alternative way for getting h'_n is to linearly interpolate the $\{h_k\}$ as follows:

$$h'_n = \frac{ah_m + bh_{m+1}}{a + b}, \quad m \leq n\beta \leq m+1 \tag{14}$$

where, coefficients a and b are determined by relative positioning of sampling points nT' $(=n\beta T)$, mT and $(m+1)T$, and are given by:

$$\left.\begin{aligned} n\beta T - mT &= a \\ a + b &= T \end{aligned}\right\} \tag{15}$$

Linear interpolation has a great advantage that the computation is far simpler than that of sampling function. In order to get information about which method is suitable here, we have examined errors due to finite L ($12 \leq L \leq 300$) and linear interpolation for several shapes of impulse response including dampled sinusoidal function with various periods in the case of $\beta = 0.5$. It is observed that linear interpolation shows at most 17% of error in the worst case and less than 5% of error in average. Although those values are a little larger than that of interpolation by sampling function with $L \geq 50$, the merit of simplicity in computation may recover the disadvantage.

Analysis-Conversion-Synthesis system as a helium speech unscrambler

Fig. 2 shows a block diagram of the proposed helium speech unscrambler. This system consists of three parts: analysis, conversion and synthesis. In the analysis part, parameters a_i of the transfer function $H(z)$ are estimated to make an inverse filter $H^{-1}(z)$ and impulse response $h(kT)$. Output of the inverse filter, residue signal, is either a sequence of impulses, spaced at the pitch periods, a sequence of white noise samples, spaced T seconds, or both. In the conversion part, the impulse response is converted to $h'(kT)$ to make a digital filter $H'(z)$. In the synthesis part, unscrambled helium speech is made by filtering the residue signal with $H'(z)$.

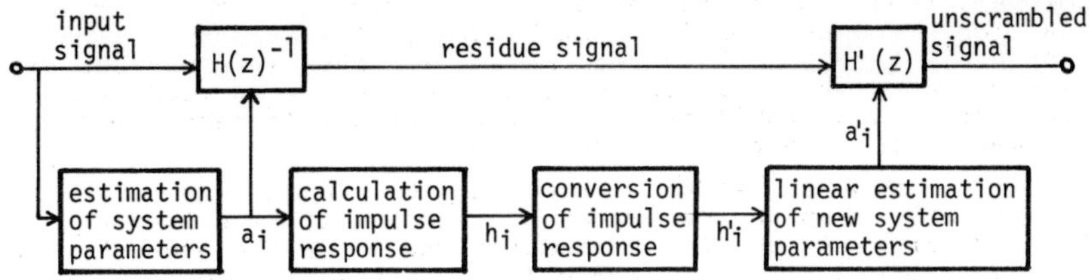

Fig. 2. Block diagram of the helium speech unscrambler.

Experiment

This unscrambling system has been implemented by a program of general purpose computer. PARCOR coefficients of Itakura and Saito [4] are used here in H'(z) instead of a'_i because of convenience in assuring the stability. Experiment was performed using words of helium speech and synthetic vowels in the case of conversion ratio $\beta=0.5$. Transfer function estimated from input signal and that of synthesized from h'(kT) with various conditions were compared in terms of formant frequencies, band width and general shape of spectral envelope.

Fig. 3 shows the broad band spectrogram for words of helium speech spoken at the depth of 450 feet. Fig. 4 shows the one for unscrambled speech. Note that the frequency scale of spectrogram in Fig. 3 is different from that of Fig. 4 while the time scales in both are the same. The linear interpolation for making h'(kT) and the linear estimation with exponential window of 15 msec width for making H'(z) in which the value of p' is 24 were used in this unscrambling system. Comparing Fig. 3 and Fig. 4, it is clear that formant frequencies and band widths are shifted downward while fundamental frequency is kept unchanged.

Discussion

i. Linear interpolation versus sampling function to obtain h'(kT): As mentioned earlier, the linear interpolation has a merit of simplicity in computation. Typical frequency responses of H'(z) for neutral vowel /ə/ made by using linear interpolation and sampling function are shown in Fig. 7 and Fig. 6 respectively. Fig. 5 shows the spectral envelope of helium speech corresponding /ə/ to be processed by the system. Major difference in those frequency response curves is that the one for linear transformation has excess resonance peaks in the frequency range above 5KHz. The difference in such a high frequency range may not, practically, have serious effect on the intelligibility of the unscrambled speech. Therefore, the linear interpolation is preferable to the sampling function.

ii. Direct Method versus linear estimation to obtain H'(z): We have not observed remarkable differences between the transfer functions obtained either by direct method or by linear estimation when the transfer function are stable. We found, however, that the direct method often makes an unstable transfer function. The unstability must be due to the errors in impulse response. Although the direct method may have an advantage of simpler computation, it is not suitable because of frequent occurrence of unstability. Therefore, we should take the linear estimation to obtain $H'(z)$ from $\{h'(kT)\}$.

iii. The shape and width of time window used in linear estimation: When parameters a_i of system $H(z)$ is estimated, Hamming window is applied to input signal. On the other hand, when parameters a'_i of system $H'(z)$ is estimated from impulse response $\{h'(kT)\}$, rectangular or exponential window should be better than Hamming window because $\{h'(kT)\}$ is essentially a damped oscillation excited at k=0 only. Tab. 1 shows a summary of spectral characteristics of synthesized transfer function for neutral vowel under the same conditions except that the different window is used. Exponential window is defined by:

$$We(kT) = \begin{cases} \exp(-\pi BkT), & \text{for } 0 \leq k \leq 300, \\ o, & \text{for elsewhere} \end{cases} \qquad (16)$$

where B=40Hz and T=0.05msec

The parameter B is chosen so that the band width of lower frequency formant in $H'(z)$ may have a proper value. Notable difference is found not in formant frequencies but in band width of transfer function $H'(z)$ in Tab. 1. Those of Hamming window and rectangular window show abnormally narrow band width but the exponential window only shows an acceptable value.

WINDOW	F_1	B_1	F_2	B_2	F_3	B_3
HAMMING	502	2	1500	5	2500	11
RECTANGULER	503	20	1506	46	2515	79
EXPONENTIAL	505	49	1510	76	2520	115

Tab. 1. Summary of spectral characteristics of synthesized transfer function in terms of formant frequencies F_i(Hz) and band widths B_i(Hz) for different windows.

iv. Value of p' in $H'(z)$: In the linear prediction model of speech production the transfer function is assumed to have a certain number of poles which is determined by taking account of the average number of formants in a given frequency band, combined effect of glottal flow and radiation, and an effect of preemphasis if used. Considering that the average number of formants of normal air speech in 5KHz band is five, we assume that the average number of formants of helium speech in 10KHz band is also five in the case of the rate of formant shift is 0.5. This requires 10 poles in estimating the transfer function. In order to compensate the reduction in higher frequency energy of helium speech preemphasis by differencing is applied to the input signal. Combined effect of glottal flow and radiation in addition to an effect of preemphasis is assumed to be represented by 2 poles. Consequently, the value of p for estimating $H(z)$ is determined to be 12. The digital filter $H'(z)$, on the other hand, must cover 10KHz of frequency band in spite of that the formant frequencies are shifted downward. For example, a neutral vowel has five formants in 5KHz band and ten formants in 10KHz band. This means that the value of p' should be about 22. To observe the effect of changing the value of p' we have examined the frequency response of transfer functions with values of p' ranging from 2 to 24. Typical ones are shown in Fig. 8. From the observation of those data we conclude that the value of p' should be at least 19.

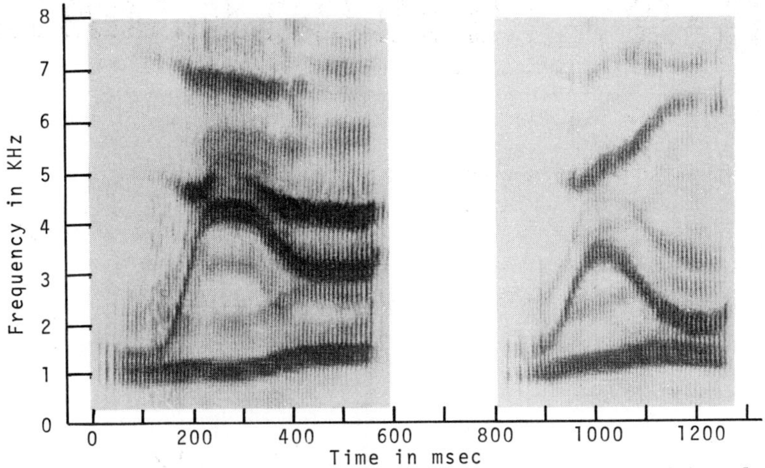

Fig. 3. Sound spectrogram for the words "we're"(left) and "will"(right) of helium speech at 450' underwater

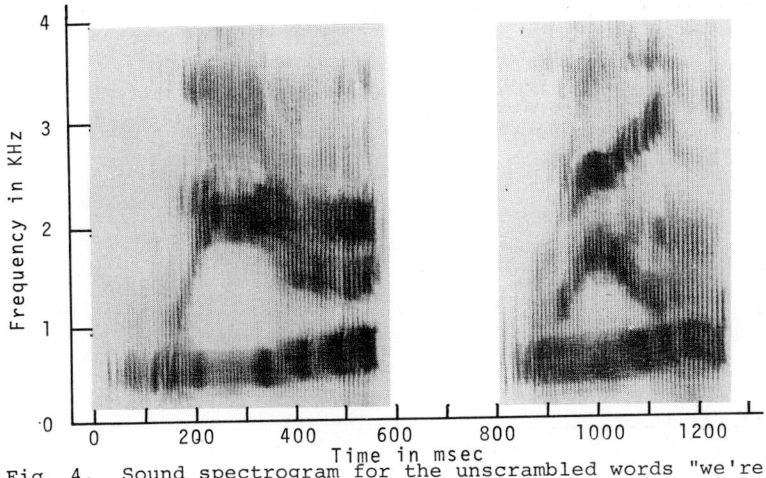

Fig. 4. Sound spectrogram for the unscrambled words "we're" (left) and "will"(right), where $\beta = 0.5$

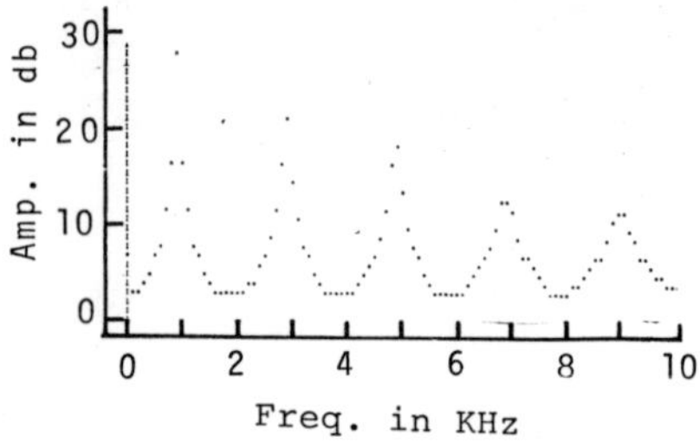

Fig. 5. Amplitude frequency response for helium speech /ə/

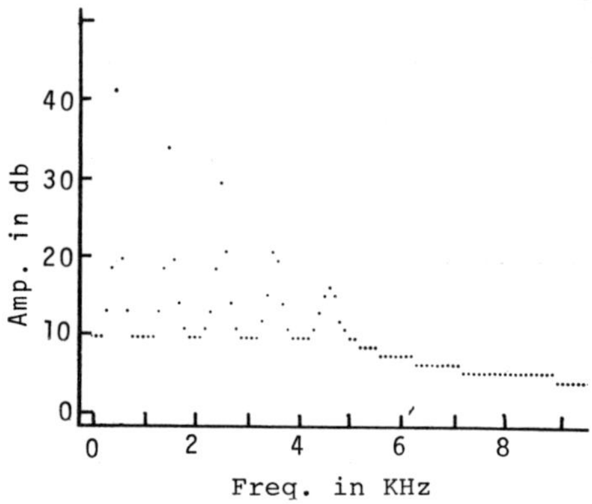

Fig. 6. Amplitude frequency response for unscrambled one by means of sampling function

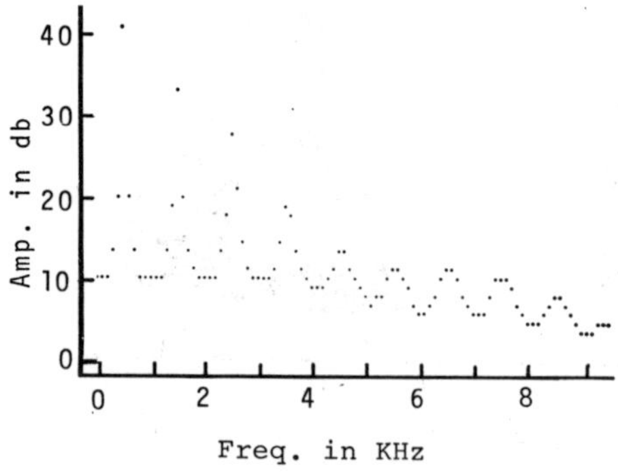

Fig. 7. Amplitude frequency response for unscrambled one by means of linear interpolation

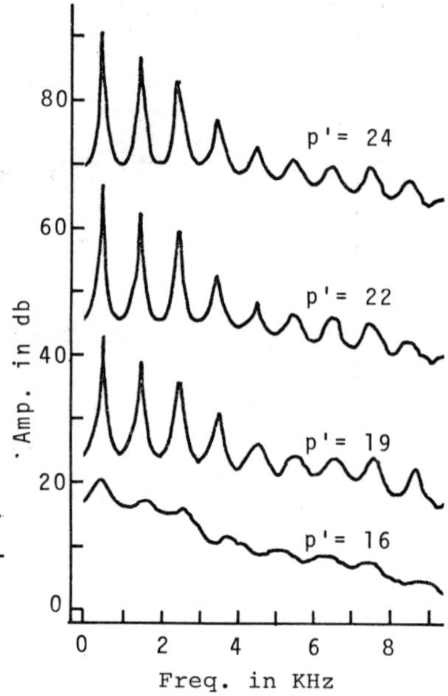

Fig. 8. Illustration of effect of changing the value of p' in estimated transfer function H'(z)

Remarks

In this paper we have successfully solved problems 1°, 3° and 4° but there remains various problems unsolved as described earlier. It is expected, however, that the level difference between voiced sounds and voiceless sounds may be compensated with the filter which is on the path for residue signal from the inverse filter $H^{-1}(z)$ in Fig. 2, and emphasizes the noise component or higher frequency component in the residue signal.

Acknowledgment

The authors wish to thank Professor H. Hollien of C. S. L., University of Florida, and Dr. J. Suzuki of Radio Research Laboratory, JAPAN for providing the material of helium speech.

References

[1] T. Giordano, H. B. Rothman, and H. Hollien; "Helium Speech Unscramblers——A Critical Review of the State of the Arts", IEEE Trans. on Audio and Elec., Vol. AU-21, No. 5, pp. 436-444, Oct., 1973.

[2] Takeshi Fukabayashi and Hisayoshi Suzuki; "Speech Analysis by Linear Prediction Taking Account of Zeros as well as Poles ", Paper for Conference of Acoustical Soc. of Japan, 2-2-5, Jun., 1974.

[3] John I. Makhoul and Jared J. Wolf; "Linear Prediction and the Spectral Analysis of Speech", BBN Report No. 2304, Aug., 1972.

[4] F. Itakura , and S. Saito; "On the Optimum Quantization of Feature Parameters in the PARCOR Speech Synthesizer", Conference Record, 1972 C. S. C. P., Newton, Mass., pp. 434-437, Apr., 1972.

Speech Communication Seminar
Stockholm. Aug. 1–3, 1974

PERCEPTION OF SPEECH UTTERED UNDER HIGH AMBIENT PRESSURE

Jouji SUZUKI and Mamoru NAKATSUI
Radio Research Laboratories, Koganei, Tokyo 184, Japan

Abstract

The problem of "helium speech", degradation of speech intelligibility under high ambient pressure, is very serious in the underwater speech communication. Acoustical characteristics of helium speech have been well studied but the perceptual effects have been hardly known. This article studies the perceptual nature of helium speech through the articulation tests of Japanese CV-syllables uttered at simulated dives.

Confusion of phonemes in the helium mixture is quite different from that in the normal air, for example, helium vowels show uni-directional confusion. The confusion is discussed with respect to the helium distortions observed in the acoustic analyses and to the results shown in English tests. It is revealed that the non-linearity in upward shift of formant frequency caused by increase in the gas density is very important in explanation of the perceptual nature of helium speech.

1. Introduction

Territory of human being is expanding into the inner space. His activity in the hyperbaric environment is indebted to utilization of helium-rich breathing gas mixture for preventing him from nitrogen narcosis and oxygen toxicosis. The use of helium, however, yields some troubles because physical characteristics of helium are different from those of the normal air. The most serious problem is deterioration in intelligibility of speech uttered in the helium mixture (this speech is well known as helium speech). It is said that verbal communication is hardly possible when man goes down into the deep sea.

Acoustical characteristics of helium speech have been relatively well studied and a lot of attempts have been made in order to translate the helium speech into intelligible one, however, perceptual effect of helium speech distortion has been almost unknown. The purpose of this article is to understand the perceptual nature of helium speech through the articulation tests of Japanese CV-syllables uttered under high ambient pressure.

2. Characteristics of helium speech

Physical characteristics of helium speech are relatively well studied. These are summarized as follows in comparison with the normal speech:

(a) Expansion of the frequency spectrum (upward shift of resonance frequency of vocal tract)[1~4,8~10,12],

(b) The extra high rate of the expansion in the low frequency range;[4~6,10,12]

(c) Reduction of the unvoiced sound level relative to the voiced sound;[3,5,6,8,10,11]

(d) Increase in the fundamental frequency of glottal excitation source;[1~4,9~11]

(e) Decrease in speaking tempo;[5,6,10,11]

(f) Daily variation of speech factors such as formant frequency, speaking tempo and fundamental frequency during several days' stay in the helium stmosphere;[4,7,10]

(g) No difference in the long-term spectrum of the helium and the normal speech.[8,10,11]

It is generally accepted that the distortion of helium speech mainly stems from (A) increase in the sound velocity and (B) increase in the gas density. As the secondary effect, it is considered that (C) speaker's adaptation to the exotic speech also contributes to the change of helium speech. Now, (a) stems from (A), (b) and (c) are elucidated by (B),[5,6] and (d), (e) and (f) by (C).

It is considered that the most important distortion is related to the expansion of spectrum. Relation between F_{He} resonance frequency of vocal tract in the helium mixture and F_a that in the normal air is represented by Eq. (1).

$$F_{He} = k^2 F_a{}^2 + k' F_{wo}{}^2 \qquad (1)$$

where F_{wo} is the lowest resonance frequency of the vocal tract in the normal air, k is the ratio of sound velocity of helium mixture and that of the normal air, and k' the constant specified by gas composition and pressure. Typical relations between F_{He} and F_a are calculated and drawn in Fig. 5(Chapter 4.3).

3. Speech materials and test procedure

Speech materials used in this article were recorded in simulated dives. Physical characteristics of breathing gas and experimental condition are indicated in Table 1. In this table, authors' data are written in Roman numerals and the refered data in capitals, and suffix 0 means control data at 1 atm.

Table 1 Experimental conditions of recording; k and r are the ratios of sound velocity and density to the normal air

Data	Pressure (atm)	Gas Composition He	N_2	O_2	k	r	S/N (dB)	List of Utterances
I-0	1.0	0.9*	78.0	21.0	1.0	1.0	20	67 CV-syllables
I	3.9	62.5	30.0	7.5	1.55	1.79	30	"
III	6.9	89.4	7.5	3.1	2.22	1.59	8	"
IV	10.6	91.3	6.0	2.7	2.31	1.93	6	"
V	3.9	0.9*	78.0	21.0	1.0	3.9	25	"
S(1)	1.0	80.0	0.0	20.0	1.84	0.33	1**	Fairbanks Rhyme
M(2)	6.9	79.0	17.0	4.0	1.88	2.20	-	Cambell

* Ar, ** addition of white noise

(1) by Sergeant[13], (2) by Murry[14] (see Chapter4.4)

CV-syllable lists (a list consists of 67 CV-syllables[5]) were read in a deck decompression chamber (Data I-0, I, III and IV) and in a hyperbaric tank for medical use (Data V). The speech was recorded through a high quality non-directional dynamic microphone (Sony FP-1). Pause time between utterances was adjusted to 2 -3 seconds by splicing and the order of syllables was rearranged by edition. The sound was presented to listeners trained for syllable articulation test through a headphone (DR 305) and the level was adjusted by each listener.

Table 2 Factors of articulation tests

Data	Pressure (atm)	Utterance Speaker	Times	Listening Listener	Times	Lists
I-0	1.0	3	2	7	1	3x2x7
I	3.9	3	4	7	1	3x4x7
III	6.9	1	1	7	3*	7x3
IV	10.6	2	1	7	3*	2x7x3
V	3.9	3**	1	7	1	3x7

* presented three times durinq four months,
** different from other speakers.

Factors of these articulation tests are listed in Table 2. These factors are not common throughout tests because of the experimental restriction of simulated dive.

4. Results and discussions

4.1 Deterioration of speech under pressure

Articulation score of syllables and vowels are listed in Table 3. It is clearly understood that the greater the pressure becomes, the lower the intelligibilty. Articulation score of Data V is compromise between those of the normal speech and the helium speech at the same pressure. These results are similar to mono-syllabic word intelligibilty in English[6] as shown in Fig. 1.

At Data I and I-0, the speech was recorded four times during

Table 3 Articulation score of CV-syllables and vowels.

Articulation (%)	I-0	I	III	IV	V
CV-syllable	96.1	85.6	38.2	22.0	91.6
Vowel	100.0	99.5	86.7	68.2	100.0

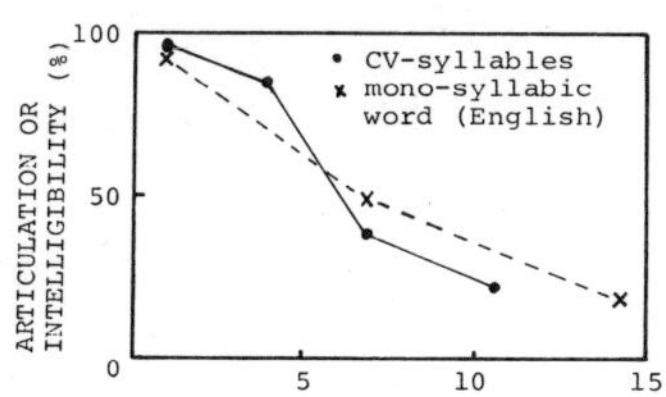

Fig. 1 Articulation of CV-syllables and word intelligibility (after Hollien et al) as a function of pressure.

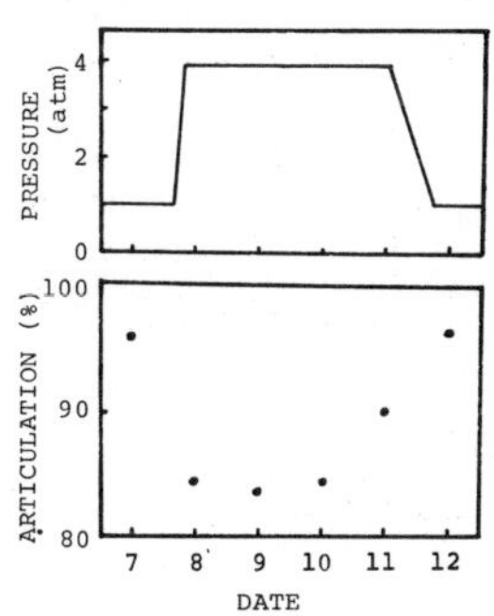

Fig. 2 Change of articulation score during dive. (Data I and I-0)

four days under pressure and twice in the normal air. Change of articulation and pressure are shown in Fig. 2. No difference between scores before and after the dive is observed, but five percent rise at the fourth day under pressure was measured. This rise is statistically meaningful and suggests speaker's adaptation to exotic speech environment.

Listener's adaptation to the helium speech is generally experienced but it is not shown in this study.

4.2 Perception of vowels

Table 4 show the confusion matrix of vowels in Data IV and the structure of confusion is schematically drawn in Fig. 3(a). Confusion of vowels, processed by several types of distortions such as low-pass-filtered, high-pass-filtered[7] and added noise, is also schematically drawn in the same figure. Those confusion are easily explained by missing of formant information due to filtering or masking with noise. On the other hand, confusion in the helium speech is completely different from that in the normal speech. It is remarkable that confusion occurs unidirectionally, that is, the matrix is unsymmetrical.

Fig. 4 shows the first and second formant frequencies (F_1 and F_2) of typical Japanese vowels (written in small letters) and those of helium vowels (in capitals). In this case, formant frequencies of helium vowels are calculated by Eq. (1) under the condition of Data IV. Fig.4 is supported by spectrographic analyses of Data I-0 and IV.

Refering to Fig. 4, it is seemed that confusion I → e, U → e and O → a occur between vowels whose F_1 and/or F_2 are close to each other. While, in the case of U → e or O → a, both vowels have the common F_1/F_2. Perception of vowels uttered by male,

Table 4 Confusion matrix of vowels (Data IV)

Stimulus	Response *i*	*e*	*a*	*o*	*u*	x	Sum
i	232	185	2	4	65	16	504
e	10	484	32		3	27	546
a	2	9	589	2		19	630
o		4	180	281	102	21	588
u	18	213	22	12	277	10	546
Sum	256	885	834	299	447	93	2814

x: unidentified vowel.

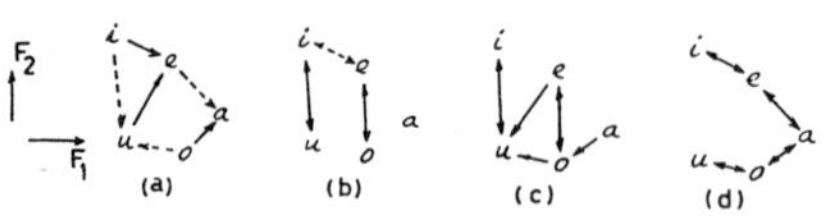

Fig. 3 Confusion in perception of vowels.
(a) Helium speech (Data IV)
(b) Speech of low signal to noise ratio
(c) Speech low-pass-filtered
(d) Speech High-pass-filtered

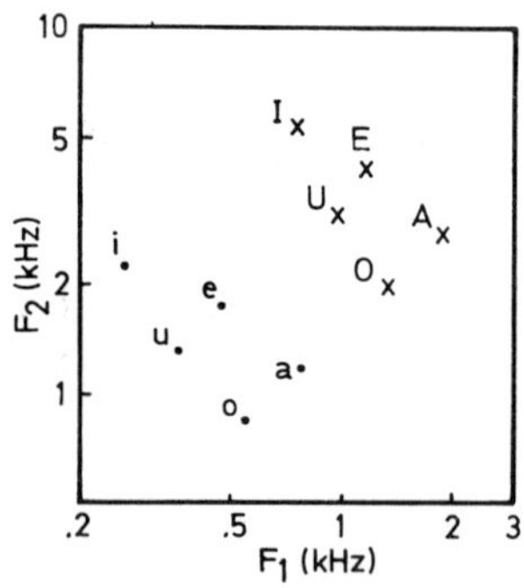

Fig. 4 Formant frequency transposition from normal vowel(small letter) to helium vowel(capital) by Eq.(1) under the condition of Data IV.

female and children is sometimes explained by normalization in the frequency scale (it equals normalization of the length of vocal tract)[18,19]. Furthermore, the similar normalization is used in the automatic recognition of speech. This idea, however, is useless for explanation of the perception of helium vowel.

It was revealed that the specific relation was required between the fundamental frequency and the length of vocal tract in order to synthesize vowels with good phonemic and prosodic quality.[19] According to this experiment, helium vowels stand out of range specified for natural vowels, because the fundamental frequency of helium speech is a compromise between male and female voice, and the length of vocal tract in the helium mixture is assumed shorter than childrens one in the normal air. We have never experienced such unfamiliar and exotic sound like helium speech. It is supposed that perceptual mechanism for the helium speech is quite different from that for the normal speech.

4.3 Perception of consonants

Table 5 is the confusion matrix of Data IV. Semivowel /y(j)/ is most correctly responded as high as 85 %. Nearly half of isolated vowels, /h/, /k/, /w/ and /n/ are recognized in correct. On the other hand, error rate of /m/, /r/ and plosives except for /k/ are greater than 75 %. Generally, plosives, fricatives, nasals and glide /r/ are difficult to be recognized and confusion occurs frequently in the order of nasals, unvoiced plosives, unvoiced fricatives and voiced plosives within phoneme groups consisting of the same manner of articulation.

Trend of confusion is rather systematic. For example, vowels and /y/ substitute for voiced consonants and /r/, and /h/ for unvoiced consonants.

With regard to place of articulation, consonants whose articulatory points are front are most difficult to be identified in the phoneme groups of plosives and nasals. On the contrary,

Table 5 Confusion matrix of consonants(Data IV)

		Response															
		Vow.	*w*	*r*	*y*	*b*	*d*	*g*	*z*	*m*	*n*	*p*	*t*	*k*	*s*	*h*	x	Sum
	Vowel	118		6	2	2		3	2	4	2	1	5	23		36	6	210
	w	1	23	2	6												9	42
	r	49	2	47	68	5		1		9	22			1		1	5	210
	y	8	4	2	109						1		1				1	126
	b	77	2	22	10	17	21	15	5	7	7	1	8	1	1	6	10	210
	d	19	1	4	22	7	26	6		8	5		12	3	1	1		126
Stimulus	*g*	54		14	34	4	18	41	9	1	2		5	14	1	5		216
	z	53	6	13	90	2	11	7	5	3	5			1	1	1	12	210
	m	19	2	20	11	7	2	6	1	55	71						6	210
	n	12		4	10	3	3	8		28	124	1		3		2	12	210
	p	13				1		3		3	3	11	27	83	1	60	5	210
	t	12		1		2	6		1	1	8	5	33	38	29	71	3	210
	k	2				1	1				2		21	107	19	50	7	210
	s	4		2	2	4	3	1		5	13	7	34	24	36	59	14	210
	h	14	1	2	1	2				1	3	4	19	50	5	104	4	210
	Sum	455	51	139	365	57	91	91	23	125	268	30	165	354	97	399	104	2814

x: unidentified consonant.

phonemes whose articulation is in back are responded rather correctly or frequently.

As shown in Fig. 5, relation of F_{He} and F_a is non-linear, that is, the rate of shift of formant frequency in the low frequency range is greater than k the ratio of sound velocity. Transitions of the second and the first formant frequency are the most important cue for identification of plosives and nasals.[20] In the case of phonemes whose place of articulation is in front, it is considered that frequent errors cause by the fact that transition of F_2 and F_1 are upward and the range of transition is compressed by the said non-linearity.

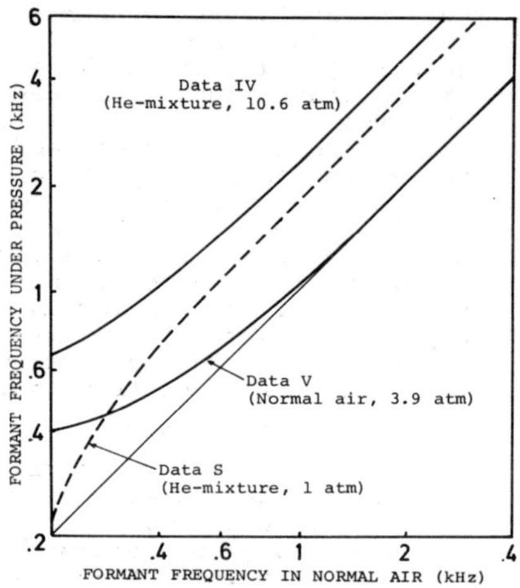

Fig.5 Elevation of formant frequency in helium mixture and in normal air under pressure.

Confusion of Data III is very similar to Data IV. In Data I, it is remarkable that /r/ substitutes for voiced plosives and nasals, less errors are ovserved in fricatives, and confusion into /y/ hardly occurs. The other tendency of confusion is similar to Data IV. The perception of Data V is relatively in common with that of Data I though the error rate is low.

4.4 Comparison with other experiments

None has studied the perception of vowels uttered in the helium mixture. It is supposed that the confusion of vowels in English, French, Swedish and Russian will be complicated one, because the number of vowels in those languages is more than in Japanese.

In the case of consonants, only two perceptual analyses have been made by Sergeant and Murry. Their experimental conditions are listed in Table 1 as Data S and M. Sergeant summarized his results as there was a marked similarity between helium speech and normal speech. While, Murry did not discuss the perception of helium speech in comparison with the normal speech, but he stated the features of confusion as follows: "The majority of confusion occurs among unvoiced sounds produced within the same manner of articulation category....With regard to the place of articulation the types of substitution are approximately at random..." Their results are summarized in Table 6 together with the authors' data. They don't always agree with each other.

There exists basic difference among these experiments. For example, Data S was recorded at normal pressure and was so intelligible that noise was added. Variety and concatenation of

Table 6 Summarized results of perception of consonants

Data	Most correct	Most frequent*	Most incorrect
S**	*l,m,b,g,n*	*t,l,p,k,r*	*s,ʃ,w,t,k*
M**	*h,r,ŋ,s,n*	*l,n,r,k,t*	*w,θ,f,ts,ð*
I	*y,w,s,z,r*	*r,n,h,s,b*	*b,m,p,h,n*
IV	*y,n,w,k,h*	*h,y,k,n,t*	*z,p,b,t,s*
V	*w,s,k,g,y*	*r,p,n,b,s*	*b,p,m,d,t*

* except correct responses. **English(see Table 1)

phonemes are also the important difference between English and Japanses. For instance, /w/ is only followed by /a/ in Japanese, but it can concatenate with many phonemes in English. /w/ is correctly recognized or frequently responded in Japanese but is the most errorneous phoneme in English. Fairbanks list is similar to Japanese CV-syllable list from the view point of position and variety of consonants. On the other hand, Cambell list contains a lot of phonemes and their position is not fixed in a word. If common consonants between English and Japanese are extracted from Cambell List, the similar tendency will be obtained in the perception of consonants.

Sergeant's results show that most of unvoiced sounds are in error. This reflects the low signal-to-noise ratio in speech materials. Amazingly, however, /m/ and /b/ are identified correctly (furthermore, /p/ is the most correct phoneme in the unvoiced plosives though it is not listed in Table 6), and some phonemes whose articulation is in back are faultly identified. These results completely disagree with authors' experiments. The cause stems from the difference of gas density, that is, Data S is obtained in the helium mixture at 1 atm (see Table 1).

As shown in Fig.5, upward shift of resonance frequency for Data S in proportion to the sound velocity is partly canceled in the low frequency range owing to the low density. Therefore, upward shift of transition of formant frequency which is cue for identification of phonemes whose articulatory point is front is emphasized in Data S. This is supported by the contrary side. That is, transpostion curve of Data V which is also drawn in Fig. 5 is only affected by increase in the density and Data V shows the similar perceptual characteristics to the helium speech under pressure.

5. Conclusive remarks

The helium speech was analyzed perceptually through CV-syllable articulation tests. The principal results are as follows:

(1) Articulation score of CV-syllables decreases to 85, 38 and 22 percent at 3.9, 6.9 and 10.6 atm respectively, and it indicates that the verbal communication will be lost in the environment under high pressure.
(2) During four days' dive, articulation score rises five percent on the fourth day. It is statistically significant. This result suggests the speaker's adaptation to the exotic sound.
(3) It is remarkable that confusion of vowels occurs unidirectionally such as /i/ → /e/, /o/ → /a/ and /u/ → /e/.
(4) In the perception of consonants, remarkable confusions are from foiced consonants to vowels or /y/(or /r/), and from unvoiced consonants to /h/. Errors frequently occurs in the identification of plosives, fricatives and nasals.

8–742577 *Volym I*

(5) With regard to the place of articulation, consonants whose articulatory point is in front are most in error among the phonemes with the common manner of articulation.
(6) It is speculated that perception of phonemes whose articulation is in front is greatly affected by non-linear shift of formant frequency owing to the increase in the density of breathing gas on the basis of these articulation tests and perceptual tests in English.

Relations between perception and physical characteristics of helium speech give many suggestions about the mechanism of speech perception. Further analyses and perceptual tests by synthetic stimuli will be needed to resolve this problem.

This study also contributes to designing a helium speech unscrambler and to selecting words understandable in underwater speech communication.

References

1) R. G. Beil: JASA, 34, p.347(L), 1962.
2) K. Holywell JASA, Harvey: JASA, 36, P.210(L), 1964.
3) R. S. Burbaker and J. W. Wurst: JASA, 43, p.798, 1968.
4) D. J. MacLean: JASA, 40, p.625, 1966.
5) G.Fant and B. Sonesson: QPSR, 1964/1, Royal Inst. Tech., p.9, 1964.
6) G.Fant and J. Lindqvist: QPSR, 1968/1, Ibid, p.7, 1968.
7) W. Wathen-Dunn and S. B. Michaels: Ann. New York Acad. of Sci., 155, p.368, 1968.
8) R. A. Flower: Final Tech. Report on Helium Speech Investigation, Singer-General Precision Inc., 1969.
9) C. T. Morrow: JASA, 50, p.715, 1971.
10) M. Nakatsui, J. Suzuki, T. Takasugi and R. Tanaka: 2nd Int. Ocean Dev. Conf., C-3, P.1615, 1972.
Ibid: Trans.of Inst. of Elect. and Comm. Eng. of Japan, 57-A, P.200, 1974 (in Japanese).
11) R. Tanaka, M. Nakatsui, T. Takasugi and J. Suzuki:"Source characteristics of speech produced under high pressure", Jour. Rad. Res. Labs., (in press).
12) R. Tanaka, M. Nakatsui and J. Suzuki: Formant frequency shifts under high ambient pressure", Ibid.
13) R. S. Sergeant: JASA, 41, p.66, 1967.
14) T. Murry: CSL/ONR, No.24, Comm. Sci. Lab., Univ. of Florida, p.1, 1968.
15) J. Suzuki: Jour. Rad. Re. Labs., 17, p.223, 1970.
16) H. Hollien and C. L. Thompson: CSL/ONR, No.20, Comm. Sci. lab., Univ. of Florida, p.2, 1967.
17) S. Saito: Reports of ECL,NTT, 7, p.207, 1959.
18) H. Kasuya, H. Suzuki and K. Kido: Jour. Acoust. Soc. Japan, 24, p.355, 1968.
19) N. Umeda and R. Teranishi: Ibid, 22, p.195, 1966.
20) P. C. Delattre, A. M. Liberman and F. S. Cooper: JASA, 27, p.769, 1955.

Speech Communication Seminar
Stockholm. Aug. 1–3, 1974

DIGITAL CODING OF SPEECH *) **)

J. L. Flanagan, Acoustics Research Department, Bell Laboratories, Murray Hill, New Jersey 07974, USA

Abstract

Our motivations and objectives in digital coding of speech fall into three general categories, illustrated in the figure.

In *Category I* we are interested in coding techniques for broad-band transmission facilities where the overriding concern is low terminal costs. In *Category II* we are interested in coding techniques for limited channel capacity, or limited bandwidth, and where one is willing to invest in more sophisticated terminal equipment. In *Category III* we are interested in coding for very low bit-rate storage of speech, a typical objective being automatic answer-back services and computer voice response applications. Data rates associated with these categories of coding are indicated along the x-axis in the figure; the scale is logarithmic in bit rate.

In *Category I* the rates begin, literally, from the megabit range and go down to the order of 20 kilobits. Coding techniques here are typified by linear delta modulation (LDM), PCM, differential PCM, and adaptive versions of delta modulation (ADM) and differential PCM. In this category we do not resort to *source coding*; that is, we do not exploit any of the acoustic features of speech production to achieve a low bit-rate coding. The fidelity criterion for the coding depends purely upon how the signal waveform is perceived by the human ear. Applications here involve digital interoffice trunks, digital rural service, such as the subscriber loop multiplexer system, and within-central office processing, where time-division switching and digital filtering may be of importance.

* not published in the preprint version.

** Based upon material presented to the International Zürich Seminar on Digital Communications, April 1974.

In *Category II* the bit rates range from about 10 kilobits down to the order of 1 or 2 kilobits. In this range we do resort to source coding and try to exploit the *acoustic characteristics of speech production*; that is, the properties of sound generation and the acoustics response of the human vocal tract. This range is typified by devices which are generically called *vocoders*. Some vocoders require automatic pitch tracking of the voice, and some, by signal-processing methods, avoid the problems of pitch tracking and voiced-unvoiced decisions. I have labelled two examples of each along the bit-rate axis; the voice-excited vocoder (VEV), the phase vocoder (øV), the linear prediction vocoder (LPV), and the well-known channel vocoder (CV). Applications in this category include mobile radio, satellite and deep-space communication, and digital encryption for secure transmission over voice-grade circuits. The growing importance of privacy techniques in civil telephony, combined with the rapidly-expanding capabilities of integrated digital circuitry, lend continuing interest to encoding methods of this complexity.

In *Category III* the bit rates range from the order of a kilobit down essentially to teletypewriter speed; 75 bits/second. In this category we are studying techniques for the *synthesis of speech* from low bit-rate data. One technique we call *formant synthesis*, where information about the resonances of the vocal tract are the stored data. A second technique is *text synthesis* where we attempt, literally, to synthesize speech from printed information. Applications of these techniques include computer voice response for systems that will provide a broad range of automatic information services, and aim to make every TOUCH-TONE telephone a small computer terminal.

I will illustrate state of progress for several points along this bit-rate axis by tape recordings of the coding techniques.

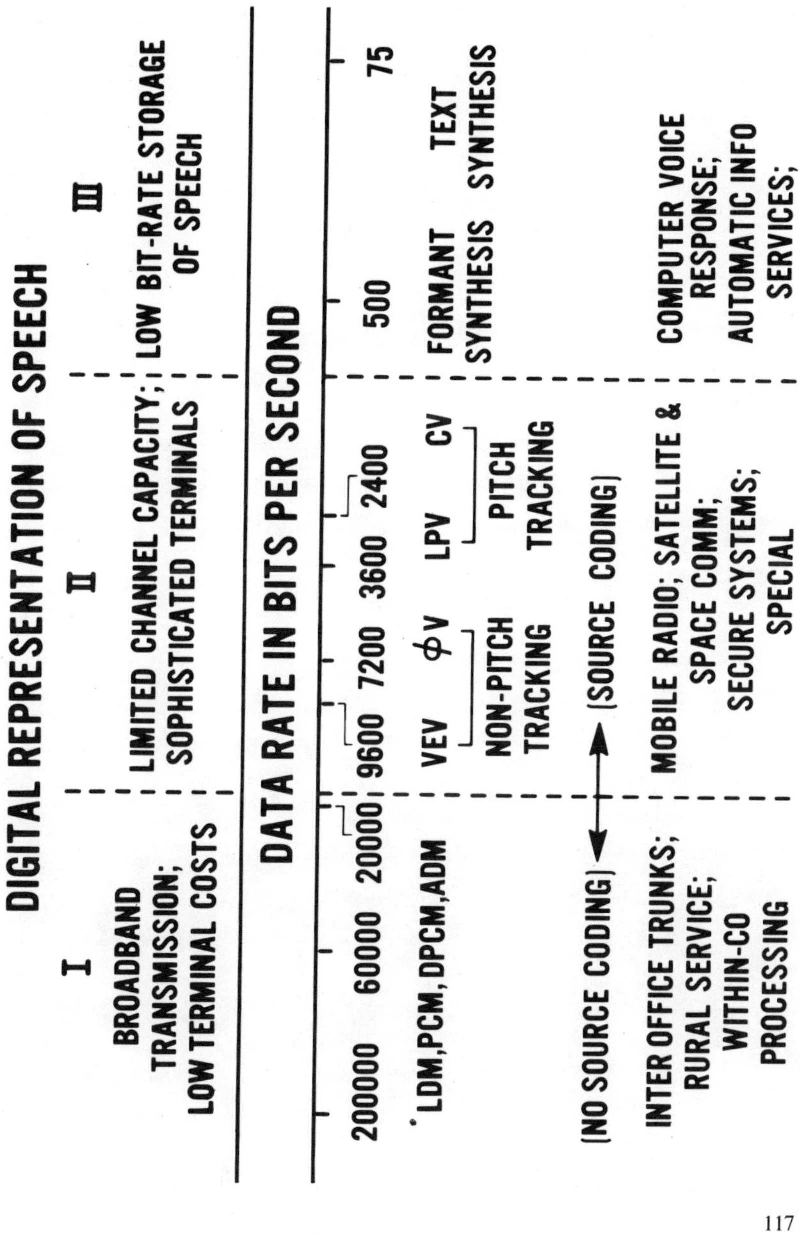
DIGITAL REPRESENTATION OF SPEECH
I
BROADBAND TRANSMISSION; LOW TERMINAL COSTS
II
LIMITED CHANNEL CAPACITY; SOPHISTICATED TERMINALS
III
LOW BIT-RATE STORAGE OF SPEECH
DATA RATE IN BITS PER SECOND
200000
60000
20000
9600
7200
3600
2400
500
75
LDM, PCM, DPCM, ADM
VEV
φV
NON-PITCH TRACKING
LPV
CV
PITCH TRACKING
FORMANT SYNTHESIS
TEXT SYNTHESIS
(NO SOURCE CODING)
(SOURCE CODING)
INTER OFFICE TRUNKS; RURAL SERVICE; WITHIN-CO PROCESSING
MOBILE RADIO; SATELLITE & SPACE COMM; SECURE SYSTEMS; SPECIAL
COMPUTER VOICE RESPONSE; AUTOMATIC INFO SERVICES;

Speech Communication Seminar
Stockholm. Aug. 1–3, 1974

IDENTIFICATION OF SPEECH PARAMETERS USING A RECURSIVE METHOD *

Bruno GARDINI - Angelo SERRA

Istituto di Elettrotecnica del Politecnico - Centro per l'Elaborazione Numerale dei Segnali - Istituto Elettrotecnico Nazionale Galileo Ferraris - Politecnico - 10129 TORINO, Italy.

Abstract

A recursive identification method is presented which can handle all types of sounds, allowing a unified approach to both the problems of speech analysis and synthesis. Poles as well as zeros of the model transfer function, voiced-unvoiced decision and pitch-detection, are obtained.

Some experimental results on synthetic speech are presented.

Introduction

A useful model for speech analysis and synthesis has been developed by Flanagan [1] and Fant [2]. The speech signal is modelled as the output of a dynamic system, having a discrete transfer function which can be expressed as:

$$H'(z) = \frac{Y(z)}{U'(z)} = \frac{\sum_{o}^{q} {}_i\, b'_i\, z^{-i}}{\sum_{o}^{p} {}_i\, a'_i\, z^{-i}} \tag{1}$$

where $Y(z)$ and $U'(z)$ are the z-transforms of the discrete speech waveform y_k and input u'_k.

Such a general model can handle all sounds, either voiced or unvoiced, in particular it can take into account the possible zeros of the transfer function, due to nasal and fricative sounds and glottal source.

The input u'_k, not measurable in practice, can be modelled, in first approximation, as a quasi-periodic sequence of pulses for voiced sounds or as a white noise sequence for unvoiced ones.

A reduced transfer function can be considered. Putting

$$\frac{b'_o}{a'_o} = G \qquad \frac{b'_i}{b'_o} = b_i \qquad \frac{a'_i}{a'_o} = a_i \tag{2}$$

and introducing a scaled input $u_k = u'_k \,.\, G$ we get :

* not published in the preprint version.

$$H(z) = \frac{Y(z)}{U(z)} = \frac{1 + \sum_{1}^{q}{}_{i} \; b_i \, z^{-i}}{1 + \sum_{1}^{q}{}_{i} \; a_i \, z^{-i}} \qquad (3)$$

The characteristic parameters we have to identify are:

1) a_i, b_i coefficients or another set of parameters connected with them, such as resonance frequencies and bandwidths
2) a decision parameter to distinguish between voiced or unvoiced sounds.
3) a pitch measure for voiced sounds
4) the mean-square value of the input u_n, characterizing the source energy.

Further more, as long as the speech production system is typically time-varying, the parameter estimate, must be adaptive, thus permitting the continuous parameters tracking and the necessary adaptation of the model to the voiced or unvoiced sounds.

A well known method, used in recent years in speech analysis, is the linear predictor algorithm. This is a Least-Square estimation procedure, giving an unbiased, efficient estimate of the a_i coefficients, only when the speech signal can be modelled as the pulse response of a system without numerator dynamics or as the output of the same system, excited by a white noise sequence.

This case is restrictive and typical of voiced sounds, for nasal or fricative ones the predictor technique is no more adequate.

The present work deals with a recursive identification method for the general model described by (3), handling all cases, and flexible enough to allow parameter tracking.

The values so obtained are a good set of features for speech recognition and can be directly used for speech synthesis, because the model adopted for this purpose is the same as for the identification procedure [3].

Identification method

In the presented model the input is considered as an uncorrelated sequence of random variable with zero-mean value and variance σ^2 almost everywhere, except in same points, where a higher-value deterministic input is present.

Let's consider a stationary system first.

Out of the points where the deterministic signal is present, the problem can be viewed as an ARMA (Auto Regressive Moving Average) model identification, because the system (3) can be described by the following difference equation:

$$y_k = \sum_{1}^{p} {}_i\, a_i\, y_{k-i} + \sum_{1}^{q} {}_i\, b_i\, u_{k-i} + u_k \qquad (4)$$

To resolve this problem, methods have been proposed in the time series theory.

One is based on the autocorrelation function of the speech signal; it uses the Yule-Walker equation to determine the a_k coefficients and solves a non linear equations system to find the b_k coefficients [4].

The estimates so obtained are unbiased but not statistically efficient.

Another more efficient method, recursively formulated, is suggested by Young [5]; this seems to be more adapted for the specific speech analysis.

Rewriting the (4) equation in vectorial notation, we have:

$$y_k = \left[-y_{k-1}, -y_{k-2}, \dots, -y_{k-p}; u_{k-1}, u_{k-2} \dots, u_{k-q}\right] \cdot \begin{bmatrix} a_1 \\ a_2 \\ \vdots \\ a_p \\ b_1 \\ b_2 \\ \vdots \\ b_q \end{bmatrix} + u_k =$$

$$= X_k^T \; c_k + u_k \qquad (5)$$

If the $(u_{k-1}, u_{k-2}, \dots, u_{k-q})$ were measurable, an unbiased minimum variance estimate of the parameter vector c_k is given by the Least Square algorithm.

As the input u_k is unmeasurable in our case, we have to estimate it in the simplest way possible:

$$\hat{u}_k = y_k - \hat{x}_k^T \hat{c}_{k-1} \qquad (6)$$

where:

$$\hat{x}_k^T = \left[-y_{k-1} - y_{k-2} \dots - y_{k-p}, \hat{u}_{k-1}, \dots \hat{u}_{k-q}\right] \qquad (7)$$

and $\hat{c}_{k-1}$ is the previous parameter estimate.

We get the following formulas:

$$\hat{c}_k = \hat{c}_{k-1} - H_k \left[\hat{x}_k^T \hat{c}_{k-1} - y_k \right] \tag{8}$$

$$H_k = P_{k-1} \hat{x}_k \left[1 + \hat{x}_k^T P_{k-1} \hat{x}_k \right]^{-1} \tag{9}$$

$$P_k = P_{k-1} - P_{k-1} \hat{x}_k \left[1 + \hat{x}_k^T P_{k-1} \hat{x}_k \right]^{-1} \hat{x}_k^T P_{k-1} \tag{10}$$

The initial values for this method, in the absence of other indications, are:

$$\hat{u}_{-1} = \hat{u}_{-2} = \ldots = u_{-q} = 0 \qquad \hat{c}_o = 0 \qquad P_o = I \delta^2 \tag{11}$$

It is preferable to choose δ^2 high enough to signify that the initial estimate of $\hat{c}_k$ is uncertain; even so, the method is poorly sensitive to δ^2. Higher values of δ^2 let the algorithm move faster, giving a good estimate of c_k, but with less reliability.

After few samples, the method converges quickly, both for the $\hat{c}_k$ and for the $\hat{u}_k$ estimate.

The $\hat{c}_k$ covariance matrix is given, in an asintotically approximate way, by $(\sigma_k^2 P_k)$, and this expression is also significant for a small value of k, provided that the method is fast converging.

The σ_k^2 value is obtained, taking out an initial number of wrong samples, from the $\hat{u}_k$ estimate of u_k, with the recursive formula:

$$\sigma_k^2 = \sigma_{k-1}^2 \cdot \frac{N-1}{N} + \frac{u_k^2}{N} \tag{12}$$

To consider of the samples of pitch period, we usually assume $N \simeq 80 \div 100$.

The described algorithm is immediately applicable for system with white noise input, whereas when pulses are present a detection method is needed to modify the identification algorithm. The simplest test we can think of is to compare the estimate $\hat{u}_k^2$ with a given threshold ;

when $$\hat{u}_k^2 \geq \beta \tag{13}$$

it is convenient simply to stop the identification process, avoiding the use of the (8), (9), (10), and continuing to estimate the following $\hat{u}_k$, while the $\hat{c}_{k-1}$ estimate is kept constant. The threshold value β is usually fixed to $(2 \div 3)\sigma_k^2$, corresponding to the required error probability.

Time varying parameters

From the previous exposition it turns out that the method structure is easily extendible to the non-stationary case. A simple way of doing this is to model the parameters variations with a stochastic matrix difference equation :

$$c_k = \emptyset \cdot c_{k-1} + \Gamma \cdot q_{k-1} \tag{14}$$

where $\emptyset$ is a (p + q) x (p + q) transition matrix and q_{k-1} is a (p + q) vector of indipendent random variables with zero-mean value and covariance matrix Q :

$$E\left\{q_k\right\} = 0 \; ; \qquad E\left\{q_k \, q_j^T\right\} = Q \cdot \delta_{kj} \tag{15}$$

where δ_{kj} is the kronecker delta.

When no more information is available, as in our case, possible values are: $\Gamma = \emptyset = I$ (identity matrix); $Q = D$ (diagonal matrix with d_i elements) so we get the following equations:

$$c_k = c_{k-1} + q_{k-1} \tag{16}$$

$$u_k = \hat{x}_k^T \, c_k + u_k \tag{17}$$

To such a system is applicable the Kalman filter algorithm, which gives the best linear estimation of the c_k vector:

$$\hat{c}_k = \hat{c}_{k-1} - H_k \cdot \left[\hat{x}_k^T \cdot \hat{c}_{k-1} - y_k\right] \tag{18}$$

$$H_k = P^*_{k,k-1} \, \hat{x}_k \left[\hat{x}_k^T \cdot P^*_{k,\,k-1} \, \hat{x}_k + \sigma_k^2\right]^{-1} \tag{19}$$

$$P^*_{k,\,k-1} = P^*_{k-1} + D \tag{20}$$

$$P^*_k = \left[I - H_k \hat{x}^T_k \right] P^*_{k,\, k-1} \tag{21}$$

where P^*_k is the covariance matrix of the error $(c_k - \hat{c}_k)$:

$$P^*_k = E\left[(c_k - \hat{c}_k)\,(c_k - \hat{c}_k)^T \right] \tag{22}$$

In the stationary case, where D = 0, in the above written equations, we can normalize the covariance matrix P^*_k by σ^2_k, obtaining the equations (8), (9), (10).

In the present case adding the matrix D prevents the matrix P^*_k from becaming too small, allows the continuous parameter updating and ensures convergence. It is important to notice that the ratios d_i/σ^2 must be keeped low.

Results analysis

The recursive identification technique discussed previously has been tested over synthetic speech signals obtained from systems similar to those used by Rabiner [3].

We treated "s" and "m" phonemes representative of fricative and nasal sounds, which have zeros in the model transfer function.

The values of the p, q, a_i, b_i parameters are shown in Tab. 1, together with the related frequencies and bandwiths. The sampling frequency was chosen 10 KHz. The exciting inputs used are white noise for the "s" and white noise with superimposed pulses for the "m". In the latter case, the two real poles at z_1 = - 0.2 and z_2 = + 0.8 have been used for the pulse excitation, as indicated in [3].

As we can see from Tab. 1, the zero frequency is very close to the second formant and this implies a partial cancellation between pole and zero. When there is a total cancellation, such a system is not identifiable, even having input and output observations, so the present example is a critical one.

A linear predictor identification has also been carried out and a comparison between the two methods is possible. For the predictor a window of 250 samples has been used.

The spectrum of the true model of the "m" is shown in Fig. 1 and in Fig. 2-3 are reported the spectra of the models obtained by the predictor and the recursive method respectively.

The output y_k and the estimated input $\hat{u}_k$ are plotted in Fig. 4. This shows the accuracy of the pulses detection. Finally in Fig. 5 is reported, the parameter E_k so defined:

$$E_k = \left. \frac{\sum_{1}^{p+q}{}_i (c_i - \hat{c}_i)^2}{\sum_{1}^{p+q}{}_i c_i^2} \right|_{k \text{ iteration}} \tag{23}$$

In Tab. 2 are shown the final $\hat{c}_i$'s extimate of the recursive method and the predictor.

It is apparent comparing the three spectra, the frequencies and related bandwiths, that in this case the results of the predictor are not so good as those obtained by the recursive method. For the "s" phoneme the results are not so different, as seen in spectra reported in Fig. 6, 7, 8 and from Tab. 3. This is because here the zero is farther from the poles and has a larger bandwidth than in "m" sound.

Conclusion

From the above, it may be seen that a good estimation is obtained even for complex systems. For simpler ones, without zeros, the algorithm proposed can be simplified, taking out from the parameter vector $\hat{c}_k$ the numerator coefficients b_i and maintaining the same structure for the computation.

Acknowledgments

This work was carried out at the "Centro di Elaborazione Numerale dei Segnali" Turin, Italy and was supported by the Consiglio Nazionale delle Ricerche. The authors are grateful to Profrs. R. Sartori, A.R. Meo and V. Mauro for the useful suggestions and discussions.

References

[1] J.L. Flanagan: "Speech Analysis Synthesis and Perception", Springer-Verlag, 1965.

[2] G. Fant: Acoustic Theory of Speech Production, Mouton & Co., 1960.

[3] L.R. Rabiner: "Speech Synthesis by Rule: an Acoustic Domain Approach", B.S.T.J., vol. 47, pp. 17-37, Jan. 1968.

[4] J.C. Chow: "On the Estimation of the Moving-Average Parameters", Trans. I.E.E.E. AC, vol. 17, pp. 268-269, Apr. 1972.

[5] P.C. Young: "Comments on "On-Line Identification of Linear Dynamic Systems with Application to Kalman Filtering"", IEEE Trans. AC-17, pp. 269-271, April 1972.

	a_1	a_2	a_3	a_4	a_5	a_6	a_7	a_8	a_9	a_{10}	b_1	b_2	p	q
[illegible]	-0.1624	-0.8237	0.1507	0.0940	-0.3313	0.2912	-0.1629	-0.6970	0.3736	0.4735	0.2214	0.5010	10	2
[illegible]	-2.6642	2.9172	-1.5732	0.3943	-0.7329	1.9088	-2.3262	1.4117	-0.1883	-0.1250	-1.3401	0.6859	10	2
	f_{1p} (Hz)	B_{1p} (Hz)	f_{2p} (Hz)	B_{2p} (Hz)	f_{3p} (Hz)	B_{3p} (Hz)	f_{4p} (Hz)	B_{4p} (Hz)	f_{5p} (Hz)	B_{5p} (Hz)	f_z (Hz)	B_z (Hz)	z_1	z_2
[illegible]	350	150	1300	120	2200	190	4000	150	-	-	1000	600	-0.2	0.8
[illegible]	200	60	1300	100	2500	120	4000	150	4850	760	2750	1100	-	-

TABLE 1 - Parameters of "S" and "M" model

	a_1	a_2	a_3	a_4	a_5	a_6	a_7	a_8	a_9	a_{10}	b_1	b_2
Predictor	-1.4442	0.6157	-0.0087	-0.0525	-0.6227	1.0527	-0.6445	-0.0099	0.2507	-0.0388	-	-
Rec. Ident.	-2.7998	3.2796	-2.0063	0.6691	-0.8268	2.0289	-2.5935	1.7480	-0.4225	-0.0597	-0.5449	0.200
	f_{1p} (Hz)	B_{1p} (Hz)	f_{2p} (Hz)	B_{2p} (Hz)	f_{3p} (Hz)	B_{3p} (Hz)	f_{4p} (Hz)	B_{4p} (Hz)	f_z (Hz)	B_z (Hz)	z_1	z_2
Predictor	254.8	135.4	1321.9	632.9	2222.9	273	3989.4	140	-	-	-0.4956	0.1646
Rec. Ident.	351.7	117.2	1305	148.6	2197.9	183.7	3999.7	150.5	1457.7	2561	-0.0967	0.9002

TABLE 2 - Parameter estimate for "M"

	a_1	a_2	a_3	a_4	a_5	a_6	a_7	a_8	a_9	a_{10}	b_1	b_2
Predictor	-0.3180	-1.0670	0.4358	0.3797	-0.5472	0.1651	0.0225	-0.5924	0.2815	0.3945	-	-
Rec. Ident.	-0.1924	-0.8518	0.1631	0.1153	-0.3424	0.3136	-0.1709	-0.7072	0.3799	0.4829	0.2036	0.5446
	f_{1p} (Hz)	B_{1p} (Hz)	f_{2p} (Hz)	B_{2p} (Hz)	f_{3p} (Hz)	B_{3p} (Hz)	f_{4p} (Hz)	B_{4p} (Hz)	f_{5p} (Hz)	B_{5p} (Hz)	f_z (Hz)	B_z (Hz)
Predictor	194.1	28.7	1246.4	92.0	2411.1	399.8	4045.5	169.9	4939.5	789.4	-	-
Rec. Ident.	194.5	35.2	1288.5	95.3	2496	121.9	4009.2	146.4	4802.2	759.9	2720.2	967.2

TABLE 3 - Parameter estimate for "S"

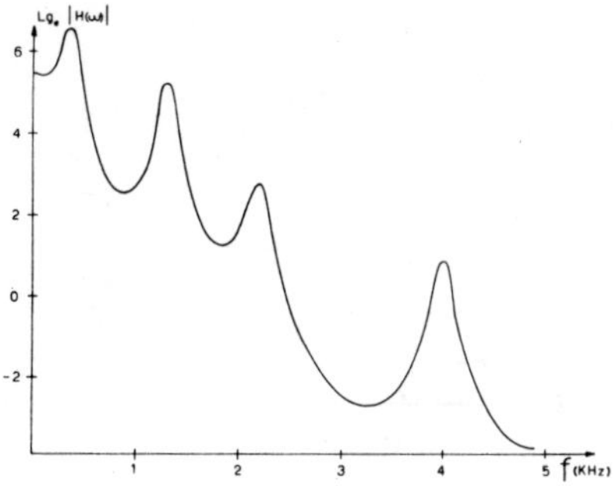

Fig. 1

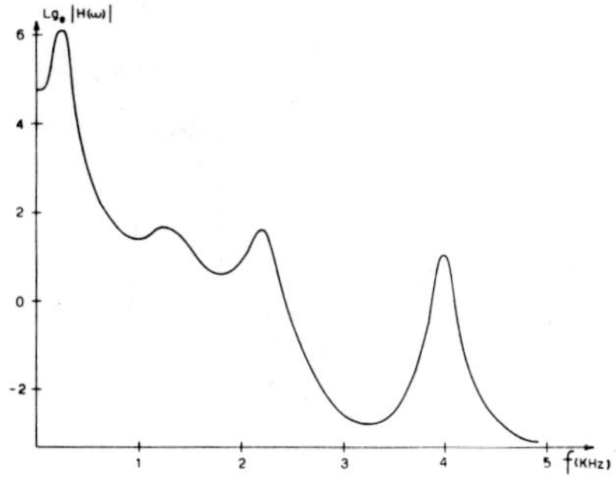

Fig. 2

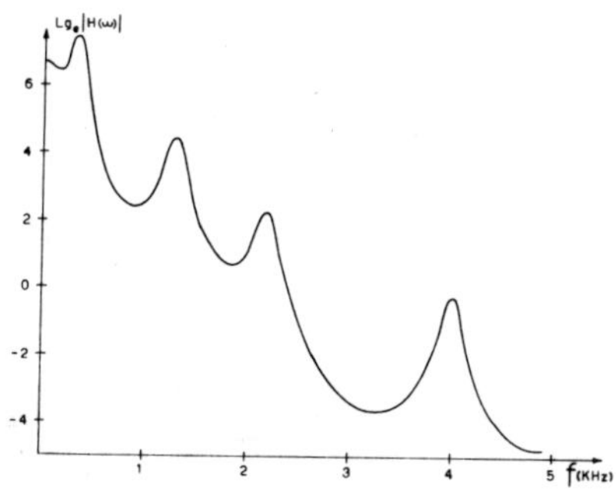

Fig. 3

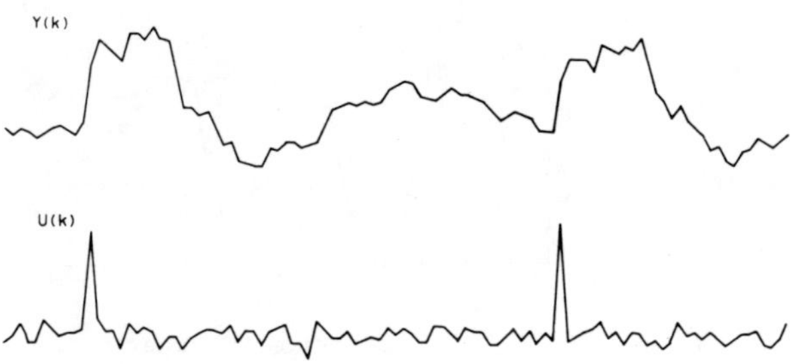

Fig. 4

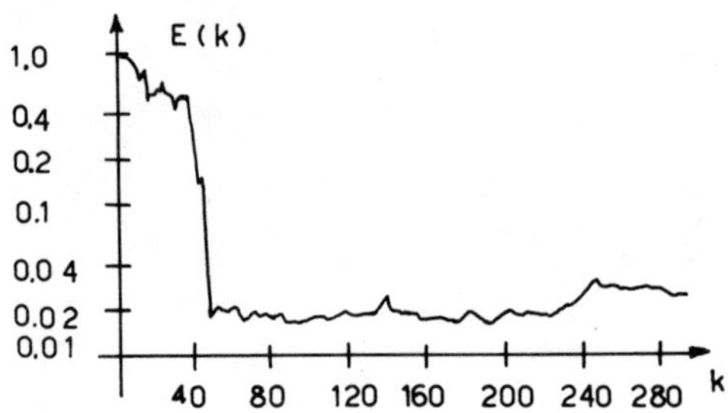

Fig. 5

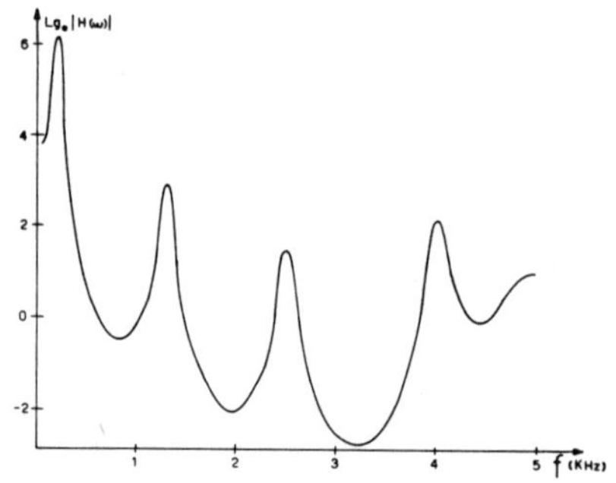

Fig. 6 - Original "S" spectrum .

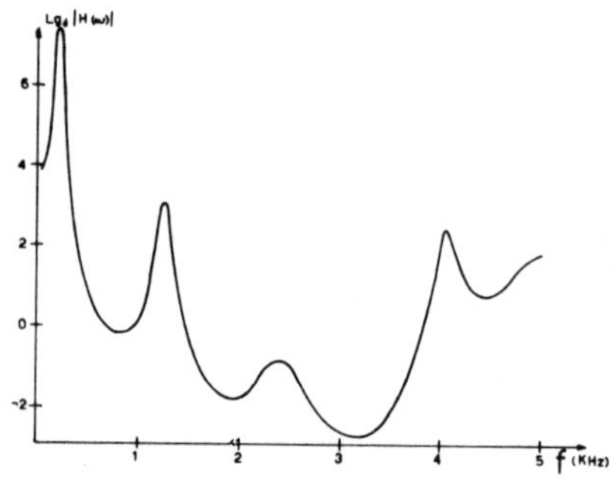

Fig. 7 - Predictor "S" spectrum .

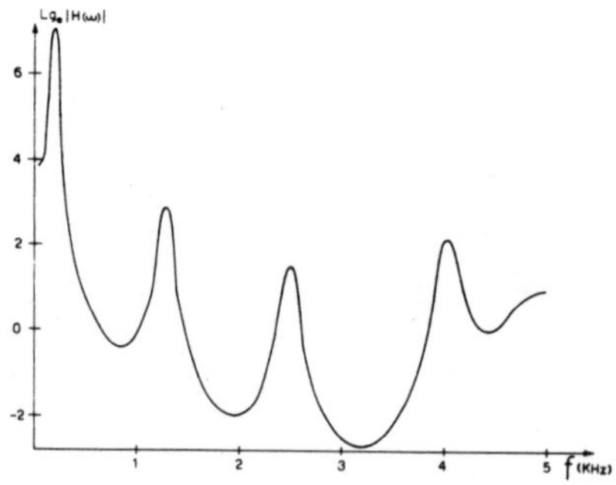

Fig. 8 - Recursive "S" spectrum .

Speech Communication Seminar
Stockholm. Aug. 1–3, 1974

SPECTRAL ANALYSIS OF SPEECH BASED ON LINEAR DELTA MODULATION *

N. S. Jayant, Acoustics Research Department, Bell Laboratories, 600 Mountain Avenue, Murray Hill, New Jersey 07974, U.S.A.

Abstract

We consider the power spectrum Y(f) of the staircase sequence $\{y_r\}$ in the linear delta modulation (LDM) of a band-limited speech sequence, $\{x_r\}$. Within the signal band, Y(f) approximates the input spectrum X(f) with an accuracy that depends on two parameters: the LDM step-size Δ and the over-sampling F (ratio of sampling rate in LDM to the Nyquist rate for the band-limited input). We demonstrate Y(f) dependencies on Δ and F (or C) using a low-pass-filtered speech input in a computer simulation. We consider the specific problem of preserving, in Y(f), the formant frequencies of a short-term input spectrum X(f). We observe, for example, when F = 9, that input resonances are shifted by amounts not exceeding perceptual limens, in an average sense, if Δ is within an estimated ± 6 dB of a step-size Δ_{OPT} (which minimizes the mean-square-quantization error in the delta-modulation of $\{x_r\}$).

The fact that y_r is a summation of r binary quantities makes the computation of Y(f) much simpler than that of X(f), in general; specifically, Y(f) can be computed without any MULTIPLY operations. Therefore, in problems where the power spectrum is the desired end result (for example, in the visual monitoring of formant frequencies), Y(f) can provide a useful and simply computed approximation to the input spectrum. With such special applications in mind, we consider the problem of implementing a Y(f) analyzer, and note two specific analyzer configurations.

I. Linear Delta Modulation

The principle of linear delta modulation (LDM) [1] is well-known. Briefly, LDM is a quantizing technique (Fig. 1) where a band-limited input signal sequence $\{x_r\}$ is approximated by a sequence of staircase function amplitudes $\{y_r\}$. The staircase function is made up of steps that follow, in polarity, the sign of the difference (x_r-y_{r-1}):

$$y_r = y_{r-1} + \Delta \cdot b_r; \quad b_r = \mathrm{sgn}(x_r-y_{r-1}) \qquad (1)$$

The step-size Δ is constant, by definition, in LDM. The quantization error variance in delta-modulation has two components: slope-overload (which is a monotonically decreasing function of Δ) and granularity (which increases monotonically with increasing Δ). Consequently, for a given input, there is an optimum step-size Δ_{OPT} that minimizes the error variance. Abate [1] has proposed a rule-of-thumb expression for Δ_{OPT}:

* not published in the preprint version.

$$\Delta_{OPT} = (\ln 2F) \left\langle (x_r - x_{r-1})^2 \right\rangle^{1/2} \tag{2}$$

denotes the expected value, and F is the ratio of the DM sampling frequency to the Nyquist frequency for the band-limited input. The input is usually over-sampled (F>>1) for useful delta modulation. The unfiltered staircase function y_r has the desirable mathematical property of being the summation of binary quantities; and we shall be concerned, in this paper, with the utilization of this property in a simple computation of the frequency spectrum Y(f). We shall also be concerned with showing how Y(f) can usefully approximate the input spectrum X(f) within the signal band, under certain conditions.

II. Speech Spectra

The speech signal used in our simulations was a low-pass-filtered male utterance of "Have You Seen Bill," which was band-limited to 3.3 kHz, and sampled for LDM at 60, 40, and 20 kHz. Spectrum computations were carried out on a weighted input sequence. The weighting was done with a Hamming window whose duration N was always set equal to that of an input section which was being transformed: This weighting function is given by

$$W_r = 0.54 - 0.46 \cos\left[\frac{2\pi r}{N-1}\right]; \quad r = 0,1,2,\ldots N-1 \tag{3}$$

Spectra will be displayed for the frequency range 0 to 5 kHz. Spectral information from 3.3 kHz to 5 kHz will be essentially due to the quantization error spectrum in that range.

III. Short-Term Spectra

Most of our results will be on the short-term spectrum of a short voiced segment which has clearly defined resonances corresponding to /bI/ in the input utterance. The criterion for the goodness of spectrum approximations will be the preservation of formant locations within the perceptual limens reported by Rosenberg, et al. [2]. These are approximately 55, 130 and 170 Hz for the first three formants. For the voiced segment in consideration, the formants in the original utterance are located approximately at 430, 1620, and 2300 Hz.

Figure 2 shows the input power spectrum X(f) and the spectrum Y(f) as a function of Δ, for F = 9 (sampling rate = 60 kHz) and an input sequence length of N = 1024. One notes that a useful range of step-size Δ for formant preservation appears to be in the order of 10 to 15 dB, centered on an optimum step-size Δ_{OPT}. When speech amplitudes were scaled for a nominal peak value of $(x_r)_{MAX} = 2048$, it was found that $\Delta_{OPT} = 70$.

Figure 3 displays spectra of the quantization error

$$e_r = y_r - x_r \tag{4}$$

for the step-sizes of Fig. 2. Notice that except during severe slope-overload (Fig. 3b) the error spectrum E(f) tends to be white (in an average sense) across the signal band.

Useful ranges of Δ decrease rapidly for smaller values of F. We present, in Fig. 4, the input spectrum X(f), and the plots of Y(f) for F = 9, 6, and 3. The step-size in each case is equal to a respective Δ_{OPT}, as determined in separate simulations. (For a peak speech amplitude $(x_r)_{MAX} = 2048$, these values of Δ_{OPT} are 70, 95 and 145, respectively.) The input sequence length is given by N. The values of N imply a sequence that includes several pitch periods; this injects fundamental frequency information in the form of the rapidly varying component in the short term spectrum.

To supplement visual location of resonances in spectrograms, formant frequencies were automatically computed in a linear-prediction-based technique which fitted short-term spectra to a four-pole model. Results are summarized in Table I where entries were average values of formant shifts in Y(f), the averages being over five locations along the test utterance. It is expected that the effect of quantization noise is such as to make automatic formant location in Y(f) more difficult than visual peak-picking. Nevertheless, the results of Table I can be combined with the visual observations in Figs. 2, 3, and 4 to arrive at the following conjectures: If the signal oversampling is of the order F = 9, input resonances are shifted by amounts not exceeding perceptual limens, on the average, if the step size Δ is within an estimated ± 6 dB of Δ_{OPT} $(0.5\Delta_{OPT} \leq \Delta \leq 2\Delta_{OPT})$. If, on the other hand, F is as small as 6, it seems necessary to use a step-size that is almost exactly equal to Δ_{OPT}.

IV. The Expression for Y(f)

We shall now formally compute the power spectrum of the staircase function in LDM, and express it as a simple function of the bit sequence b_r. The notation employed in this section is summarized below:

$$\mathcal{Y}(f) = \sum_{r=1}^{N} y_r \exp(-j2\pi rk/N) \tag{5}$$

$$Y(f) = |\mathcal{Y}(f)|^2 \tag{6}$$

$\mathcal{Y}$ is the transform of the time sequence $\{y_r\}$ and Y is the power spectrum. Explicitly, for values of k = 1,2,...N,

$$\mathcal{Y}(f)\Big|_{f=\frac{k}{NT}} = \sum_{r=1}^{N} y_r \exp(-j2\pi rk/N) \tag{7}$$

$$= \sum_{r=1}^{N} \left[\sum_{u=1}^{r} \Delta \cdot b_u \right] \exp(-j2\pi rk/N) \tag{8}$$

Expanding, grouping terms involving a given b_r, and summing resulting geometric series, we obtain:

$$\begin{aligned}
Y(f) = {} & \Delta \cdot b_1 \; \exp(-j2\pi k/N) \left[\frac{1-\exp(-j2\pi k)}{1-\exp(-j2\pi k/N)} \right] \\
& + \Delta \cdot b_2 \; \exp(-j2\pi 2k/N) \left[\frac{1-\exp(-j2\pi k[N-1]/N)}{1-\exp(-j2\pi k/N)} \right] \\
& + \ldots\ldots\ldots\ldots \\
& + \Delta \cdot b_n \; \exp(-j2\pi Nk/N) \left[\frac{1-\exp(-j2\pi k/N)}{1-\exp(-j2\pi k/N)} \right]
\end{aligned} \tag{9}$$

Upon further re-grouping of terms,

$$Y(f) = \frac{\Delta}{1-\exp(-j2\pi k/N)} \left[\sum_{1}^{N} b_r \exp(-j2\pi kr/N) - \exp(-j2\pi k[1+\tfrac{1}{N}]) \cdot \sum_{1}^{N} b_r \right] \tag{10}$$

Multiplying the numerator and denominator by $[1-\exp(j2\pi k/N)]$, and noting that $\exp(-j2\pi k) = 1$ for all k,

$$Y(f) = \frac{\Delta[1-\exp(j2\pi k/N)]}{4\sin^2 \frac{\pi k}{N}} \left[\sum_{1}^{N} b_r \exp(-j2\pi kr/N) - \exp(-j2\pi k/N) \cdot \sum_{1}^{N} b_r \right] \tag{11}$$

The following are the real and imaginary parts of $Y(f)$:

$$\mathrm{Re}[Y(f)] = \left\{ \left[(1-\cos \frac{2\pi k}{N}) \cdot P(k) \right] - \left[(\sin \frac{2\pi k}{N}) \cdot Q(k) \right] \right\} \cdot \Delta \tag{12}$$

$$\mathrm{Im}[Y(f)] = \left\{ \left[-(1-\cos \frac{2\pi k}{N}) \cdot Q(k) \right] - \left[(\sin \frac{2\pi k}{N}) \cdot P(k) \right] \right\} \cdot \Delta \tag{13}$$

where

$$P(k) = \sum_{1}^{N} b_r \left(\cos \frac{2\pi kr}{N} - \cos \frac{2\pi k}{N}\right) \tag{14}$$

and

$$Q(k) = \sum_{1}^{N} b_r \left(\sin \frac{2\pi rk}{N} - \sin \frac{2\pi k}{N}\right) \tag{15}$$

Consequently,

$$Y(f)\Big|_{f=\frac{k}{NT}} = \left|\mathcal{Y}(f)\right|^2 = \frac{\Delta^2}{4\sin^2\frac{\pi k}{N}}\left[[P(k)]^2 + [Q(k)]^2\right]; \qquad (16)$$

where k = 1,2,...N.

V. Conclusion

The multiplications involved in (14) and (15) are trivial in that b_r is a binary number = ± 1. The computation of P(k) and Q(k) can in fact be regarded as a succession of sign assignments and additions. (It is assumed, as in conventional transform techniques, that the cosine and sine terms are known, or alternatively, can be efficiently computed.) Then, if N is sufficiently large, the computation of Y(f), for any given value of f (or k), is essentially no more complicated than an operation which involves the 4N additions needed to determine P(k) or Q(k). This is demonstrated in Fig. 5(a). The implementation is simple in that it is based on ADD operations rather than MULTIPLY operations of the form $[x_r \cdot \cos(2\pi rj/N)]$. Furthermore, it can be shown that the implementation can also be faster than conventional transformation (in spite of the oversampling factor F) if

$$2F < T_{MA} \qquad (17)$$

where T_{MA} is the ratio of MULTIPLY time to ADD time. For F = 9, (17) is true of many software implementations where average T_{MA} values can be as high as 50 [3].

If our spectral analysis technique is used in conjunction with an FFT type algorithm, basic computations can be performed on conveniently short signal sequences of length N_0; where N_0 is a factor of a composite number N, the length of the sequence whose spectrum is desired. The advantage of using shorter sequences is that for any given k, all (of the 2^{N_0}) possible P(k) and Q(k) values can be stored in read-only-memory (ROM) elements; with each pair of P, Q values corresponding to one of the (2^{N_0} possible) bit sequences b_r of length N_0. This leads to a fast implementation as depicted in Fig. 5(b).

We are unable at this time to make any quantitative assessments about the utility and costs of LDM-based spectral analysis. It is reasonable to assume, however, that application of this technique would be most appropriate when accuracy requirements are not the most stringent, and when the speech spectrum itself (rather than target values of formant or fundamental frequency) is the desired end result.

References

1. J. E. Abate, "Linear and Adaptive Delta Modulation," Proc. IEEE, March 1967, pp. 298-308.

2. A. E. Rosenberg, R. W. Schafer and L. R. Rabiner, "Effects of Smoothing and Quantizing the Parameters of Formant-Coded Voiced Speech," J. Acous. Soc. Am., Vol. 50, No. 6 (Part 2), December 1971, pp. 1532-1538.

3. J. L. Butler, "Comparative Criteria for Minicomputers," Instrumentation Technology, Vol. 17, October 1970, pp. 67-82.

Table I

Formant shifts due to delta-modulation. Entries are in Hz, and are averages over five voiced segments along test utterance. Numbers in parentheses are the respective perceptual limens.

Sampling Frequency (KHz)	60			40	20
Step-size: $20 \log_{10} (\Delta/\Delta_{OPT})$	-10	0	+10	0	0
F1 (55)	20	23	28	27	21
F2 (130)	147	36	54	37	229
F3 (170)	264	113	223	161	348

Figure Captions

Fig. 1 - Schematic block diagram of a linear delta modulator.

Fig. 2 - Short term spectra for voiced speech (N = 1024, F = 9). (a) Input spectrum X(f); (b) Y(f); $\Delta = \Delta_{OPT}/\sqrt{10}$; (c) Y(f); $\Delta = \Delta_{OPT}$; (d) Y(f); $\Delta = \Delta_{OPT} \cdot \sqrt{10}$.

Fig. 3 - Short term power spectra for speech and quantization error (N = 1024, F = 9). (a) Input spectrum X(f); (b) E(f); $\Delta = \Delta_{OPT}/\sqrt{10}$; (c) E(f); $\Delta = \Delta_{OPT}$; (d) E(f); $\Delta = \Delta_{OPT} \cdot \sqrt{10}$.

Fig. 4 - Short term power spectra for voiced speech ($\Delta = \Delta_{OPT}$). (a) Input spectrum X(f); F = 9, N = 2048; (b) Y(f); F = 9, N = 2048; (c) Y(f); F = 6, N = 2048; (d) Y(f); F = 3, N = 1024.

Fig. 5 - Block diagram of a spectral analyzer based on linear delta modulation. (a) Straightforward implementation; (b) Implementation based on an FFT Type algorithm (N_0 is a factor of a composite number N which represents the signal sequence length).

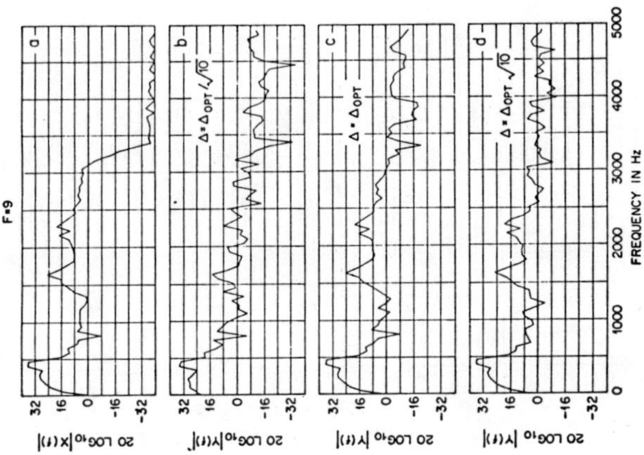
F=9
20 LOG10 |X(f)|
20 LOG10 |Y(f)|
Δ = ΔOPT/√10
Δ = ΔOPT
Δ = ΔOPT √10
FREQUENCY IN Hz

FIG. 2

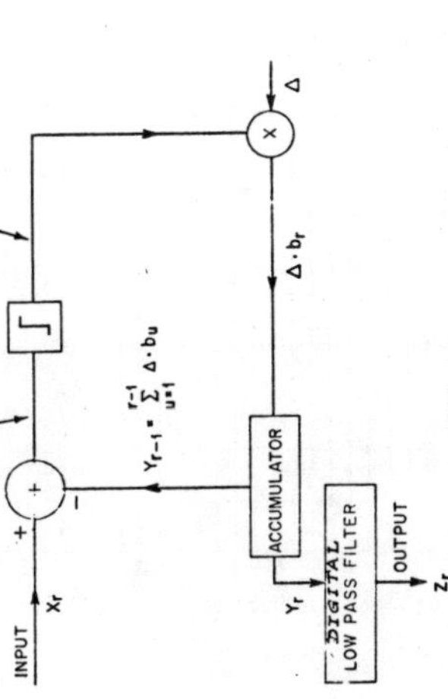
INPUT
ACCUMULATOR
DIGITAL LOW PASS FILTER
OUTPUT

FIG. 1

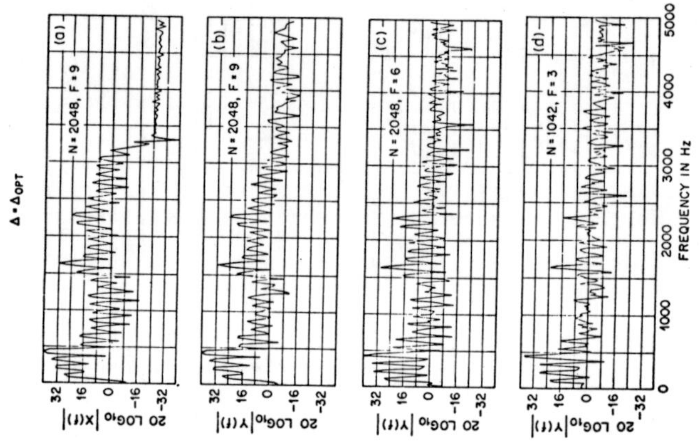

Δ = Δ_OPT
N = 2048, F = 9
(a)
N = 2048, F = 9
(b)
N = 2048, F = 6
(C)
N = 1042, F = 3
(d)
20 LOG10 |X(f)|
20 LOG10 |Y(f)|
FREQUENCY IN Hz

FIG. 4

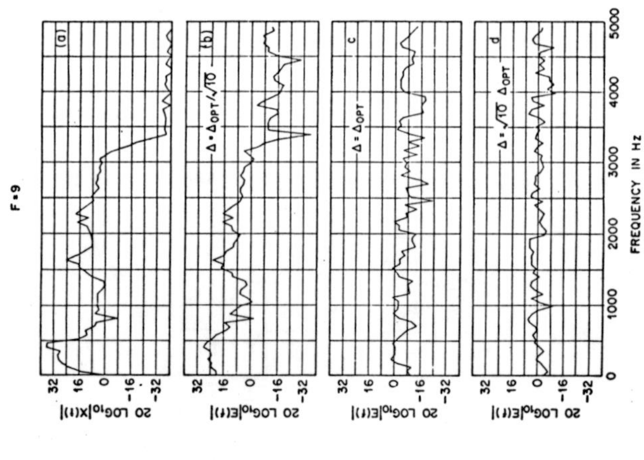

F = 9
(a)
Δ = Δ_OPT/√10
(b)
Δ = Δ_OPT
c
Δ = √10 Δ_OPT
d
20 LOG10 |X(f)|
20 LOG10 |E(f)|
FREQUENCY IN Hz

FIG. 3

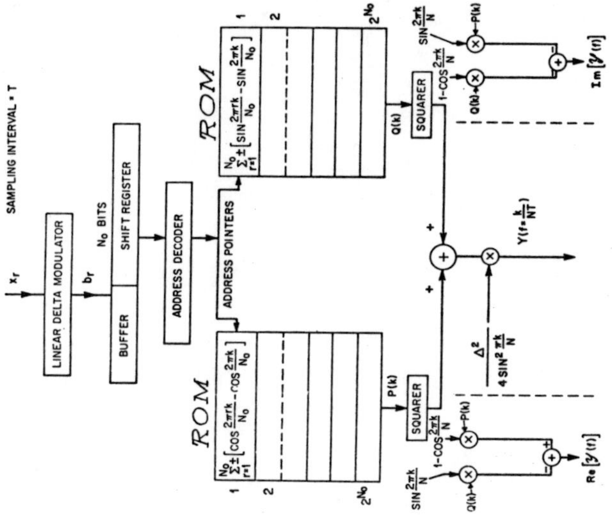

FIG 5b

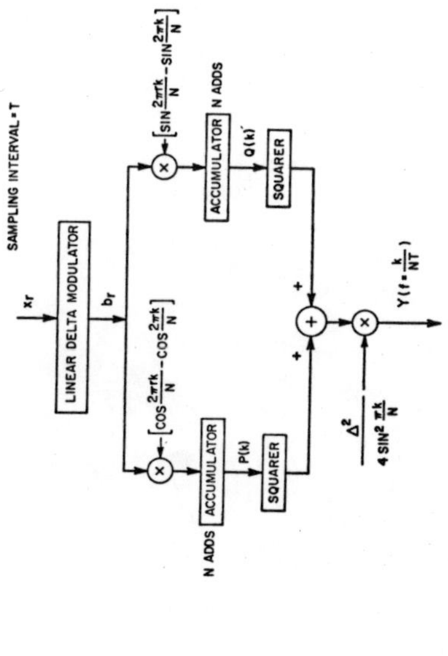

FIG. 5a

FIG. 5a

Speech Communication Seminar
Stockholm. Aug. 1–3, 1974

EFFICIENCY AND ACCURACY IN VOCAL PITCH DETERMINATION BY SOME METHODS USING DIGITAL COMPUTER *

G. LUKATELA, T. TOMIĆ, D. DRAJIĆ
Faculty of Electrical Engineering, Belgrade, Yugoslavia

Abstract

The adaptive autocorrelation method as proposed in the previous paper /1/ has shown the possibility of determining with small probability of failure, the pitch of connected speech, particularly during rapid pitch inflections and transitions. These features of the adaptive autocorrelation are useful for general linguistic research, automatic speech recognition, speaker verification etc.

This paper compares the adaptive autocorrelation with the "Cepstrum" /2/ as far as the accuracy in pitch tracking and the efficiency in exploiting the computer time are concerned.

2. PRINCIPLES OF THE ADAPTIVE AUTOCORRELATION

The short-time autocorrelation function of the speech signal is the convolution of three components:

$$R(\tau,t)= R_{PP}(\tau,t)*R_{FP}(\tau,t)*R_{AP}(\tau,t) \qquad (1)$$

The first component, R_{PP}, takes account of pitch periodicities; the second component, R_{FP}, of formant (basically first-formant) periodicities; and the third component, R_{AP}, reflects the presence of aperiodicities. Assuming that the width of the lag window through which a part of the input speech signal is viewed is comparable to the pitch period, T_o, one may observe some typical shapes of the"R-pattern", i.e., of the short-time autocorrelation function as plotted against the delay τ. Over the quasi-periodic intervals of speech, when the pitch periodicity is dominant, the R-pattern shows an absolute maximum for zero delay (τ=o) and the heights of the subsequent maxima at $\tau = mT_o (m=1,2,3,\ldots)$ are usually less than for zero delay. Incidentally, it may be noted that R(0,t) represents the mean square value of the weighted input signal.

* not published in the preprint version.

For $\tau>0$, the aperiodic component R_{AP} in (1) vanishes rapidly, and the formant component R_{FP} behaves like a damped oscillation of a relatively high "Q-factor". Hence, the R-pattern usually displays several large-amplitude oscillations at the formant period T_F. When a particular voiced segment lacks periodicity, as it happens during fast pitch variations and formant glides in the transition from one speech sound to the next, the R-pattern can show multiple false peaks, and the tracking of the "pitch peak" that corresponds to the true pitch period may become a difficult task.

In studying the distribution and relative values of peaks in the R-pattern of low-pass filteres speech, it was noticed that the voiced segments of speech start with a rapid build-up of the R(0,t) value and that the peak at $\tau=T_o$ is well defined, provided the width of the lag window is large. Since this initial build-up behaviour of voiced speech segments has shown small variance across many speech samples, it was designated as an invariant feature of the speech signal. During the Initial-Build-Up (IBU) period it was possible to locate the true pitch peak of the short-time autocorrelation function (for$\tau=T_o$) even if the inflection is fast because the speech signal energy increases rapidly, and the previous maximum is easily updated by the subsequent one.

Therefore, by the end of the IBU period, there is a reliable value for the true pitch peak, which makes it possible to follow closely the subsequent movement of this peak. This involves narrowing the lag window to the minimum width consistent with the running pitch period. This narrow lag window allows updating of the pitch peak position even during the rapidly decreasing speech level, usually found at the end of phonation.

3. OUTLINE OF THE SYSTEM

A block diagram of the adaptive autocorrelation system for pitch determination is shown in Fig. 1. It consists basically of a preprocessor, correlator, maxima selector, postprocessor, and control unit.

The input speech signal, s(t), is first prefiltered by low pass filter with a cutoff frequency f_g=1 kHz. After sampling the filter output at a high sampling rate, v=8 kHz, the speech samples are shifted through a delay line. At each output tap of the

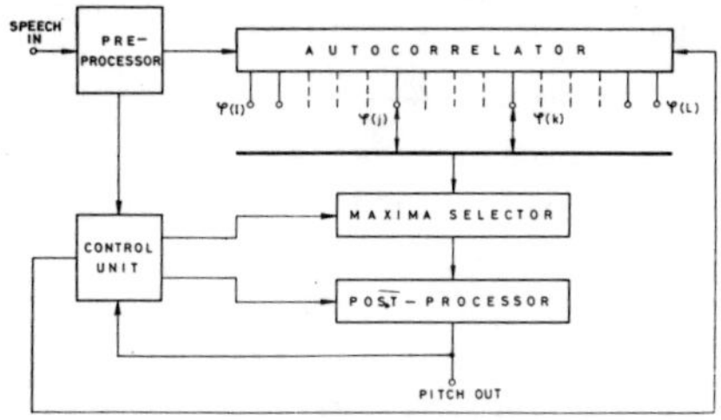

Fig. 1 Block diagram of the adaptive autocorrelation system

delay line a short-time autocorrelation function is calculated. Thus, the autocorrelator transmits to the maxima selector a discrete spatial R-pattern. This unit finds and stores a number of maxima, while the postprocessor checks and compares the heights and delays of the stored maxima and determines which maximum represents the true pitch peak. With this information, and considering also the mean square value of the input signal, the control unit makes appropriate changes in the time constants of the autocorrelator and in the position and width of the "spatial window" through which the maxima selector views the spatial R-pattern.

4. THE AUTOCORRELATION ALGORITHM

The choice of the autocorrelation window function w(t) was governed by some mutually exclusive requirements. In order to minimize the effect due to the inclusion of the nonintegral number of the pitch period the window function should gradually decrease toward both ends. This requirement is almost perfectly satisfied by the Hamming time window /3/. Unfortunately, under variable window width conditions the Hamming window is hardly conceivable in hardware, and in software it consumes additional computer time and storage. Hence, for the sake of simple implementation the asymmetrical exponential window

$$w(t) = \begin{cases} \exp\left[-\frac{t}{\tau}\right] ; & 0 \leqslant t < \infty \\ 0 ; & t < 0 \end{cases} \qquad (2)$$

was used. With this window the short time autocorrelation function defined by Fano /4/ is of the form:

$$R(\tau,t) = \frac{1}{\gamma} \int_{-\infty}^{t} s(x)s(x-\tau)\exp\left[-\frac{t-x}{\gamma}\right] dx \qquad (3)$$

The integration can be carried out by means of a simple RC integrator with a time constant .

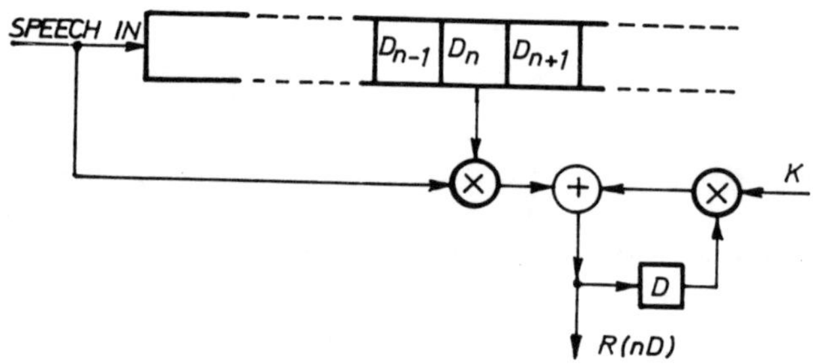

Fig. 2 Algorithm for computation of an autocorrelation function

A straightforward implementation of the short time autocorrelation function as given by /3/ is possible. A block diagram of the corresponding autocorrelation algorithm is shown in Fig. 2. The delay line, (DL), consists of N cells, the equivalent delay introduced by each cell being D=1/v. The speech sample in the n-th cell is multiplied with the content of the "Zero Delay Cell"(ZDC), the product is added to the weighted sum of the previous products and the resulting short time autocorrelation function, R(nD), is transferred to the corresponding n-th cell of the R-pattern line (RPL). Thus, the calculation of the each R(nD)-value requires two multiplications and one addition, or 2N multiplications and N additions for each R-pattern. The number of R-patterns per second equals to the sampling rate v and therefore the total number of necessary operations per second, if one neglects the relatively short subroutines of peak peaking etc., roughly ammounts to 2Nv multiply and Nv add operations.

During the initial Build-Up (IBU) period the length of the R-pattern line is constant. Since it was noticed that the voiced segments of speech start at relatively higher value of F_o, the number of cells in the R-pattern line during the IBU period is N=80, within the range (2,12)ms.

During the post-IBU period the short time autocorrelation functions R(nD) need to be computed only in the neighbourhood of the previous pitch peak and, therefore, the number N depends on the pitch of the analysed utterance. For a low-pitched male speaker on the average it is N=40 and for a high-pitched female speaker it is on the average below N≐20.

Further reduction of the computer time could be achieved by diminishing the sampling rate,v. With regard to the cutoff frequency of the input lowpass filter (f_g=1kHz) the sampling frequency could be as low as 2000 Hz. However, in order to ensure sufficient time scale resolution for accurate determination of the pitch peak position in the R-pattern, the sampling rate was not altered, i.e. it remained at v=8000 samples/sec., and another approach that will be designated as "interlacing techniques" was chosen.

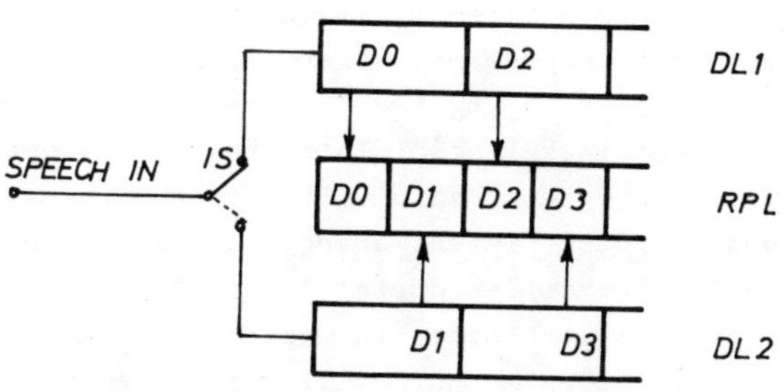

Fig. 3 Principle of the interlacing techniques

The delay line,(DL), in Fig. 2 could be imagined consisting of the odd and even cells that constitute two separate delay lines,

DL1 and DL2 as shown in Fig. 3. The input speech samples are directed either to DL 1 or DL2 via a 2-position "interlacing switch" (IS), that changes its position once-per each sampling interval. Thus, the N/2 autocorrelation functions are calculated and transferred to the corresponding odd or even cells of the R-pattern line, once per sampling interval. Actually, the adaptive autocorrelation algorithm uses an 8-position interlacing switch with 8 equivalent delay lines each oonsisting of N/8 cells thus reducing by a factor of 8 the number of necessary operations.

The interlacing step could be probably further increased. The preliminary experiments with the 16-fold interlacing techniques gave satisfactory results.

5. EXPERIMENTAL RESULTS

In order to investigate the capabilities and limitations of the adaptive autocorrelation as compared with the cepstral analysis a program was written in Fortran IV language for the IBM-1130 computer. A statistically significant number of purposely difficult utterances was analysed.

In adaptive autocorrelation method there are two possible kinds of errors: regular and nonregular. The regular error is a small deviation from the true value. It arises because the adjacent formant peaks may shift the true pitch peak in the R-pattern from its position at T_0 to a false position at $T_o \pm T_F$. Nonregular error, on the other hand, represents a serious failure in pitch determination. It arises if during the IBU- period the wrong maximum in the R-pattern is selected. In contrast, the cepstral analysis was accurate in determination of the pitch when the voiced segments possessed sufficient energy, but it failed in the most of the analysed examples during the fast pitch variations at low power level as it happens in voiced stops and fricatives, when the autocorrelation method still worked. A typical example will demonstrate this point.

A pitch contour of the sentence "Palm trees grow very tall", as obtained by the visual inspection of waveforms and sonograms, is plotted by solid line in Fig. 4. The dots indicate F_o estimates obtained with the cepstral analysis, and the crosses -with adaptive autocorrelation.The points are shown in 20 ms increments, The pitch contour in the voiced fricative /v/ in the word "very" was adequately traced by the adaptive autocorrelation, whereas

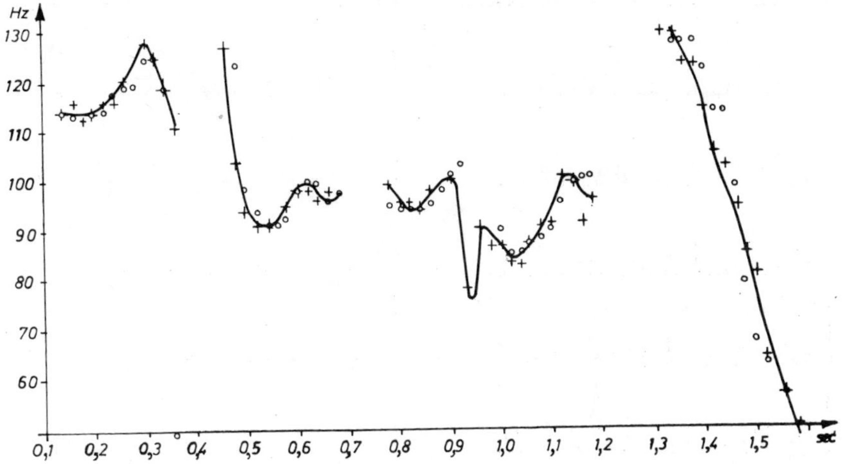

Fig. 4 Pitch contour of the sentence "Palm trees graw very tall".

the cepstral analysis failed completely. The critical part of the speech waveform is shown in Fig. 5, and the corresponding 512-point cepstral and adaptive autocorrelation patterns are

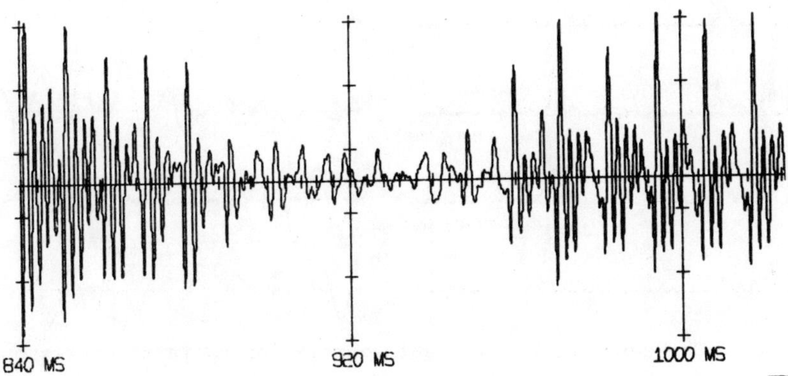

Fig. 5 A crtitical part of the input waveform "grOW VEry..."

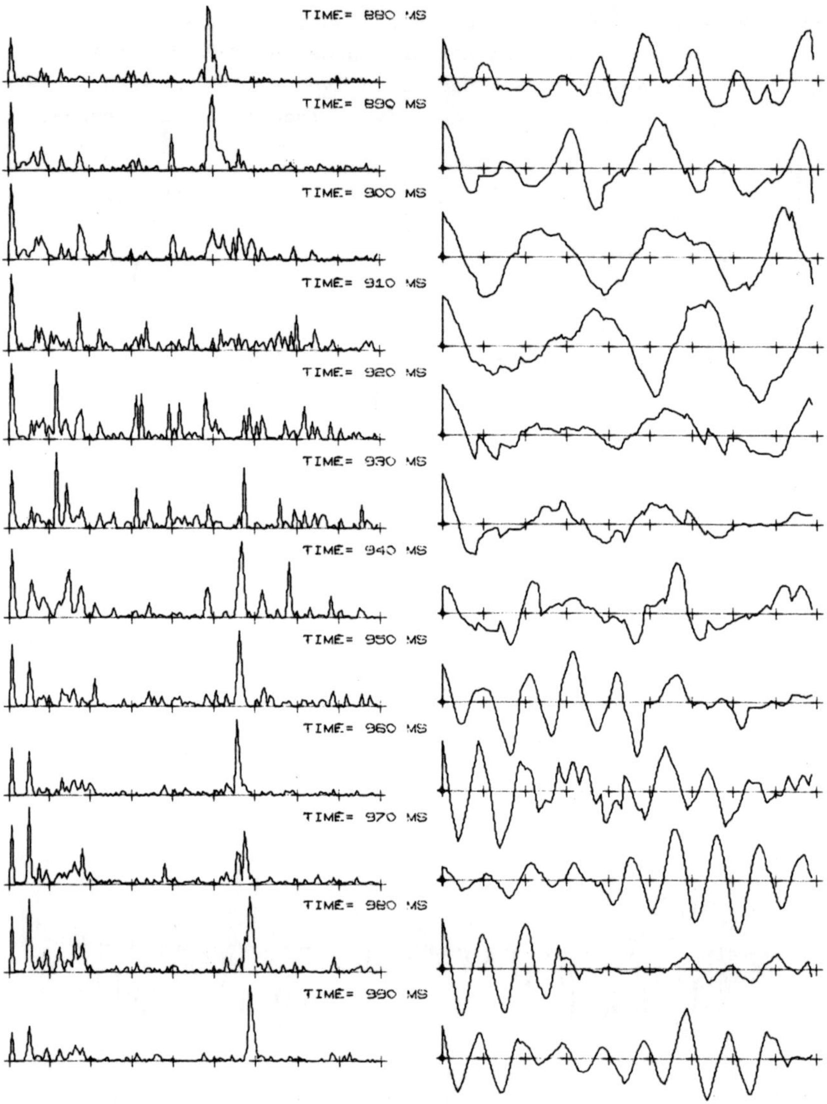

Fig. 6 The cepstral and the autocorrelation patterns corresponding to the waveform in Fig. 5

shown in Fig. 6

It was found that the adaptive autocorrelation algorithm is on the average 2 times faster than the cepstral analysis when the cepstral patterns are computed for each lo ms.

CONCLUSION

It has been experimentally demonstrated that the adaptive autocorrelation algorithm compares favourably with the cepstral analysis as concerns the accuracy in pitch determination during fast pitch variations at a relatively low power level as well as concerns the number of necessary computer operations.

Presently the experiments are being conducted to compare the adaptive autocorrelation with the simplified inverse filter tracking algorithm /5/.

REFERENCES

/1/ G.Lukatela: Pitch Determination by Adaptive Autocorrelation Method.Haskins Laboratories: Status Report on Speech Research, SR(1973),185-193.

/2/ A.M.Noll:Short-Time Spectrum and"Cepstrum" Techniques for Vocal Pitch Detection. J.Acoust.Soc.Am.,36(1964)296-302.

/3/ J.W.Cooley and J.W.Tukey:An Algorithm for the Machine Calculation of Complex Fourier Series.Math.Computation, 19(1965), 297-301.

/4/ R.M.Fano:Short-Time Autocorrelation Functions in Power Spectra.J.Acoust.Soc.Am., 22(1950),546-550.

/5/ J.D. Markel:The SIFT Algorithm for Fundamental Frequency Estimation. IEEE Trans. on Audio and Electroacoust..AU-2o, No. 5(1972), 367-377.

Speech Communication Seminar
Stockholm. Aug. 1–3, 1974

UNDERWATER SONAR SYSTEMS (PASSIVE) IN HUMANS *

Hollien, H., Feinstein, S.H., Rothman, H. and Hollien, P.,
Communication Sciences Laboratory, University of Florida, Gainesville, Fla. U.S.A.

Abstract

Man may be able to utilize his passive SONAR system when attempting to navigate underwater. In order to study this possibility, we have carried out a number of experiments on underwater sound localization. The results of these studies are reported; their implications to auditory function and, especially, underwater directional capability are discussed.

A. Introduction. It has been established that divers can hear underwater; they do so, however, at acuity levels that are reduced when compared with those in air. But having heard a sound, can the diver localize the direction from which it is coming? As we know, in air, man has a reasonably well developed directional sense of hearing to aid him in locating the source of sounds, to warn him of approaching objects, to help differentiate among competing signals and so on. Does he have these same capabilities when submerged? Some workers would answer in the negative. For example, Bauer and Torick (1965) suggest that when an individual is submerged "Sounds appear to arrive from nowhere. The location of a friend or foe becomes a matter of dangerous conjecture and reverberant sounds mix with direct sound into an unintelligible jumble."

B. Arguments For and Against Man's Ability to Localize Sound Underwater. Theoretically, three relationships would argue against underwater sound localization; they are: 1) the speed of sound is much greater in water than it is in air; 2) in water there is no appreciable impedance mismatch between the head and the surrounding medium (as there is in air) and 3) underwater hearing is accomplished primarily by bone conduction rather than via the middle ear (Hollien, 1973). In any case, many divers and scientists argue that the ears simply are not isolated enough,one from the other, to permit use of passive SONAR by humans in that milieu. Other than the work by Bauer and Torick, there are only two experiments which argue against human underwater sound localization. First, Kitagewa and Shintaku (1957) report that they were unable to demonstrate such localization by using "high percussion sounds" underwater. They report no systematic localization capability. Usually the Image was fixed in front of the forehead; if the subject occluded his ears with his fingers, the sound image shifted to the occipital region. Secondly, Reysenbach de Haan (1957) reported an experiment in which divers were unable to localize sounds underwater. In this study, the subject floated on the surface of the water three meters above and 25 meters distant from a sound source; in order to hear the stimulus, he ducked his head below the surface. However, it is clear from the geometry of this experiment that there was little likelihood that subjects could have been expected to localize the sound. Nevertheless, it may be seen that there is, at least, some evidence that underwater sound localization is not possible. Opposed to these negative findings and the subjective reports of some divers, there are allegations to the contrary (see Feinstein, 1966) plus a very powerful early study by Ide (1944). Ide found that the sound produced by an ammonia jet could be localized immediately by

* not published in the preprint version.

some divers and by others after a few hours practice.

In any case, when we undertook to study passive underwater SONAR in humans (in the middle 1960's), considerable controversy existed concerning whether or not humans possessed such capability. Our early pilot work ultimately developed into a rather extensive program of research designed first to obtain reasonable data on basic auditory function in this area and then on whether or not man could utilize passive SONAR (if, indeed, it existed at all) in order to navigate underwater. Two major methodological approaches were used: 1) the multiple sound source procedure and 2) the minimum audible angle technique.

C. The Multiple Sound Source Approach. The first study in this series of investigations was pivotal in nature and provided the basic methodologies for the others. First, a Diver Auditory Localization System (DALS) was designed and constructed. In general, DALS is an open framework diving cage, constructed of polyvinylcloride tubing; five 3-meter arms project from the top of this system. These arms allow J-9 projectors to be placed at ear level at a reasonable distance from the center of the subject's head at angles of 0°, 45°, 90°, 270° and 315°. The J-9's were selected because of their omnidirectional characteristics and because it is possible to calibrate them in a very precise manner. In order to do so, an F-36 Hydrophone was fixed to DALS at a position corresponding to the center of the diver's head and calibrations conducted in order to assure that subjects would not receive cues from intensity differences.

Experiment 1a: The experimental stimuli selected for the Experiment 1a were 250, 1000, 6000 Hz sinusoids and thermal noise. The stimulus presentations consisted of five pulses of the particular experimental frequency delivered in 500 msec bursts at 110 dB SPL (re: 0.0002 dynes/cm^2) or 40 dB re: average underwater hearing threshold for the diver/subjects. Subjects were 17 adults (10 males and seven females) who were competent divers and had experience taking hearing tests in air (all had essentially normal hearing).

DALS was lowered by winch to an ear depth of 40 feet; the diver/subjects, wearing open/circuit SCUBA equipment were positioned in DALS in such a manner that they were free to move their heads but not their bodies. The experimental signals were presented to diver/listeners five times from each of the five transducers, for a total of 25 presentations of each stimulus.

The results of Experiment 1a may be seen in Table 1 (first half), which will reveal that the overall performance of the 17 subjects was significantly above chance as, on the basis of chance alone, the scores should cluster around 20%. Only 10 of the 68 scores were close to chance, only one individual had an overall score of less than 30%, and the overall mean of 43.8% (based on 1700 S-R presentations) is more than double chance. Thus, it was concluded that humans show better ability to localize sounds underwater than theory would predict -- and, incidentally, that localization is best for low frequency or broad-band signals.

Experiment 2a: Once the validity of the underwater localization response had been established, it appeared appropriate to investigate specific parameters related to this auditory ability in order to better understand its nature and extent. In this second experiment, the basic protocols were followed with one exception: subjects were immobilized by having them replace their dive mask with one that was directly attached to DALS. The results of Experiment 2a also may be seen in Table I. From the data, it may be observed that subjects appear to be able to localize sound underwater as well with their head immobilized as they could when they were free to scan. An exception is found for the 250 Hz condition; here the differences between the two scores are statistically significant with the fixed head responses the poorer. However, it should be remembered that the 250 Hz condition was always presented first and that divers are notoriously uneasy when their freedom of movement is curtailed; thus they appeared to be attending (at first) as much to life support considerations as they were to the experiment. Another interesting result was a dramatically reduced response latency for this experimental procedure when compared with any of the others. Indeed, in this case the diver/subjects responded to the stimuli at rates that were about four times quicker than for the other procedures. In any event, it can be tentatively concluded that divers do not have to avail themselves of head scanning in order to localize sound underwater.

Table I. Percent correct localization re: each of four stimuli by subjects in two experiments. In the first study, 17 subjects were permitted to move their head; in the second, the procedure was replicated for seven subjects re: a condition of no head movement.

Condition		Stimulus			
		250 Hz	1000 Hz	6000 Hz	Noise
A. Experiment 1a (N=17)					
Movable Head					
	Mean	50.6	38.8	33.4	52.5
	S.D.	14.0	11.9	16.3	12.9
B. Experiment 2a (N=7)					
Fixed Head					
	Mean	37.1	37.7	38.2	58.3
Movable head					
	Mean	61.1	37.7	34.8	54.8

Experiment 3a: In the third experiment, two major changes were made: 1) the stimuli were presented at 95 dB (SPL) and 2) only 15 presentations of each stimulus were provided. The purpose of this study was to investigate different classes of signals in order to ascertain whether or not different stimuli might enhance the passive SONAR response. Pulses, frequency "glides" and dolphin whistles were included among stimuli. The results suggested that some stimuli were better for underwater localization than were others. For example, high scores (52 to 60% correct responses) were obtained for a 50 pps pulse train and the low and middle frequency "glides." Hence, this research provided additional indication that certain signal classes may have potential for enhancing acoustic localization underwater.

Experiment 4a: The fourth experiment in this series focused on signal strength with trials replicated at 80, 95 and 110 dB. Six subjects were presented the stimuli in random order. The results suggested some confounding of the localization response with signal strength, the highest intensity condition exhibited the greatest overall localization scores and the middle intensity the lowest (i.e., 80 dB: 43.8%; 95 dB: 38.8% and 110 dB: 52.8%). It is suggested that this relationship could be due to 1) the effects of training - improvement in scores correlated with number of trials or 2) tactile cues for the 110 dB condition. In summary, however, it appears that divers can localize soft and loud underwater sound sources albeit with slightly different levels of success.

Experiment 5a: Determination of the effects of training on seven divers who had little or no experience with underwater sound localization constituted the thrust of the fifth experiment. In this case, subjects were given a pre-training test of two stimuli (25 pps and 1000Hz) at 95 dB. Following this test, they received two sets of 30 training trials (for each stimulus) in which the correct location of the sound source was provided immediately after a response to the stimulus and while the stimulus was still being presented. Once training had been completed, subjects received a post-test similar to the first one. Improved scores were noted for both stimulus conditions. Statistical analysis indicated improvement for the 1000 Hz condition to be significant at the 5% level of confidence but the 25 pps condition barely failed to reach that level of significance. It is possible that 1) a greater number of training trials would have provided a more marked improvement and 2) ease of training is a function of type of signal. In any case, it can be tentatively concluded that "training" appears to improve and individual's ability to localize sounds underwater.

Experiments 6a and 7a: It is of some importance to investigate the underwater sound localization abilities of divers at distances other than the relatively close range (i.e., three meter) situation employed in the experiments cited above. Even more important is the need to obtain at least preliminary data about divers' ability to localize sounds in the open sea. Accordingly, a set of two related experiments were carried out during TEKTITE-2, U.S. Virgin Islands.

Procedures basic to the previous experiments were followed with certain exceptions. Transducer distance was 40 feet and subjects were placed in a mini-DICORS in 30 feet of sea water. The J-9 transducers were positioned at ear depth (15 feet) on taut lines; they were rigged to face the diver. This arrangement prevented the equipment from varying in distance or position due to the effects of currents, etc. The divers' bodies were fixed in relation to the transducers but they were free to move their heads. The first study duplicated the four stimuli utilized in Experiment Ia; the second employed two pulse trains, four glides and dolphin whistles; signal level was 100dB/SPL.

The results of the first study yielded lower scores than were expected (250 Hz: 38.4%; 1kHz: 32.8%; 6 kHz: 20.8%, and thermal noise: 40.0%). However, these depressed scores appear to be due to several extraneous conditions. First, three of the five subjects had not participated in underwater sound localization experiments of any type. Secondly, the experimental site was much noisier than Bugg Springs and the stimuli sometimes were difficult to hear. Finally, a number of barracuda were feeding on schools of small fish in the vicinity of the project; they distracted the divers. In any case, except for the 6000 Hz condition, the mean responses were clearly above chance.

The results of the second study appeared to confirm the notion that divers possess ability to localize underwater sounds in the open sea. Three of the four subjects in this experiment were those who exhibited the poorest scores on the first study; the fourth was a diver who had not participated previously in investigations of this type. Nevertheless, the resulting scores were of the same magnitude as those obtained from similar experiments at Bugg Springs. Indeed, they are quite high -- especially those for the pulse trains and the dolphin whistles (range: 46.6-50.0% correct). In short, it appears that, once divers are in command of the task, they will localize sounds at sea at approximately the same level as in the relatively benign environment of fresh water springs. The development of appropriate skills in this regard is of special importance to diver navigation by means of acoustic beacons.

D. Minimum Audible Angle (MAA) Experiments. Mills (1958) described a procedure which provides an index of the acuity of the auditory localization system, i.e., the Minimum Audible Angle (MAA). In this procedure, one sound source is located in the intersection of the coronal and midsagittal planes of the head and the second to the right or left of center. The experimental stimuli are presented in succession as pairs of pulses; the first always coming from the central position and the second from either side. The subject reports whether the sound came from the right or left speaker and the difference in degrees between the standard and comparison (which can be detected 75% of the time) becomes the Minimum Audible Angle (MAA). Investigators who have worked with marine mammals have changed this procedure slightly; i.e., the standard source is omitted and the animal indicates whether it hears a signal to its right or left. Thus, the MAA can be defined as the difference in degrees between the place of the sound source and an imaginary line extending tangentially from a point between the eyes.

Experiment 1b: In the series of MAA experiments reported here, the procedure was as follows: diver/subjects were situated in an underwater equipment configuration similar to DALS. The J-9 projectors were set at a predetermined angle and the diver seated with his head against a positioning ring. Subjects held their breath and listened for the stimulus, responding either "right" or a "left" on each trial. The experimenter energized one of the projectors according to a pre-determined random sequence of 15 "right" and "left" responses; the number of angles tested on a dive (in blocks of 30 trials) depended on the temperature of the water. Responses were expected within 15 seconds of the stimulus onset and, with the exception of the first few trials and the smallest angles, nearly all responses were initiated well within this limit. Three signals 3500 Hz, 6500 Hz and thermal noise) constituted the experimental stimuli; they were pulsed (100 msec duration at 1/pps) and the intensity level was 40 dB re 1 μbar. Six divers served as subjects. Figure I summarizes performance at each angle tested for each stimulus and indicates the MAA's were: 1) 21.5° at 3500 Hz, 2) 14.5° at 6500 Hz and 3) 9.75° for thermal noise.

Experiments 2b and 3b: Since divers do not normally depend on auditory information to orient themselves underwater, it was hypothesized that their performance would be less than asymptotic in the MAA task until they learned to utilize the available auditory cues effectively. In order to test that hypothesis, the second experiment was designed to provide them a large number of trials (300) with feedback at an azimuth greater than the point at which correct responses occured only 50% of the time (3°) but smaller than the MAA

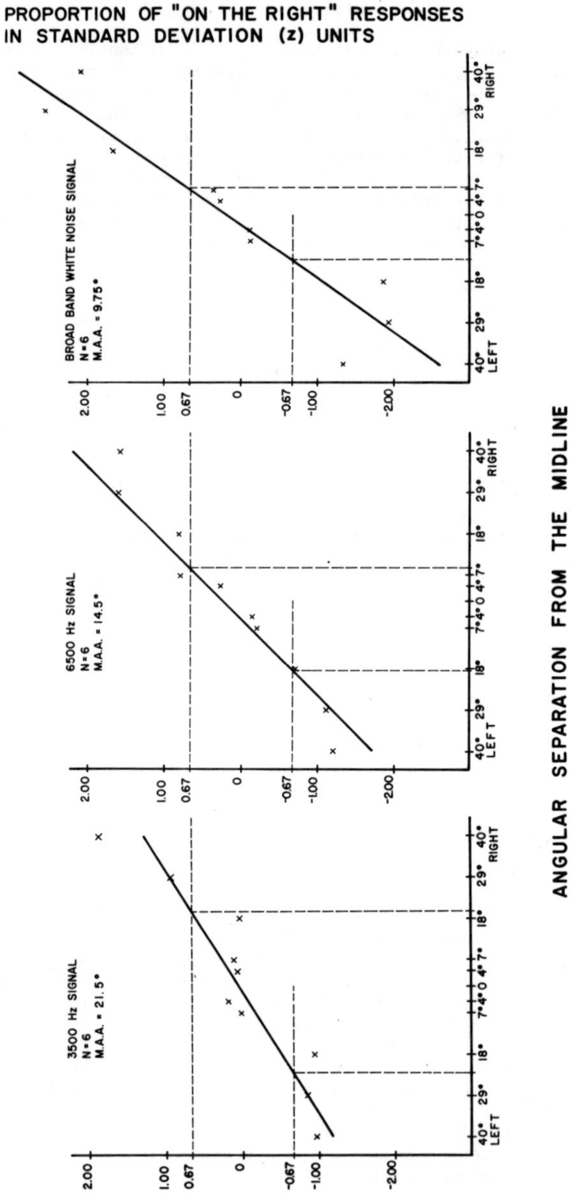
PROPORTION OF "ON THE RIGHT" RESPONSES
IN STANDARD DEVIATION (z) UNITS
BROAD BAND WHITE NOISE SIGNAL
N=6
M.A.A. = 9.75°
6500 Hz SIGNAL
N=6
M.A.A. = 14.5°
3500 Hz SIGNAL
N=6
M.A.A. = 21.5°
2.00
1.00
0.67
0
-0.67
-1.00
-2.00
40° LEFT
29°
18°
7° 4° 0 4° 7°
40° RIGHT
ANGULAR SEPARATION FROM THE MIDLINE

(9.75°). In order to monitor the immediate effects of this training procedure, a block of feedback trials was always followed by a block of no-feedback trials. In Experiment 2b, two blocks of 30 trials were run at 7° on each dive. In Experiment 3b, the MAA was redetermined using the same procedure as in Experiment 1b. Four divers who had participated in the preceding experiment served as subjects; the mean MAA's of these four subjects, obtained from that experiment, were compared with their post-training scores. Performances improved significantly after training and these data demonstrate that training improves the acuity of sound localization underwater. It should be noted furtherthat, in Experiment 1b, the MAA was larger for the 3.5 kHz signal than it wasfor the 6.5 kHz signal. After training, this difference disappeared -- a result which may indicate that the earlier difference in MAA at these frequencies was a function of the audibility of the signal. A further implication may be that human sound localization underwater is not wavelength dependent at these frequencies. This conclusion seems to be a reasonable one in light of the compelling evidence that human hearing underwater is a bone conduction phenomenon (Brandt and Hollien, 1967; Hollien and Brandt, 1969; Smith, 1965).

Experiment 4b: A fourth MAA experiment was required because the earlier ones were carried out in the cold and relatively noisy waters of a Canadian harbor (Feinstein, 1969). The divers had to wear hoods while being tested and the combination of these hoods, and the ambient noise level, made it necessary to use a very intense sound source (40 dB re: 1μbar). Thus, it was possible that the obtained MAA's could have resulted from both auditory and nonauditory (tactile cues. Therefore, a replication of the earlier experiments was carried out at Bugg Springs. In this experiment, the seven divers who served as subjects wore full wet suits (except for the hood) and stimulus intensity was 26 dB re: 1μbar. The results demonstrated no remarkable differences between the performance of these subjects and that of divers from the earlier experiments. In particular, the data indicate that MAA's are relatively insensitive to a wide range of conditions, e.g., level of background noise, water temperature, water salinity and absolute loudness of the stimulus. Finally, it appears as if the presence or absence of a neoprene diving hood is not likely to effect the capacity of divers to localize sounds, provided that the signals are loud enough to be heard.

E. Current Research on Human Underwater SONAR. Some evidence has been offered as confirmation that tactile cues play a role in underwater sound localization; we wished to test this relationship. In order to do so we developed two procedures by which tactile cues were maximized and auditory cues minimized. In the first procedure, we presented all stimuli at 55 dB SPL. Of course, these signals were below auditory thresholds but we reasoned that, while not audible to the diver, they might be strong enough to be felt. In the second experiment, we wanted to utilize a signal at an intensity level that we knew could be felt by the submerged diver. Hence, in this study, stimuli were presented at 110 dB SPL. Naturally, a signal of this strength could be heard clearly; hence, all divers wore either one or two hoods (depending on preference) and received (via underwater phones) a sawtooth noise emitted at a high enough intensity level to effectively mask the experimental stimuli. The multiple sound source procedure was used; subjects wore only a bathing suit, a face mask and SCUBA gear.

The results of the first study yielded only chance levels of localization responses (250 Hz: 22.4%; 1000 Hz: 14.4%; 6000 Hz: 16.8% and thermal noise: 18.4%). In this case, it could be concluded that the stimuli were not presented at levels intense enough for either tactile or auditory localization. The scores for the second experiment were slightly higher (250 Hz: 30.0%; 1000 Hz: 16.5%; 6000 Hz: 22.8% and thermal noise: 16.0%); however, none of these scores were significantly above chance. Moreover, the diver/subjects reported 1) that while they often could "feel" the signal, they could not tell (from these tactile cues) where the sound was coming from and 2) that sometimes for the 250 Hz condition, they could hear the stimulus over the masking signal; in such cases they went ahead and localized by means of these sensations. In summary, it appears that the diver wishing to locate underwater sound sources or navigate by means of acoustic signals may be able to do so via the auditory modality but probably cannot depend on any supplemental information processed tactilly.

E. Diver Acoustic Navigation. There are a number of reasons for studying diver sound localization. For example, such research: 1) adds to our basic understanding of binaural hearing, 2) may allow a diver to determine the location of objects or individuals emitting acoustic signals of one kind or another and 3) is directly relevant to the implementation of acoustic diver navigation systems. Indeed, it has been apparent almost from the inception of SCUBA that one of the major limitations to diver effectiveness is the absense of adequate and efficient methods of directing him from one specific location to another. The traditional solution to such navigation problems has been the use of an underwater compass to permit him to use a "dead reckoning procedure; this approach proves to be a poor one at best!

Two relatively new approaches to the navigation-retrieval problem are presently evolving; one approach is to develop electronic devices for active SONAR; the other is to study, and possibly develop, human biological SONAR capabilities. The former has resulted in a proliferation of devices, usually large and cumbersome, which the diver carries in his hands or on his person. The second approach is the one to which we subscribe; it is based on the possibility that man can auditorily localize underwater sounds with considerable precision -- and without the aid of electronic listening devices. Specifically, our assumption is that in most cases the human auditory system can be used underwater to provide the necessary information for effective navigation.

In our first navigation experiment we utilized a J-11 transducer (in deep water) which was placed one meter above a thermocline (average depth: six meters) at the center of one end of a large barge anchored in 45 meters of water. The diver/subject entered the water at a predetermined point approximately 270 meters from the barge, descended until he could hear the signal and then attempted to swim toward it. A second (safety) diver in a tender maintained contact with a float via a long safety line.

Four divers completed a total of 22 acoustic navigation runs; of that total, 69% succeeded in reaching the barge. Moreover, all of the misses were in the general vicinity of the target and the diver never swam a course away from it. Thus, these results were much the same as those reported by Ide.

Subsequently we have run an additional 23 subjects for a total of 70 trials, in various other marine and fresh water environments, using different signals and different sources. Of that total number of trials, the subject reached the sound source nearly 93% of the time. These results would appear to indicate that the variability found in diver sound navigation is determined to a great extent by extra-aural perceptual parameters.

To date, all of the acoustic navigation experiments that we have completed have utilized a beacon consisting of a single sound source. It is possible, however, that an array of two or more sound emitters in the proper temporal and spatial relationship could prove to be a more effective target for the diver than will the single source. Accordingly we now propose that a line array of multiple transducers energized in sequence to produce an apparent auditory movement (the Phi phenomenon) is likely to be more effective than a single pulsed source. In theory, the array will provide the same kind of phonomenal motion cues as are utilized in landing light systems for aircraft runways. A diver listening to the beacon would be able to orient himself so that, for example, the sound would move first from right-to-left and then from left-to-right. The impression of spatial location should be so strong that deviations from a true course would be recognized immediately. Experiments which examine the utility of the Phi approach to underwater acoustic navigation are presently in progress. In addition to these experiments, we are continuing to work with and improve the single source concept for a number of reasons. First, we need more information about both the stimulus and the response variables related to this approach. More importantly, however, we wish to determine how effective it is as an aid to human underwater acoustic navigation.

References

Bauer, B.B. and Torick, E.L., (1966), Analysis of underwater earphones, J. Acoust. Soc. Amer., 39, 35-39.

Brandt, J.F. and Hollien, H., (1967), Underwater hearing thresholds in man, J. Acoust. Soc. Amer., 42, 966-971.

Feinstein, S.H. (1966), Human hearing underwater: are things as bad as they seem?, J. Acoust. Soc. Amer., 40, 1561-1562.

Feinstein, S.H., Human underwater sound localization, doc.dis., Dalhousie University, Hallifax, N.S., 1971.

Hollien, H. (1973), Underwater sound localization in humans, J. Acoust. Soc. Amer., 53, 1288-1295.

Hollien, H. and Brandt, J.F. (1969), The effect of air bubbles in the external auditory meatus on underwater hearing thresholds, J. Acoust. Soc. Amer., 46, 384-387.

Ide, J.M., (1944), Signaling and homing by underwater sound for small craft and commando swimmers, NRL Sound Report No. 19.

Smith, P.S., (1965), Bone conduction, air conduction, and underwater hearing, U.S. Naval Submarine Medical Center, Groton, Connecticut, Memorandum Report No. 65-12.

Vol. 1 ERRATUM

J. Makhoul: "Linear prediction vs. analysis-by-synthesis"

Equation (5) on p. 36 should be read as follows:

$$G^2 = R_o + \sum_{k=1}^{p} a_k R_k . \qquad (5)$$